Shepherding the Family of God
the Spirituality of Diocesan Priests in St. John of Avila

Father Gustavo Castillo

The Institute for Priestly Formation
IPF Publications

NIHIL OBSTAT: Father Matthew J. Gutowski, JCL

IMPRIMATUR: Most Reverend George J. Lucas
                             Archbishop of Omaha, Nebraska
                             June 3, 2019

THE INSTITUTE FOR PRIESTLY FORMATION
IPF Publications
2500 California Plaza
Omaha, Nebraska 68178-0415
www.IPFPublications.com

Printed in the United States of America
ISBN-13: 978-0-9981164-7-1

Cover design by Timothy D. Boatright
Vistra Communications
Tampa, Florida

THE INSTITUTE FOR PRIESTLY FORMATION
MISSION STATEMENT

The Institute for Priestly Formation was founded to assist
bishops in the spiritual formation of diocesan seminarians
and priests in the Roman Catholic Church. The Institute
responds to the need to foster spiritual formation as the
integrating and governing principle of all aspects for priestly
formation. Inspired by the biblical-evangelical spirituality of
Ignatius Loyola, this spiritual formation has as its goal the
cultivation of a deep interior communion with Christ; from
such communion, the priest shares in Christ's own pastoral
charity. In carrying out its mission, the Institute directly
serves diocesan seminarians and priests as well as those who
are responsible for diocesan priestly formation.

THE INSTITUTE FOR PRIESTLY FORMATION
Creighton University
2500 California Plaza
Omaha, Nebraska 68178-0415
www.priestlyformation.org
ipf@creighton.edu

To Reverend Monsignor Juan Esquerda-Bifet

who has brought St. John of Avila to the twenty-first century
through his writings, retreats, and his own priestly witness

TABLE OF CONTENTS

Acknowledgments

The older I get, the more I realize the truth that all is grace. Pope Benedict XVI had it right when he wrote in his *Introduction to Christianity* that the Christian religion is not so much about what we do, but about what we receive. God is the author of all good gifts, and I have received so many of his blessings!

The present work is part of a dissertation I completed during my doctoral studies in Rome. First of all, then, I thank my bishop, Archbishop Jose H. Gomez, for having sent me to study there. Being in the Eternal City gave me a greater insight into the universality of the Church and the importance of the Christian community. I also could not have completed my studies without the help and the support of so many different people: my professors at the *Angelicum*, my family and friends here in Los Angeles who encouraged me in every step of the way, and my brother priests at Casa Santa Maria.

God had also prepared a special gift for me in Monsignor Juan Esquerda-Bifet, Professor Emeritus at the Pontifical University Urbaniana in Rome. I learned about the more than six decades of study he has dedicated to the works of St. John of Avila soon after I began my research. He not only became an invaluable resource; but, in his kindness, he agreed to be my spiritual director during those years of my doctoral studies. If my study helps to point to the writings of this humble and dedicated man who has, by now, personified the Apostle of Andalusia, it will be enough reward for me. No one studying the works of St. John of Avila can do so without drinking from Monsignor Esquerda's fountain of knowledge. It is to him that I dedicate this book.

Other individuals deserve to be mentioned: Deacon James Keating from The Institute for Priestly Formation in Omaha, Nebraska and Father Ron Knott from the Institute for Priests and Presbyterates at St. Meinrad, Indiana for facilitating resources and nudging me in the right direction. Also, Father Peter Addai-Mensah from Ghana, Africa and Father Ray Carey from Portland, Oregon for sharing their work with me.

My diocesan brothers studying in Rome made things easier for me while I was there. It is a blessing to have them as my colleagues now at St. John's Seminary. The seminarians there have offered encouraging and constructive feedback for the improvement of this writing. I thank them for their openness and support.

And last, but not least, I would like to thank the members of the Apostolic Union of the Clergy at Casa Santa Maria and in our newly formed group in Los Angeles. Their fraternal support has been a true gift. I pray other priests may also experience the rewards of belonging to a group like this.

My gratitude to you, kind reader, and all the People of God, especially those in ministry. I pray the following pages make sense to you and contribute to the collaboration God wants to see in the Church for the good of all. May the Lord continue to make us docile to the action of the Holy Spirit in our lives so that we can employ our gifts to serve and support one another on our path to holiness and advance God's kingdom as we build up His family wherever He places us.

Father Gustavo Castillo, STD

FOREWORD

    This is an important book, and it comes at a crucial moment when there is growing awareness that we are living in a time of reform and renewal in the Catholic Church. The troubles of the Church in our times are not unique. In fact, we see striking similarities between our times and those of St. John of Avila in pre-Reformation Europe. What Pope Francis has said about our times also applies to St. John's times: "We are not living in an era of change but a change of era." As in John's time, the Church carries out her mission today in an emerging global society marked by rapid and profound changes—technological, economic, political, and cultural. These changes challenge the Church's moral authority and institutional structures and call into question her truth claims in a secularizing society. As in John's time, in our day, we also see symptoms of moral weakness and spiritual confusion, a decline of faith and discipline, a diminishing confidence in the Church's identity and mission.

    In every period of the Church's history, the key to her reform and renewal is the reform and renewal of the priesthood. Reform means returning to the original "form" and correcting what has been "de-formed." And as Dante, the great Christian humanist, wrote in the 14th century *De*

Monarchia: "The form of the Church is nothing else than the life of Christ in word and in deed." As established by Jesus Christ, the form of the Church reflects His priestly identity and mission. In the New Testament, the Church herself is called a "kingdom and priests for our God" (Rv 5:10) and a "royal priesthood, a holy nation, a people of his own, so that you may announce the praises of him who called you out of darkness into his wonderful life" (1 Pt 2:9). There is a common priesthood of all the faithful that participates in the priesthood of Jesus Christ and His mission. But Christ Himself willed also an ordained ministry that would offer sacrifice in His name—and in His very person.

The Church is built on these apostolic and priestly foundations, with Jesus Christ Himself as the cornerstone. So, the Church's mission depends on the priestly ministry of preaching and sanctification that Christ entrusted to the bishops, as the successors of the Apostles, and to their co-workers, the priests. The priest alone is ordained to stand *in persona Christi*, mediating between heaven and earth, uniting the world to the salvific mystery of Christ—His person and mission, His Life, Death, and Resurrection for us and for our salvation.

This sacred character of the priest and His essential identification with Christ lies at the heart of St. John of Avila's vision for Church reform. "The priest . . . is the face of the Church," he wrote, "and just as in the face is reflected the beauty of the entire body, likewise the clergy must be the principal beauty of the Church."

In retrieving John's heroic vision of priestly dignity and sanctity, Father Gustavo Castillo has performed an important work of "ressourcement"—introducing the English-speaking world to a giant of Hispanic theology and spirituality and a true pioneer of authentic renewal and reform in the Church.

To encounter John of Avila is to enter into the diverse and rich streams of revitalization and renewal that flowed in the Church during the years prior to the Protestant Reformation. It is a still-too-common misunderstanding that Church reform began with Martin Luther's protests against indulgences and other ecclesiastical abuses in 1517. The truth is that decades before Luther, a broad groundswell had already begun, with Catholics in almost every country working to reform Church structures, revitalize the Liturgy, and revive the fervor, devotion, and virtue of the clergy and lay faithful.

These movements were fragmented and not embraced evenly by Church authorities, as Carlos Eire writes in *Reformations: The Early Modern World, 1450–1650,* his towering history of this period. But Eire notes that already in the late Middle Ages, there was talk of a broad agenda for *reformatio in capite et in membris*—the reform of the Church in her head and in her members. The late Fordham University historian John Olin made an important distinction between what he called "the Catholic Reformation" and the Protestant Reformation, on the one hand, and the Counter-Reformation, on the other. As distinct from these movements, the various projects of Catholic reform shared two common concerns—reform of believers' moral and spiritual lives and renewal of the Church's pastoral mission of teaching and sanctification. "The state of the clergy loomed large in the Catholic reform," Olin wrote in *Catholic Reform from Cardinal Ximenes to the Council of Trent, 1495–1563.* "If their ignorance, corruption, or neglect had been responsible for the troubles that befell the Church, as nearly everyone affirmed, then their reform required urgent attention and was the foundation and root of all renewal."

John of Avila's reform mission can be understood only in this larger context of Catholic reform. St. John was born within a decade of the first voyages to the New World; and during St. John's formative years, Europe was being transformed by these discoveries and the expansion of global trade and the political upheavals they brought about, not to mention the revolution in the distribution of knowledge and spirituality ushered in by the new printing press technology. Studying at the University of Acalá, outside Madrid, John was immersed in the spirit of Christian humanism inspired by Erasmus of Rotterdam and the vision of one of the Church's great reformers, Cardinal Francisco Jiménez de Cisneros, a Franciscan friar and Archbishop of Toledo. Cardinal Jiménez sought to build a new Christian humanism, grounded in a return to Greek and Roman sources and the writings of the Church Fathers and the study of the Scriptures in their original languages. He also believed there could be no true and lasting reform in the Church or in the wider society without holy priests and a virtuous and educated laity. Jiménez restored a strict priestly discipline, emphasizing the vow of celibacy. He required priests to abandon common-law wives and to live in parishes and to preach and teach, especially to the young, and to go to confession frequently. He also encouraged lay holiness and spirituality, using the new printing technology to publish spiritual and devotional works that until then had been available only for priests and religious.

These same priorities can be traced in the reform ministry of St. John of Avila. Ordained in 1526, John worked among the poor in southern Spain, concentrating his ministry on preaching and teaching. He taught the catechism to children, using poems and songs, and instructed adults in the ways of contemplative prayer. Later, he founded a priestly movement in Granada, sending out priests, two by two, to preach and hear confessions. He envisioned a new breed of "holy and working" priests whose spirituality would be centered on the Passion and Cross of Christ and the Eucharist.

Many of John's priestly protégés went on to join the Jesuits. His teaching was greatly admired by the Jesuits' founder, St. Ignatius of Loyola; and his preaching is credited with the conversion of two men who went on to become saints—St. Francis Borgia and St. John of God. The list of those who sought his spiritual counsel reads like a who's-who of 16th-century Hispanic saints and mystics—St. Peter of Alcántara, St. John of Ribera, St. Thomas of Villanova, and St. Teresa of Avila.

In his day, St. John of Avila's influence cut across the Catholic reform movements in Europe. St. Francis de Sales praised his teaching, as did Pierre de Bérulle of the French School of spirituality. His teaching helped shape the ministries of such priestly reformers as St. John Eudes, St. Vincent de Paul, St. Alphonsus Marie de Liguori, and St. Anthony Marie Claret.

St. John suffered for his vision of renewal, which was far ahead of the ecclesial thinking of this time. He was jailed by the Inquisition for a year, 1532–1533, in part for encouraging contemplative prayer and the striving for holiness among the laity. While in prison, he studied St. Paul's letters and translated into Spanish Thomas à Kempis's classic work of spiritual renewal, *The Imitation of Christ*. He later told his

biographer that he learned more about Christian living while
he was in prison than in all his days of study.

This book by Father Castillo is a tour de force, drawing
from John of Avila's sermons, letters, and treatises. Much of
this material is being presented for the first time in English.
In my opinion, it should be required reading in seminaries
and rectories and among all who work for the formation
of priests.

Already during his lifetime, John was referred to as "the
Master" or "the Teacher." And in 2012, Pope Benedict XVI
declared him a "Doctor of the Church," commending the
entire Church to study his teaching, especially on the universal call to holiness and priestly spirituality. This book is the
first comprehensive study of the Master's teachings on the
priesthood to appear in the English-speaking world, where
he is still, unfortunately, a virtual unknown. Father Castillo
has given us a great gift in bringing St. John's teachings into
fruitful conversation with the teachings of the Second Vatican Council and the magisterium of the postconciliar popes,
especially St. John Paul II, Benedict XVI, and Pope Francis.

St. John of Avila was a spiritual doctor who keenly diag-
nosed what ailed the Church in the years before the Council
of Trent. John knew that without holy priests, the Church
cannot be what Christ intends her to be and cannot fulfill the
salvific mission entrusted to her. In this, St. John anticipates
the needs of our present moment in the Church as we continue to implement the reform vision of Vatican II.

While he opposed all expressions of clerical privilege
and any efforts to place priests "on a pedestal," St. John did
not hesitate to call priests to a renewed appreciation of their
sacred dignity and mission in God's plan of redemption. In

this spontaneous prayer that he makes in his *Treatise on the Priesthood* (1563), we see John's grand vision of the priest as ordained to continue in history the Lord's own sacrifice of love:

> May You be forever blessed! Your immense goodness compelled You to descend from heaven to earth. After You announced the way of heaven with many labors and did many favors, this same goodness . . . compelled You to mount the cross. . . .

> You lost Your life, so that by Your dying, we would regain the life that we had lost through the sin of Adam and by our own sins. Seeing the great signs of love that You showed exteriorly, we would know the great fire of love for us that was burning within Your heart. Being loved, we would love You.

> You knew, Lord, the hardness of our hearts and how soon they forget the favors already received. Therefore, You magnified Your unbounded love and wonderfully ordained how, even though You went to heaven, You would be here with us.

> You did this by giving power to priests, so that they might call You with the words of consecration, and You Yourself would come in person into their hands and be there really present.

> Thus, we are participants in the good things You gained by Your Passion, and we remember it with profound gratitude and consolation, loving and obeying the One that did such a great work, which was to give His life for us.

St. John gives us a beautiful and thrilling vision of the ministerial priesthood rooted in the priesthood of Christ and the Sacrament of Love, the Eucharist. The priest must be "on fire with the love of God," St. John said, and filled with a great zeal to bring souls to God. In his vision, the priest is a pastor of souls, a spiritual leader called to sanctity and service, a sign of Christ and a mediator between God and His people, speaking His Word and bringing all into contact with His saving mysteries.

St. John of Avila preached continual conversion of life for priests. And, most importantly, he modeled it in his own priesthood. Priestly spirituality, as St. John taught it, is the imitation of Christ, High Priest and Good Shepherd. "There must be between Christ and the priest a very deep interior friendship, similarity of customs, a love and hatred of the same things, and a love that is so endearing to the point that, from two, there can remain only one," he said.

In canonizing the Master of Avila in 1970, St. Paul VI called him a "prophetic figure," and he prayed:

> May this Saint, who we are happy to exalt before the Church, be her favorable intercessor for the graces that the Church evidently needs now more than ever: firmness in the true faith, authentic love for the Church, the holiness of her clergy, fidelity to the Council, and the imitation of Christ as it should be in these modern times.

This prayer is more timely than ever in this year, which marks the 450th anniversary of St. John of Avila's death on May 10, 1569. I pray that in this jubilee year, this fine book will stir the hearts of every priest and seminarian, reminding them of the great dignity of their calling. May God grant us holy priests and holy bishops. And through their ministry, may Jesus Christ bring about the reform and renewal of His Church—that all of us may hear His call to holiness and play our part in His great mission of proclaiming salvation to the ends of the earth.

Most Reverend José H. Gomez
Archbishop of Los Angeles
February 21, 2019
Memorial of St. Peter Damian, Bishop and Doctor

Introduction and Biography

When Pope Benedict XVI bestowed the title of Doctor of the Universal Church on St. John of Avila in 2012, many were asking themselves who this saint might be. Outside his native Spain, very little was known about him. Upon learning that he was a spiritual master contemporary with St. Ignatius of Loyola and St. Teresa of Avila, that he had been declared Patron Saint of Spanish Secular Priests by Pope Pius XII in 1946, and that he was the first Doctor, among the thirty-four others (at the time), who chose to remain a diocesan priest, it was obvious that he had something to offer to all priests in the universal Church, especially diocesan priests.

The concept of a diocesan priestly spirituality has been debated for a long time, and many authors and theologians have expressed different views on the subject. While most agree that it does, in fact, exist, there is no clarity as to what that spirituality entails. For some, diocesan spirituality has to do with being well informed of the different "spiritualities" available in the Church to help people grow in their faith. When it comes to diocesan priests themselves, some affiliate with religious communities as oblates or third-order members in order to have something "substantial" to offer their people. Many just go through the motions and respond to what is asked of them without giving too much thought to their inner life or to the steps they can take to grow and seek the holiness to which every Christian is called.

Most authors agree that up to the seventeenth century, there was no mention of a priestly spirituality.[1] People spoke only of Christian spirituality, which was seen as just being one, one in which all the baptized shared.[2] However, just as theology is divided up into different branches for the sake of study despite the fact that it is one science, in the same way, one can speak of different "spiritualities" within the Church's tradition.[3] By spirituality, it is meant "any religious or ethical value that is concretized as an attitude or spirit from which one's actions flow."[4] Since Christian spirituality can be defined as "a participation in the mystery of Christ through the interior life of grace, actuated by faith, charity, and the other Christian virtues,"[5] it is certain that all those incorporated into the Body of Christ will have similar approaches in the way that they live out their faith.

However, this does not mean that one cannot speak of a Franciscan or Jesuit or Dominican or Benedictine spirituality. One can see this variety at the parish level in most churches. It would be unwise to have only one prayer group in which to address all the different spiritual needs of the faithful, regardless of their age or their vocation. There are reasons for having groups for the youth, for married couples, for those in the charismatic renewal, for men, for women, and so forth. There is no question that different groups of people have different needs and concerns, depending on their vocation and their state in life. The same applies to diocesan priests. As in the case of religious orders, they, too, have their own unique "spirit from which their actions flow."[6]

As a "secular" priest, one who is in the world in the midst of his people, a diocesan priest will have a spirituality that resembles that of the lay faithful for, as the Church teaches, the common and ministerial priesthood are "ordered one to another."[7] In the post-synodal exhortation on the laity, *Christifideles Laici*, one reads:

> The unity of life of the lay faithful is of the greatest importance: indeed they must be *sanctified in everyday professional and social life*. Therefore, to respond to their vocation, the lay faithful must see *their daily activities* as an occasion to join themselves to God, fulfill his will, serve other people and lead them to communion with God in Christ. . . .

> To such an end the lay faithful must accomplish their *work* with professional competence, with human honesty, with a Christian spirit, and especially *as a way of their own sanctification*.[8]

When these words are compared to those found in the Second Vatican Council in regard to diocesan priests, the similarities are striking:

> Priests will acquire holiness in their own distinctive way *by exercising their functions* sincerely and tirelessly in the Spirit of Christ. . . .

> Therefore priests will achieve the unity of their lives by joining themselves with Christ in the recognition of the Father's will and in the gift of themselves to the flock entrusted to them. In this way, by adopting the role of the good shepherd they will find in the practice of pastoral

charity itself the bond of priestly perfection which will reduce to unity their life and activity.[9]

Thus, we can ascertain that it is *precisely in the faithful carrying out their functions* that both the laity and the diocesan priests will find their own sanctification.[10] Sharing in the life of Christ, they also share in His priestly, prophetic, and kingly ministry through Baptism.[11] As they proclaim the good news to others, as they sanctify the world through their prayers, and as they gather everyone together into the one family of God, they themselves are challenged and called to conversion as they seek holiness of life.

Experts on Vatican II confirm that this is the case for diocesan priests. They tell us that while the first draft of *Presbyterorum Ordinis* was entitled "Decree on the Life and Ministry of Priests," the final document reversed the order of the words to reflect what exists today: "Decree on the Ministry and Life of Priests."[12] This title truly highlights the theology discussed at the Council that it was in the loving fulfillment of his ministry, in his pastoral charity, that the priest would find meaning and personal holiness. St. John Paul II would later confirm this in *Pastores Dabo Vobis*. In that exhortation, St. John Paul II would write: "an intimate bond exists between the priest's spiritual life and the exercise of his ministry."[13]

It is common knowledge that after Vatican II, there was "a crisis in the Catholic priesthood."[14] There are many factors that converged and gave way to the crisis, but the lack of priestly identity and spirituality were paramount during those years.[15] Perhaps some priests interpreted the above texts from the Council as meaning that "their work could be their prayer," as some individuals involved in apostolic ministry were known to claim (to their own detriment and which the Magisterium of the Church has been trying to correct ever since). The Church has always emphasized the primacy of the spiritual life for priests. They are the primary spiritual leaders in the community, and their call to sanctify the people must begin with their own soul. Their ministry must flow from their prayer.

This is the great witness of St. John of Avila. Despite being formed in the somewhat monastic environment that was customary of schools of theology before the erection of diocesan seminaries mandated by the Council of Trent, he intuited the need to keep a healthy balance between one's prayer life and pastoral ministry.[16] He did not fall into the pietistic spirituality of *devotio moderna* present in his day or the errors of the Quietist movement condemned by the Inquisition.[17] Both movements showed a concern for mere spiritual gratification for the salvation of one's soul independent from the community. Master Avila, on the other hand, embraced a comprehensive approach: yes, prayer was of utmost importance but so was the care of souls, the incorporation of all the baptized into the Body of Christ so that all could "be one" (Jn 17:21). In the case of priests, then, the saint was a great promoter of priestly holiness but also of preaching and of care for the marginalized. In his own way, he was a sixteenth century precursor of the need for balance between the ministries of priest, prophet, and king for which the Church would call at Vatican II.[18]

It was precisely during the turbulent days of the priestly crisis that St. Paul VI approved the equipollent canonization of St. John of Avila in 1970. The life of this truly dedicated

Spanish priest who was confident of his own calling and who concerned himself with the formation of good, holy pastors even before the reforms of the Council of Trent was worthy of emulation, St. Paul VI thought.[19] With the bestowal of the title of Doctor of the Church by Pope Benedict XVI, the Church has also declared that his teachings have a universal appeal. Those teachings are a mine full of treasures still waiting to be discovered.

Can someone from the sixteenth century have something valuable to offer for the spirituality of diocesan priests today? After examining what has been written on the subject thus far,[20] the answer seems to be in the affirmative. In order to appreciate our saint in his own context, it is helpful to begin by knowing something about his life and his teachings as they are found in his writings.

The Early Years of St. John of Avila[21]

Juan of Avila was born in Almodóvar del Campo, Spain on January 6, 1499.[22] He was the only child of Alonso de Avila and Catalina Xixón, a devout and wealthy couple in the Archdiocese of Toledo.[23] As noted by Monsignor Juan Esquerda-Bifet, an expert on the writings of the saint, the wealth of the family came from silver mines that they owned in Sierra Morena.[24] The fact that the Avilas came from Jewish ancestry is well attested.[25] This would cause some difficulties for the young St. John as he tried to get an education and serve the Church in a country where "new Christians" were always seen as suspect.

The process of beatification for St. John of Avila provides many details about his early days. A witness from Almodóvar del Campo, the lawyer Juan Bauptista de la

Fuente, testified in 1624 that Catalina Xixón, finding herself childless, had turned to St. Bridget to intercede for the conception of the heir. The future mother would go barefoot for several days to pray at a shrine, doing other penances and promising to consecrate the child to God's service should she be granted her request. Once St. John was born, Bauptista also mentions how, growing in this devout home, the child was known for his fasts and penances, even to the point of sleeping on thorny branches.[26]

These early sources also give a window into the early charity of the saint. When St. John was a school boy, his mother bought him a new sweater, but he traded it for another one that was torn and worn out. Upon getting home and being questioned about it, he replied that his was better suited for his classmate.[27]

Most likely, besides the normal lessons on grammar and Christian doctrine, St. John also studied literature and humanities in his native Almodovar. In his future writings, he quotes Seneca, Horace, and Virgil, among others.[28]

First Conversion

The first biographer of the saint, the Dominican Friar Luis of Granada, mentions that, when St. John of Avila was fourteen years old, his parents sent him to Salamanca to study law. Shortly after that, though, being "a person already touched by God,"[29] St. John returned to his house and convinced his parents to allow him to live in solitude in their home. He lived this way for almost three years, leaving his penances only to go to church. It seems that it was at this time that his devotion to the Blessed Sacrament began, for he would spend many hours in the church in prayer. He would go to confession often and in so doing, edified the priests and parishioners with his example.[30]

Some authors mention that St. John of Avila was a friar for some time,[31] but it is possible that they may have misunderstood some of the letters written between St. Ignatius of Loyola and Ignatius's vicars. The two saints enjoyed a great affinity for each other, and they even discussed the possibility of St. John entering the Jesuits. While this point will be addressed later, this relationship may be the source of the confusion. Sala and Martín, the editors of Master Avila's *Obras completas*, point to a letter from St. Ignatius to one of his priests in 1550 where he mentions that if there are any impediments to entering the Jesuits, "such as having been a friar," the Pope could easily dispense those.[32] It is likely that this statement could have been taken as a fact for in 1554, a Jesuit mentions in a letter that St. John of Avila was a friar; but it was unclear whether or not he professed vows.[33] Fra Luis of Granada simply states that a Franciscan advised St. John to go to Alcala to study for the priesthood since it was obvious that God was calling him to serve in the Church.[34] This is precisely what he did.

Theological Studies

Over the next few years, the young John would enroll in preparatory courses of art, logic, and all the normal classes that other students of his age studied. In 1523, he received his bachelor's degree and remained in Alcala to continue his theological studies. The contact with the Dominicans at this university introduced him to St. Thomas Aquinas. In the future, he would often refer to Aquinas's writings, and

Aquinas's teachings would be the only doctrine taught at the University of Baeza founded by the saint.[35]

During these years, Erasmus of Rotterdam was a prominent figure in academic circles. In 1525 alone, more than five of his books were published, including his commentaries on the Gospels and the Epistles. St. John was very much attracted by his writings and later would also encourage his followers to read them.[36] However, Erasmus's positions would later take some questionable turns, especially after John had left the university.[37] The saint continued quoting him, but in a more cautious manner. John would also depart from Erasmus's teachings when he felt Erasmus was not interpreting the sacred texts correctly.[38] The prudence and good judgement of Master Avila can be seen here. He loved the Church and would not even think of ever departing from her teachings.

Ordination to the Priesthood

By the time St. John was ordained a priest in 1526, his parents had already died. He went back to his home town to offer Mass for them; and, as Granada mentions, "instead of the banquets and feasts that are usually done for such occasions, as one who already had higher thoughts, he fed twelve poor people whom he served and dressed himself."[39] He soon gave away his belongings, keeping but a simple change of clothes for himself, carrying out the Lord's command to His disciples when He sent them out to preach. Like them, St. John also trusted that he would never lack anything in life.[40]

Desire to Go on Mission to the New World

Soon after his ordination, St. John of Avila made his way to Seville. His intention was to serve where there was a greater need and where there was less recognition from the world. There, in Seville, he was hoping to meet up with the Dominican that had just been appointed as bishop of Tlaxcala in the New World so that he could accompany the bishop there.[41] Since those preparations would take some time, he remained in the city for a few months, sharing a simple house with a saintly priest, Fernando de Contreras. Together, they would help the poor, teach catechism to the children, and support each other in prayer.[42]

Decision to Remain in Spain

During those months that the two priests spent together, Contreras got to know the future saint. Spain was at a critical point in its history, having just recovered its last occupied territories from the Muslims in the last few decades and feeling the first attacks of the Reformation that Martin Luther had started in Germany. Aware that St. John had much to offer, his companion spoke with the archbishop of Seville so that he could convince St. John to stay in Seville. The archbishop had him preach in a church so that he could hear him;[43] and being impressed with him, he ordered St. John to stay in his archdiocese. Since it was under obedience that the archbishop asked him this, he complied.[44]

Apostle of Andalusia

The dedication of the young preacher was exemplary. He would preach in hospitals, schools, and even out in the open in main squares. His ministry took him to different cities throughout the archdiocese, such as Alcala de Guadaira, Jerez, Palma, and Ecija.[45] Luis of Granada dedicates a great portion of St. John's biography commenting on the preaching ministry of the saint, a great honor since Granada himself belonged to the Order of Preachers. What was so particular about St. John's method? More than a method, it was the intention: he wanted to wound hearts more than please ears, to proclaim the glory of God rather than the praise of men.[46] He sought only the salvation of souls[47] and would prepare for his preaching with prayer and tears,[48] the tears of a true father in sorrow for those who were living in sin.[49]

His sermons were clear and scriptural,[50] and they soon bore good fruit; however, they also gained him some enemies. Since he was known for preaching through his example—living a life of poverty and not accepting stipends—this caused conflicts with others. In Ecija, a rich and commercial city in Andalusia, St. John was scheduled to preach one day at the main church. Early that morning, the church was already filled with people waiting to listen to his sermon. As he was preparing to go up to the pulpit, another preacher who was commissioned to read a bull for that day told him that he was going to take St. John's place. St. John agreed to let him preach, but he went into another church in the outskirts of the city to preach the sermon he had prepared. Since most people followed St. John without waiting to hear what the bull commissioner had to say, the latter sought him out and slapped him in public in the main square of the city. The response of the saint was to kneel down and ask for his forgiveness.[51] Yet, those who were made uncomfortable with his preaching continued to persecute him, and "it was precisely clerics who denounced him to the Inquisition of Seville in 1531."[52]

A Prisoner of the Inquisition

The main accusations started in Ecija. According to those who turned St. John in, he had said in a sermon that the people burned by the Inquisition were martyrs. There were other charges as well: saying that the rich could not be saved, affirming to give a better interpretation of the Scriptures than St. Augustine, stating that Our Blessed Mother had committed venial sins, and recommending contemplative rather than vocal prayer. This last charge seems to have concerned the Inquisition the most since this was the age of the *alumbrados* (illuminated ones) in Spain. After a few months of investigations, his arrest was ordered.[53]

In 1532, St. John was sent to prison.[54] Although he did not want to defend himself, he was forced to respond. Esquerda gives a good summary of this process: "his responses are sincere, humble, clear . . . without giving in to servile fears, but trusting unconditionally the judgment of the Church (of which, as a good theologian, he was the first one to defend). He did not want to say anything against the five witnesses, but Divine Providence provided fifty-five who spoke on his behalf."[55] St. John also used these months that he was kept in custody to write and to reflect upon the Mystery of Christ. There, he said, he learned much more than in his many years of study.[56]

Eventually, the saint was absolved but not without having to clarify in his preaching, "under danger of excommunication,"[57] whatever might have been misunderstood, a decision that was customary at the time. His return to the pulpit was celebrated with music as if it were a major feast in that region.[58]

"*Maestro*" *Avila and His Priestly School*

St. John of Avila went to Cordoba in 1535 at the request of the bishop of that diocese. It was during these days that he met Fra Luis of Granada with whom he would enjoy a close friendship that would last for three decades. They both shared a passion for preaching, a ministry St. John was able to exercise freely in this diocese while he lived in a small hospital room. When another Dominican heard him preach, he said of the saint, "I have just heard St. Paul commenting upon himself."[59] Indeed, St. John always referred to the letters of St. Paul in his preaching and writings and tried to model his life after him. And, not unlike St. Paul, he also had several other priests who looked up to him for leadership and guidance.

In 1536, John of Avila moved to Granada where it is likely that he pursued the studies that would earn him the title of "Master." Starting in 1538, he is addressed as *Maestro Avila.*[60] The concept of an *escuela sacerdotal* (priestly school) associated with Master Avila was first coined by the saint's second biographer, Luis Muñoz.[61] The movement was so influential in Spain that similar currents of spirituality developed in other parts of Europe. This, in fact, seems to be what gave rise to what today we know as the "French School."[62]

What did the *Maestro's* movement look like? It certainly had some very clear characteristics. In Cordoba, where St. John gathered more than twenty disciples, he founded a center that lasted for almost ten years, until his followers found their way into religious communities. Esquerda explains, "John had given them concrete instructions: to go as a group (two by two), find lodging in hospitals or sacristies, not to receive stipends, give away whatever was offered to them, doing penance with their meals, taking with them some objects of devotion for the people (rosaries, etc.)."[63] It was a form of mission that they made available to bishops.[64] The main objective was to preach and to hear confessions.[65] The priests were known all throughout Spain "for their modesty, moderation in the way they dressed, their composure and for the outmost respect with which they carried themselves."[66] The model proved so effective that it was reproduced in the different cities of that region. It also led to the founding of several colleges.

Founding of Colleges

Given that the Church was in dire need of holy priests to respond to the Reformers—a theme that St. John really emphasized at the Council of Trent, as shall be seen later— the saint wanted to die founding colleges. In every city where he would spend some time, he tried to start one. He organized more than fifteen in cities like Jerez, Cordoba, Seville, and Ecija. The most important one was in Baeza. The Pope soon gave permission for that college to become a university; this took place in 1542. Besides instructing priests—or future priests—in academics, he was concerned about forming them as men of virtue. He wrote of this much-needed holistic formation in the recommendations he would give to the bishops at Trent.[67]

The colleges were a blessing for every city where they were founded. Granada mentions how, in Baeza, the saint's presence served to bring peace between different bands of people who had engaged in bloody encounters for generations.[68] His disciples, working at the university, continued to provide the spiritual presence that was needed there and, besides instructing the adults, they also made it a point to catechize children to sow the seeds of peace. The movement then looked very much the same wherever they went: they would try to create colleges for adults; and others, for children.[69] The children would be instructed with a special method that St. John had learned from Father Contreras.[70] He would later publish these materials under the title of *Doctrina Cristiana*.

Refusing Higher Offices

The activity of St. John of Avila through the southern part of Spain did not go unnoticed. He was admired and respected by those who knew him. In 1536, he was invited by the archbishop of Granada to minister in that archdiocese. It is said that initially, his preaching disappointed those at the university because of its simplicity. Yet, as soon as they paid attention to the content and realized his true wealth, he was even offered a canonry there. This he refused, but his preaching ministry bore abundant fruit. It was in Granada that the future saints John of God and Francis Borgia would be converted after hearing St. John's sermons.[71]

Avila renounced bishoprics and even the title of cardinal, which the Pope wanted to bestow on him. Always emphasizing the need to know oneself, he considered himself unworthy, "the worst of people," he would say. How can a person be honored, he would ask, when Jesus was reduced to humiliations and scorn on the Cross?[72] Yet, when one of St. John's disciples was chosen for a similar office, he would encourage him to trust God and to serve Him the best he could. This was the case, for example, when Francis Borgia was elected as general of the Jesuits, the second successor of St. Ignatius of Loyola. In a letter that he wrote to Borgia in 1566, he says (making reference to John 21:18, where Peter is told that he would be led where he does not want to go): "Admirable is the wisdom of the Lord, which knows how to mortify evil people with humiliations and give honor and high places to humble ones. Have patience, father, and trust in Him, who is almighty, for He will give you what you need for the position that He gave you, and us poor ones will help with our sighs, for your good is our good."[73]

St. John rejoiced when Ignatius founded the Jesuits. In a way, they were both trying to accomplish the same thing: to form holy priests who were committed to serving others and renewing the Church through their efforts and their example. He would say that he felt like a little kid who was trying to push a big rock up a hill, something that St. Ignatius had done with very little effort.[74] Many of St. John's disciples ended up joining the Society;[75] he had prepared them well to live the evangelical counsels by the way they lived together. He himself also considered joining the newly founded community, but his health did not permit it. At the end, he just continued collaborating with them.[76]

Last Years and Influence on Other Future Saints

Starting in 1551, the health of the *Maestro* began to decline.[77] He retired to a small house in the city of Montilla where he dedicated most of his time to prayer and writing. This is what his ministry consisted of in these last years of his life. It is said that his writings inaugurated the *Siglo de Oro* (golden century) of Spanish spiritual writers.[78] It is probably not an exaggeration, for St. Teresa of Avila did ask him to review the book of her *Life*[79] and recommended his sermons to some of the Carmelite priests who were working with her.[80] Traces of his thought can also be found in St. John of the Cross and in Felix Lope de Vega. Even saints like Francis de Sales, Alphonsus Liguori, and Anthony Claret make reference to his works in subsequent years.[81]

The physical ailments of St. John were many. Granada speaks of stomach and kidney problems, gout, pains in his arms and legs, and extreme fevers that did not leave him much strength.[82] Toward the end, he would get up only to preach for the solemnity of Corpus Christi or feasts of Our Lady, the two loves of his life.[83] To his disciples, though, he continued preaching through his patient example.[84] In his sermons, he had always emphasized frequent Communion.[85] Since it was in this that he found his strength, one of his disciples obtained permission from the Pope so that he could break the fast for Holy Communion due to his illness. It was granted by Paul IV in 1558.[86]

The Death of St. John of Avila

After years of suffering, St. John knew that his end was approaching. When the doctor confirmed this, he asked for someone to hear his confession and to give him the Extreme Unction. He also asked for the intercession of Our Lady and held fast to a crucifix that he was given. When one of his wealthy benefactors went to visit him to see what she could do for him, his response was, "Masses."[87] To the Jesuits who went to see him, he confided that he was afraid of the final judgment because of his many sins.[88] His humility and the knowledge that all was grace stayed with him through the end. He asked the Jesuits to bury him in their church. As

Granada writes, "since he loved them in life, he wanted to give them in death this token of his affection."[89] His *transitus* occurred on May 10, 1569.[90]

Upon hearing of his death, St. Teresa of Avila cried over the loss. She said that the Church had "lost a great column," and souls, a great refuge.[91] St. Thomas of Villanueva, the archbishop of Valencia who preceded him in death, had said of him that "ever since St. Paul there has not been another preacher of Christ who has obtained so many conversions."[92] One of his biographers would acknowledge that "never before in the history of Christian spirituality has there been a constellation of saints around one man."[93]

The Making of a Saint

Although St. John of Avila's saintly qualities were recognized by his contemporaries and the process of beatification was started soon after his death (1623-1628), it was not until 1894 that Pope Leo XIII actually enrolled him among the blessed ones. The reasons for the delay were basically financial and organizational. His disciples Francis Borgia and John of God belonged to religious communities who worked effectively for their early canonizations. In the case of St. John, the lack of coordination between the different dioceses and the change in administration within them proved to be a stumbling block.[94] In 1946, Pius XII named him Patron of the Spanish Secular Clergy; and in 1970, St. Paul VI finally canonized him. The latest honor arrived when Pope Benedict XVI declared him a Doctor of the Church on October 7, 2012.

The Witness of a Saintly Priest

There is no question that St. John of Avila exhibited heroic virtues throughout his life, yet he was always mindful of his lowly state. If there was anything good in his life, he would say it was because of the love of God. In his recommendation for the title of "Doctor" to be bestowed on the saint, Esquerda—a collaborator in the process on behalf of the Spanish bishops—mentions how St. John could be called the "doctor of the trust in the love of God and of Christian and priestly holiness."[95] St. John was very much aware of the power of God to transform the human person, and he personally could not take credit for the good he was able to accomplish. His saintly life, then, was merely a consequence of his openness to God's grace. His biographers agree that he would spend two hours of prayer in the morning and two more in the evening.[96] Strengthened by God's love, St. John could go about his duties without losing that perfect union with Him.[97]

As a spiritual guide, St. John would recommend practices to others that he himself lived. This was especially true when it came to priests, those whom he spent his life serving. It was because of his exemplary life that St. Paul VI decided to canonize him at the height of the priestly crisis. The added title of "Doctor of the Church" also tells us that his teachings are very relevant. After many years of studying the writings of Master Avila, Monsignor Esquerda can assert that "in very few other figures in the history of the Church can be found an exposition of Christian doctrine as complete as in St. John of Avila."[98] It is to his works and written ministry that we now turn.

Writings of St. John of Avila

Although St. John of Avila was a diocesan priest, the circumstances of his life allowed him to write much and to leave behind a rich legacy. After his death, his disciples would organize and publish his works.[99] Some have been translated into French and Italian, influencing the French and Italian schools of spirituality. A brief survey of his writings follows.

Treatise "Audi, filia"

Undoubtedly, the masterpiece of Master Avila is his *Audi, filia*. It has been translated into many different languages, and it is said that King Philip II of Spain kept a copy of it by his bed. According to the Archbishop of Toledo, Cardinal Astorga, with this work, the saintly priest "converted more souls than the number of letters contained in it."[100] Based on the words of Psalm 45, "Listen, my daughter, and understand" (Ps 45:11), the treatise offers suggestions for spiritual growth and discernment.

In 1527, one of Father John's disciples brought a young lady by the name of Sancha Carrillo to him so that he could hear her confession. She must have been talented and beautiful for there were plans for her to be part of the court of the newly wedded Queen Isabella. Yet, the moment she confessed to Father John of Avila, she received a new perspective on life. Instead of following through on the courtly life, she asked her parents to allow her to enter the convent or to live in a separate room of their house where she could pray and do penance. The parents opted for the latter and prepared a small house for her next to theirs, conditioned for the kind of life she wanted to live.[101] During this time, she asked the saint to give her some written suggestions for a rule of life that she could follow. He sent her a few pages; and soon after that, more pages followed. When the Master was imprisoned by the Inquisition in 1532, he gave definite shape to the work, to "his ideas on the mystery of our justification and incorporation in Christ."[102] He would continue adding to it throughout his life, even after the death of Sancha Carrillo in 1537.[103]

The troubles that the *Maestro* would face because of his ministry did not end with the imprisonment by the Inquisition. When the Count of Palma, Luis de Puerto Carrero, encouraged him to publish the treaty and offered to pay for the expenses, the saint prepared the manuscript. St. John wrote in the dedication: "The intent of this book is to give some teachings and Christian rules so that people who begin to serve God may, by his grace, carry out his will."[104] This was in 1546. However, that same year, a new session of the Council of Trent was convoked. Since it was known that the Council would treat of justification, the Master decided to wait until the final decrees were published in order to incorporate the bishops' decisions into his work. Somehow, though, a publisher obtained a copy of the work and, without the author's permission, he published it in 1556 with the title *Avisos y reglas chistianas para los que desean seruir a Dios, aprouechando en el camino espiritual. Compuestas por el Maestro Auila, sobre el verso de Dauid: "Audi, filia, et vide et inclina aurem tuam"* (Recommendations and Christian Rules for Those Who Desire to Serve God Walking the Spiritual Path. Written by Master Avila on the Verse from David: "Listen, O Daughter, See and Incline thy Ear").[105] In 1559, the *Cathalogus* of the Inquisition was published; and St. John's work was on the list of forbidden books. This was not surprising since works that considered the Sacred Scriptures, prayer, or the Sacraments lent themselves to attacks on the Church from the Reformers.[106]

Upon the conclusion of the Council, the Master promptly corrected the manuscript. In 1565, the Bishop of Cordoba gave his approval so that it could be printed; nonetheless, the Inquisition wanted to review it again before its publication. Despite their favorable review, they did offer some slight suggestions to the author. He was going to work on these revisions when death came to him in 1569. The final version was prepared by his disciples and published in 1574. There were different printings and different titles even within the same year; but since then, the final text of the *Audi, filia* was "definitively fixed."[107]

The work was soon translated into other languages. In the Foreword to *Audi, filia* within *The Classics of Western Spirituality*, Archbishop Francisco Javier Martínez Fernández, the Archbishop of Granada, mentions how the French edition had an impact on figures like St. Francis de Sales, St. Vincent de Paul, and Cardinal Bérulle. He also states:

> Most strikingly, in my view, is the English translation of 1620, almost fifty years after publication of the definitive edition of the *Audi, filia* in Spanish. Once again, the church was facing a crisis, this time in England. Not only was the unity of the church broken, but Catholics were beset by persecutions and penalties of various kinds, including confiscation of property, fines, imprisonment, and even death. . . . The translator . . . affirms that he can find no better book for their instruction and consolation "in these difficult times."[108]

It is understandable, then, that the *Audi, filia* is considered "one of the main contributions to the religious thought of the sixteenth century."[109]

Spanish Translations of Treatises and Prayers

Besides conceiving the format of his *Audi, filia* while he was in prison, the Master also translated the *Imitation of Christ* into Spanish during that time.[110] Although his name does not appear in the 1536 publication—perhaps to avoid further complications with the Inquisition—experts have identified the doctrine in the prologue as being the saint's.[111] Even though there were already translations that had come out in Spanish—the first one being in 1482—the *Maestro* explains in the prologue why he took it upon himself to offer a new edition (besides overcoming the boredom of the prison):

> Because from such a fountain comes water so clear as to bear so much fruit, it was turbid and almost full of mud for not having a clear and proper romance close to the Latin as it called for, I was moved with zeal for this precious pearl that was so darkened, and because of that so little enjoyed, to take it out again, making it closer to the Latin in which it was written by the first author. I removed what in the previous book was not conforming to Latin; I clarified that which was obscure, so that you do not stumble upon anything. I removed what was superfluous, I added what was lacking. This way, with the Lord's grace, I worked to present to you this mirror so that you can look at yourself.[112]

In later years, given his love for the Eucharist and for the feast of Corpus Christi, he would also translate the *Pange lingua* and the *Sacris solemniis* into Spanish so that they could be sung by the people.[113]

"Treatise on the Love of God"

The Apostle of Andalusia was, above all, a priest. After preaching, though, he would gather his ideas and organize them for future use. This is how most of his treatises were born.[114] In 1596, one of his disciples, Father Juan Diaz, published the saint's *Tratado del amor de Dios*. There is no question that it was his. In it can be found his famous *miradas* (gazes) that were already a theme in his writings ever since the *Audi, filia* and which would appear later in the French School of the seventeen century: the gaze of Christ to the Father and the gaze of Christ to humanity. Such a gaze was an expression of the great love that Christ the priest had for His people.[115] In the saint's own words: "The love of Christ is not born from the perfection that is found in us but in what He has, which is gazing in the Eternal Father."[116] The treatise ends with the hope that was characteristic of the Master's writings: "If you truly believe that the Father gave you His Son, trust that He will give you everything else, for everything is less . . . . In life and in death He is your true friend."[117]

Monsignor Esquerda sees this work as being a summary of St. John of Avila's teachings and beliefs. He says:

> His treatise on the love of God is a jewel of theological literature in the Spanish language. His love of neighbor was the expression of the priestly ministry; he felt the problems of others as his own and he was helped by three things: looking at himself (his own misery and God's gifts), looking at Christ the savior of all, looking at the mercies that God does for others. All the work of

John of Avila aims at this Christian charity. From there arose his preoccupation for Christian and integral human education, his concern for social problems, for the reform of the secular state (as he would say), for the reform of the clerical state and even for details like those of having invented some utensils for making easier the extraction of water from the ground.[118]

He also suggests the possibility that this treatise inspired St. Francis de Sales to write his own since he uses the same title and even quotes St. John in it.[119] Whether or not that was the case, the influence of the Master in the French movement cannot be denied.

"Treatise on the Priesthood"

The *Tratado sobre el sacerdocio* was first published in 1950. It is a copy of an incomplete manuscript that was found in Mexico, most likely where the Spanish Jesuits took it in the sixteenth century.[120] In this treatise, St. John of Avila offers a generous synopsis of the patristic theology on priesthood that was known up to his day. Following the teachings of these Church Fathers, he encourages priests to be mindful of their dignity.

Toward the end of the treatise, St. John offers specific recommendations for pastors, preachers, and confessors. He also speaks of renewal through the implementation of the decrees of the Council of Trent, emphasizing how important it is for those not to be ignored. The teachings of Master Avila found in this *Tratado* are very pertinent for the spirituality of diocesan priests.

Writings for the Council of Trent

The Council of Trent—held between the years of 1545 and 1563—took place during the mature life of St. John of Avila. When the session in 1551 was about to begin, Archbishop Pedro Guerrero, the archbishop of Granada and a former classmate of the saint during his time in Alcala, wanted to take the Master along with him as a consultant. By this time, however, Father John's health was starting to decline, and he opted for writing some recommendations for the archbishop and the council fathers. This first document— there was a second one—is commonly known as the *Primer Memorial para el Concilio de Trento*, but the author gave it the title of *Reformación del Estado Eclesiástico* (The Reform of the Clerical State).[121] The text was extremely helpful and important for the work of the Council, as St. Paul VI acknowledged in St. John's canonization homily in 1970. When Guerrero read the recommendations, the Holy Father states, there was great applause from all the participants.[122]

What were those recommendations? As the title suggested, there needs to be a reform of the Church at all levels, especially within her sacred ministers. It was important for everyone to embrace the reform since, as St. John writes, "by a drop of water, the taste of the water in the entire sea is known."[123] He suggested the founding of seminaries throughout the world to form the future clerics, something that did not yet exist in those days. And, for those seeking to enter: "may entrance be not easy nor the life without rules, so that those who seek earthly things can be excluded and those who are able to be ministers of God can be admitted."[124] He gave specific recommendations for their formation and suggested, as well, the erection of colleges for confessors and preachers similar to the ones he had founded throughout Spain. He even conceived methods for the endowment of such institutions.[125] His concern, then, was the holistic education of God's ministers. This is, in a way, the beginning of what today we call ongoing permanent formation of the clergy.[126]

The second *Memorial* came exactly ten years later, in 1561. The Master entitled it *"Causas y remedios de las herejías"* (Causes and Remedies Against Heresies) because the influence of the Reformation was being felt throughout Christendom. St. John knew that the loose life of the clergy—both of bishops and priests—was to blame; and, as Monsignor Esquerda mentions, he addresses this "with a vision that is constructive, serene, experienced and within reach. Sometimes it is noticeable that he desires a better remedy, but is content with that which is possible. He is not afraid to speak of the reform that the Pope himself must do, but he does it with the same truth, love and reverence as the same brave reforms that he proposes."[127]

Writings for the Synod in Toledo

After the Council of Trent ended, it was the duty of the bishops to implement it in their local dioceses. To this effect, the bishops of Spain gathered in Toledo in 1565 and sought, once again, the Master's guidance in their work. St. John's *Advertencias al Concilio de Toledo* was written for Cristobal de Rojas, the bishop of Cordoba who had the task of leading the synod, and was very timely in continuing the much-needed reform. Monsignor Esquerda notes:

John speaks very clearly (his writings were not for the public, but for the council Fathers), he speaks of what he knows (relationship with priests, founding of colleges, catechesis, collaborating in social issues, etc.), he speaks well documented on Scripture, Tradition, Fathers, councils, saints, theology . . . And, above all, he speaks with humility and with the sense of the Church.[128]

He emphasizes that the reform must start with bishops, who are to set an example for everyone; and then, he gives specific comments on the different decrees of the Council.[129]

Spiritual Conferences

As mentioned earlier, the formation of priests was one of the Apostle of Andalusia's main preoccupations. He would speak with them to instruct and exhort them on the way of holiness. His words were so profound that many wanted to hear them; phrases spoken by him continued to be repeated in different cities, such as when he said that "he would rather see students with callouses on their knees from praying than from bad eyes from too much studying."[130] Certainly not the only ones he gave, there are sixteen *Pláticas* that have been preserved from his works: fourteen for priests and two for religious sisters.[131]

Some of his conferences are addressed to Jesuit priests (*Pláticas* 3 and 4) and to secular priests from different dioceses. In them, he gives them recommendations for hearing confessions and for living out priesthood to the fullest. They were so valued by those who read them that his biographer Luis Muñoz enthusiastically wrote that "they should be printed on golden plaques and placed in churches' tabernacles, so that they could serve as mirrors in which priests could see themselves."[132]

Sermons

The latest collection of St. John of Avila's *Obras completas* offers a total of eighty-two sermons, which include some not present in the early editions. Many of them are on the Blessed Sacrament and Our Lady, two of the Master's favorite topics. There are others on the Holy Spirit[133] and many on saints or for major feasts. The collection closes with one St. John preached for a funeral.[134] Not surprisingly, the priestly theme comes up in many of the sermons.[135] His great love for the priesthood served St. John to see the Scriptures through those lenses.

"Christian Doctrine"

In the Master's *Doctrina cristiana* were published all the different texts he and his disciples used to instruct children in the faith.[136] The text is meant to be sung; and it covers the commandments, prayers, beatitudes, gifts of the Holy Spirit, virtues, and all the essential teachings of the Church. In the last section, he also included questions that catechists could use with different groups.[137]

The following is a sample of the original Spanish verses. The cadence and the simplicity with which the Master wrote these catechetical works are exquisite:

Oídnos vos,

por amor de Dios.

A todos los padres

y a las madres

quiero hablar

y avisar;

y a los señores,

grandes y menores,

el peligro y afán

en que todos están,

y digo con amor

en el nombre del Señor:

[Enseñar] por caridad

[la doctrina de la verdad]

a vuestros hijitos

desde chiquitos

y haceldos [sic] venir

[a saber servir]

a nuestro Señor Jesucristo . . . . [138]

Biblical Commentaries

It is said that St. Ignatius of Loyola paid St. John of Avila quite a compliment. Being informed of St. John's interest in joining the Jesuits, St. Ignatius exclaimed: "I wish he did, we would carry him on our shoulders, like the Ark of the Covenant, for being the archive of the sacred scripture, for if it ever got lost he alone would restore it to the Church."[139] Perhaps, an endearing exaggeration, but certainly a tribute to Master Avila's knowledge of Scripture. Experts have found

up to 5,298 Scripture quotations in his works; and those
who knew him all testify that, just by looking at a passage,
he could speak on it for more than two hours.[140] The saint,
however, had no ambition of being a great author and publishing his works. His concern was pastoral: he wanted people
to understand the Scriptures so that they could put them
into practice.[141]

Two major works of his biblical endeavors survive: the
Lecciones sobre la epístola a los gálatas (Commentary on the Letter to the Galatians) and *Lecciones sobre la primera canónica de
san Juan* (Commentary on the First Letter of John). Muñoz
describes how the *Maestro* would give these lectures in the
evenings at one of the parish churches.[142] The saint's explana-
tions are simple and familial.[143] Yet, the insights he would
see in the text were profound and of great value for the
life of the people and the Church. For example, commenting on Galatians 4:13-14, where St. Paul praises the people
for accepting him despite his physical ailments, St. John of
Avila says:

> [The apostle] is grateful that they overcame that
> temptation of doubting on the gospel in order not to
> receive him: seeing that the minister was sick and fragile,
> persecuted and tired, etc. This endears the Apostle
> much, and for a good reason; this lets us know how the
> Christian, in order to receive the Gospel and the other
> benefits that come from the hand of God, must not
> stumble that the minister that comes to him is a bad
> one, that bad things or inconveniences have occurred
> because of the fault of the ministers. He must look at the
> principal author, for He wanted to govern him this way.
> Those who put their eyes on the ministers and their value

> err and reject the ways of God and His providence, as we
> see in the children of Israel . . . who put their eyes on Saul
> [making reference to 1 Sm 10:27].[144]

And he continues:

> To convert the world and to preach the Gospel, He
> takes as instruments people who are so low, and these
> he puts in great tribulations, so that they and we not
> trust in human beings, but in God [and gives 2 Cor 1:9
> in Latin]. . . . And this is according to the wisdom of
> God: that we may not hang great things as one's faith and
> God's promises on people, but on who God is (1 Cor
> 1:9), and that the glory may be His: *Ut non glorietur omnis
> caro* (1 Cor 1:29), etc.[145]

Letters

Besides the *Audi, filia*, the letters of St. John of Avila
are the other works that have had the most printings. His
disciples published the first edition in 1578, nine years after
the Master's death. The collection consisted of 147 letters.[146]
Unfortunately, these editors eliminated all names, dates,
and places from the letters before they published them.
Though some of this data has been recovered, those trying
to learn more about the details of the life of St. John and his
relationships with others sometimes do not find much help
in them.[147] Letters that have been found after the work of
those first disciples do reveal more information. The latest
edition of the *Epistolario*—published in 2003—consists of
263 letters.[148]

Fra Luis of Granada sees in the saint's letters a resolute desire to save souls. Of this part of the Master's ministry, he writes:

> In these letters we will see the special faculty and grace that our Lord had given him. Because being so many and so varied the subjects of which he would write as were the needs of the people, to all of them he would respond with so much purpose as if that is all he had to do. In this way he comforts the sad, encourages the weak, awakens the lukewarm, strengthens the fainthearted, helps those who are tempted, cries for the fallen ones, humbles those who brag about themselves.[149]

St. John would write them in one sitting and without going back to correct them, yet they "expose a simple and solid doctrine, without empty phrases; it is a vibrant style, as from someone who is 'tempered' to say what is needed."[150]

Of the letters written to priests, Monsignor Esquerda explains, "almost all the priestly problems appear in his epistolary. . . . He explains plans for study, for the spiritual life, for apostolic work, for social endeavors. He adorns his recommendations with comparisons and, sometimes, with a fine humor of healthy humanism."[151] "Some of them," he goes on to say, "could deserve the title of treatises of post-conciliar reform."[152] Yet, the reform he always sought was one that could be brought about through holiness, especially that of the prelates and priests.

Other Minor Writings

The *Obras Completas* of St. John of Avila includes a series of reflections and meditations that have come to light as late as the year 2000.[153] The authorship of some of them—like the *Ecce Homo*, who some people attribute to Fra Luis of Granada[154]—is disputed, but there seem to be enough reasons for them to be included among his works. These writings—among them, brief treatises on the Blessed Sacrament and the Beatitudes[155]—as well as his compositions in verse, his prayers, and his "Rules of the Spirit" (*Reglas de espíritu*),[156] open another window into the soul and thought of the Master.

In the pages that follow, the works of St. John of Avila will be cited generously. His teachings have been relegated to the darkness of the unknown for too long. In declaring him a Doctor of the universal Church, the Church has decided that this spiritual master has something relevant to say to us today. Being the first diocesan priest among this illustrious body of doctors, St. John of Avila becomes their primary benefactor. Despite the difference in context and challenges we face in our day, the insights and the holiness of this humble witness can be very helpful for diocesan priests in understanding our own spirituality. In the Mass of canonization for St. John of Avila, St. Paul VI called him a "contemporary saint." By this, he meant that the years between the Apostle of Andalusia and us today are not an obstacle to understanding the one priestly heart that Christ has placed in those he calls to ministry in every age. Jesus, indeed, is the same "yesterday, today, and forever" (Heb 13:8).

NOTES

1.   See Louis Bouyer, *Introduction to the Spiritual Life*, trans. Mary P. Ryan (Notre Dame: Christian Classics, 2013), 271 (published originally in French in 1960); Myles Rearden, "Concerning Priestly Spirituality," *The Furrow* (Ireland, 1990): 281.

2.   This view is still held by some people in the Church today. See William H. Shannon, "Priestly Spirituality: 'Speaking Out *for the Inside*,'" in *The Spirituality of the Diocesan Priest*, ed. Donald B. Cozzens (Collegeville, MN: Liturgical Press, 1997), 88.

3.   See John Paul II, "Vita Consecrata" (1996) in *Acta Apostolicae Sedis* (*AAS*) 88 (1996), 377-486. English translation: Vatican City: Libreria Editrice Vaticana, 1996, n. 93; Paul Murray, O.P., *The New Wine of Dominican Spirituality: A Drink Called Happiness* (New York: Burns & Oates, 2006), 112.

4.   Jordan Aumann, *Spiritual Theology* (London: Continuum, 2006), 17.

5.   Ibid., 18.

6.   Ibid.

7.   "Lumen Gentium" in *The Conciliar and Post Conciliar Documents*, new rev. ed., ed. Austin Flannery, O.P., vol. 1 (New York: Costello, 1998), n. 10 (from here on, abbreviated as *LG*). All Vatican II documents are taken from this same volume.

8.   John Paul II, "*Christifideles Laici*" (1988) in *AAS* 81 (1989), 393-521, English trans. Boston: Pauline Books and Media, 1988, nn. 17, 43 (emphasis added; from here on abbreviated as *CL*).

9.   Vatican II, *Presbyterorum Ordinis* (1965), sec. 13-14 (emphasis added; from here on, abbreviated as *PO*).

10.   Pope Francis has reiterated this teaching for all the faithful in his exhortation *Gaudete et Exsultate*: "We are all called to be holy by living our lives with love and by bearing witness in everything we do, wherever we find ourselves." *Gaudete et Exsultate* (2018), sec. 14, http://w2.vatican.va/content/francesco/en/apost_exhortations/documents/papa-francesco_esortazione-ap_20180319_gaudete-et-exsultate.html (accessed May 4, 2018). See George Niederauer: Ministry "is the very 'stuff' of [the priest's] asceticism," in "A Ministerial Spirituality: Reflections on Priesthood," *Church* 7 (Summer 1991): 26.

11.   See *LG*, sec. 11-13. The threefold ministry in Christ and all the baptized goes back to Apostolic times. Even at the Council of Trent, we find references to it. It seems that the Church avoided mentioning it in the future because Calvin and some of the other Protestants emphasized it in their preaching and their writings; it was not until Vatican II, with the new ecumenical movement, that the Church began to refer to it again.

See David Bohr, *The Diocesan Priest: Consecrated and Sent* (Collegeville, MN: Liturgical Press, 2009), 22, 63.

12.   See Most Rev. Erio Castelucci, Archbishop-Abbot of Modena-Nonantola: *"Presbyterorum Ordinis*: Fifty Years On. Origin, Development and Current Relevance," Address, Convention "One Vocation, One Formation, One Mission," Congregation for the Clergy, Rome, Italy, November 19-20, 2015.

13.   John Paul II, *Pastores Dabo Vobis* (1992) in *AAS* 84 (1992): 657-804. English trans. London: Catholic Truth Society, 1992, sec. 24 (from here on, abbreviated as *PDV*). There are also similarities in what the Pope says about priests and married couples when it comes to their faithfulness to their vocations and the graces found within them. In *Pastores Dabo Vobis*, he speaks of "*a vocation 'within' the priesthood* . . . [for] God continues to call and send forth, revealing his saving plan in the historical development of the priest's life and the life of the Church and of society" (sec. 70, emphasis in the original). In *Familiaris Consortio*, he writes: "God, who called the couple *to* marriage, continues to call them *in* marriage. In and through the events, problems, difficulties and circumstances of everyday life, God comes to them, revealing and presenting the concrete 'demands' of their sharing in the love of Christ for His Church in the particular family, social and ecclesial situation in which they find themselves." See John Paul II, *Familiaris Consortio* (1981), sec. 51 in *AAS* 74 (1982), 81-191. English trans. Boston: Pauline Books and Media, 1981 (emphasis in the original; from here on, abbreviated as *FC*).

14.   Thomas McGovern, *Priestly Identity: A Study in the Theology of the Priesthood* (Dublin: Four Courts Press, 2002), 7.

15.   Ibid., 8-9. In the United States, the national conference of bishops commissioned a comprehensive series of studies that could help them address the crisis during those years. See Andrew Greeley, *The Catholic Priest in the United States: Sociological Investigations* (Washington, D.C.: United States Catholic Conference, 1972); John Tracy Ellis, ed. *The Catholic Priest in the United States: Historical Investigations* (Collegeville, MN: Saint John University Press, 1971); *Spiritual Renewal of the American Priesthood* (Washington, D.C.: United States Catholic Conference, 1973); *The Report of the Bishop's Ad Hoc Committee for Priestly Life and Ministry* (Washington, D.C.: United States Catholic Conference, 1974). At the universal level, St. Paul VI also responded by including "The Ministerial Priesthood" as one of the topics at the 1971 Synod of Bishops to address the crisis, a synod that was originally supposed to touch only on "Justice in the World." It is the only Synod that has addressed two different topics at the same time. The theology and the spirituality of the diocesan priest would later be developed by St. John Paul II in his Post-Synodal Exhortation *Pastores Dabo Vobis* contributing this way to a renewed and more solid understanding of the priesthood.

16. See Francisco Martín Fernández and José Carlos Martín de la Hoz, *La formación sacerdotal: Historia y vida* (Madrid: San Pablo, 2014), 81-101.

17. See Jordan Aumann, *Christian Spirituality in the Catholic Tradition*, 153-56, 162-68, 233-34 (from here on abbreviated as *Christian Spirituality*). In Spain those who subscribed to the ideas of Quietism were known as *alumbrados* (the "illuminated ones"). See Biographical information by Sala and Martín in *San Juan de Ávila: Obras Completas*, eds. L. Sala Balust and F. Martín Hernández, vol. 1, 2000, Reprint (Madrid: Biblioteca de Autores Cristianos, 2007), 276-80 (from here on, abbreviated as *OC*).

18. See *PO*, sec. 4-6, 13-14.

19. See Apostolic Act for the canonization of St. John of Avila: "Porque si la Iglesia, afligida por aquel entonces con muchas dificultades, al surgir las herejías por todas partes, y también caídas en cierta languidez la piedad y la disciplina, se robusteció sobre todo en España con la virtud de este bienaventurado varón, confía que su santidad, proclamada por la suprema Silla de Pedro, animará a los Sacerdotes, para que conscientes de su dignidad acomoden su vida según todas las exigencias, criterios y normas de la virtud. De este modo podrán iluminar a los fieles como luz puesta sobre el candelero y apartarlos de la corrupción de las malas costumbres," n. 2 (May 31, 1970), in *OC*, vol. 1, 349.

20. An effort has been made to see how the spirituality of the diocesan priest is understood and spelled out in the different continents. The research was limited to sources in English and Spanish and, to some degree, Italian. Spain seems to be the country that has done more reflection on the subject, which probably points to the fruit of the saint's work in that land. Besides having had congresses on the writings and the spirituality of St. John of Avila on multiple occasions ("Semanas Avilistas" in 1952 and 1969, and international congresses in the years 2000 and 2013), scholars from that country also held a congress specifically on the spirituality of the diocesan priest. See Ignacio Oñatibia Audela, "La espiritualidad presbiteral en su evolución histórica," in *La espiritualidad del presbítero diocesano secular* (Madrid: EDICE, 1987), 23-58. Another serious exposition was published in 2005 in that country by Florentino Muñoz Muñoz. See "Espiritualidad del sacerdote diocesano secular (I)," *Seminarios* 175 (2005): 65-102. (Parts II-IV were published in subsequent issues: II in 176, pp. 175-216; III in 177, pp. 321-367; IV in 178, pp. 463-489). Writings in other countries include: (Italy) Erio Castellucci, ed., *La Spiritualità Diocesana: il cammino nello Spirito della Chiesa particolare*, Unione Apostolica del Clero (Roma: Elledici, 2004); (India) Fr. Abraham Kadaplackal, S.D.B., *The Spirituality of the Diocesan Priest* (Bandra: St. Paul Press, 2010); (Australia) Frank Devoy, *The Spirituality of Diocesan Priests: Bearers of the Incarnate Face of God*, Australian Catholic Bishops Conference (Fyshwick: Kings Printing, 2012); (Ghana) Peter Addai-Mensah, *Do Diocesan Priests Have a Spirituality?: A Ghanian View* (Takoradi: St. Francis Press, 1997); (Argentina) José

María Recondo, "La vida espiritual del sacerdote diocesano secular. Rasgos para un perfil," *Pastores* 11:31 (Diciembre 2004): 60-85; (Mexico) Rafael González, "Hacia una espiritualidad del clero diocesano, a la luz de las enseñanzas de San Rafael Guízar y Valencia, Quinto Obispo de Veracruz, *Ecclesia* 21:1 (2007): 33-41; (United States) George A. Aschenbrenner, S.J., *Quickening the Fire in Our Midst: The Challenge of Diocesan Priestly Spirituality* (Chicago: Loyola Press, 2002) and Donald B. Cozzens, ed., *The Spirituality of the Diocesan Priest* (Collegeville, MN: Liturgical Press, 1997).

21.   Most of the content on the life and works of St. John of Avila in this section is taken from chapters one and two of the thesis "Diocesan Priestly Spirituality in the Writings of St. John of Avila with Special Application to the Church in the United States" presented for the Licentiate Degree by the author of this work at the Pontifical University of St. Thomas Aquinas (Angelicum) in June 2014.

22.   The year of his birth is debated. Some sources say 1500. His *Obras completas* settle for 1499 and point as evidence to a picture of the saint in the monastery of *Encarnación* in Granada, a place where he often ministered. The inscription on the picture says that he died in 1569 at the age of 70. See Sala and Martín in *OC*, vol. 1, 17. The "Estudio biográfico" offered in this first volume of St. John's works is the most reliable one. Luis Sala Balust was the author who published the first edition of the *Obras completas* in 1952. Francisco Martín Hernández continued building on Sala's research to produce this final critical edition.

23.   Ibid., 15, 18.

24.   *San Juan de Ávila: Escritos Sacerdotales*, ed. Juan Esquerda Bifet (Madrid: Biblioteca de Autores Cristianos, 2012), xvi (from here on, cited as *Escritos Sacerdotales*). See Sala and Martín, *OC*, vol. 1, 18.

25.   See Sala and Martín, *OC*, vol. 1, 19, 32, 132, 150, 152, 275. The family's name also points to this. Jewish converts in Spain would often take on the name of a city as their family name.

26.   José Luis Martínez Gil, ed. *Proceso de beatificación del Maestro Juan de Ávila* (Madrid: Biblioteca de Autores Cristianos, 2004), 123-24. The witness also says that both parents were "christianos viejos limpios"—that is, that they did not have Jewish roots. This, however, is something that he had only heard from others. Bauptista was sixty years old when the testimony was taken in 1624, so there is no way he could have known them since they were both deceased by the time the saint was ordained in 1526. It was probably customary for people to hide their Jewish ancestry, given the environment they lived in; and it is also not unlikely that the family's history was "purified" by the faithful as not to "stain" the name of such a noble man who was being put forward for canonization.

27.   See Sala and Martín, *OC*, vol. 1, 20.

28.   Ibid., 22-23.

29. Luis de Granada, O.P., *Vida del padre maestro Juan de Ávila*, 2nd ed. (Madrid: Edibesa, 2010), 32 (the biography first appeared in 1588. Since then, it has gone through multiple reprints. The present edition is acknowledged to come from Granada's *Obras completas*, vol. 16). Unless otherwise noted, all translations from Spanish to English are the author's. NB: Both Granada and Avila write in sixteenth century Spanish. Quotes from these authors will necessarily reflect some differences from today's usage.

30. Ibid.

31. See Sala and Martín, *OC*, vol. 1, 25.

32. Ibid.

33. Ibid. It is possible that St. John of Avila might have professed simple vows with the Dominicans when he was intending to go the New World with the newly appointed bishop of Tlaxcala (Mexico), the Dominican Julián Garcés. See Sala and Martín, *OC*, vol. 1, 29, 31. However, this is unlikely. Dominicans are called to live in community, and the saint never lived with Dominicans. If he had professed vows with them, Fra Luis of Granada would have mentioned that in the biography he wrote or in some of his other writings. The fact that he refers to him as a friend and a spiritual father and not as a fellow Dominican discards that possibility.

34. Granada, 32.

35. Sala and Martín, *OC*, vol. 1, 26-27.

36. Ibid.

37. Sala and Martín, *OC*, vol. 1, 27. Jordan Aumann also explains: "The humanism of Erasmus, Lefèvre and their companions has been severely criticized by many Catholic historians, in spite of the fact that educated Catholics of the sixteenth century found much sound instruction and guidance in the devotional treatises composed by these men. . . . There are, however, several good reasons for the criticism of the Christian humanists. First, in their zeal for a 'new theology' which was based exclusively on Scripture and the Fathers of the Church, they rejected all the theological wisdom of the Middle Ages and also weakened, unwittingly perhaps, the authority of the magisterium of the Church. Secondly, through their intensive study of the Greek and Latin classics they formed an erroneous opinion concerning man's inherent goodness, with the result that they underestimated the effects of original sin and man's need for mortification and self-denial. Thirdly, the very fact that Luther spoke approvingly of some of the theses of the humanists was sufficient to discredit them, just as Tauler and Gerson became somewhat suspect among Catholics because Luther quoted from their writings. Thus, by an odd twist of events, the Christian humanism that attempted to reform the Church and renew the Christian life became a victim of its own excesses and helped to set the scene for the division of the Church." *Christian Spirituality*, 184.

38. See Lope Rubio Parrado and Luis Rubio Morán, *San Juan de Ávila, Maestro y Doctor* (Salamanca: Ediciones Sígueme, 2012), 25.

39. Granada, 33.

40. Ibid., 37.

41. Ibid., 129.

42. Sala and Martín, *OC,* vol. 1, 29-31.

43. Ibid., 31-32.

44. Granada, 130. Some authors see this as another consequence of Avila's Jewish background since the Spanish Crown had decreed that no "new Christians" should go to the Indies as missionaries. See Sala and Martín, *OC,* vol. 1, 32. However, this cannot be ascertained. The country presented enough reasons to keep such a preacher there.

45. Granada, 131.

46. Ibid., 55.

47. Ibid., 37.

48. Ibid., 65.

49. Ibid., 46.

50. Esquerda, *Escritos Sacerdotales,* xxv.

51. Sala and Martín, *OC,* vol. 1, 33, 35.

52. Esquerda, *Escritos Sacerdotales,* xix. See Sala and Martín, *OC,* vol. 1, 35.

53. Sala and Martín, *OC,* vol. 1, 35-38.

54. Ibid., 38.

55. Esquerda, *Escritos Sacerdotales,* xix.

56. Granada, 118.

57. Esquerda, *Escritos Sacerdotales,* xx.

58. Sala and Martín, *OC,* vol. 1, 47.

59. Esquerda, *Escritos Sacerdotales,* xxi.

60. Sala and Martín, *OC,* vol. 1, 68.

61. Luis Muñoz, *Vida y virtudes del venerable varón el P. Maestro Juan de Ávila, predicador apostólico; con algunos elogios de las virtudes y vidas de algunos de sus más principales discípulos* (1635), in *Vidas del padre maestro Juan de Ávila,* ed. Luis Sala Balust (repr., Barcelona: Flors, 1964), Biblioteca Virtual Miguel de Cervantes: http://bib.cervantes-virtual.com/servlet/SirveObras/78038402103470573565679/index.htm (accessed March 15, 2014).

62. Juan Esquerda Bifet, "Escuela sacerdotal española del siglo XVI. Juan de Ávila (1499-1569)," *Anthologica Annua* 17 (Roma, 1969), 52-54 (from here on cited as "Escuela sacerdotal").

63. Esquerda, *Escritos Sacerdotales,* xxxi. See Sala and Martín, *OC,* vol. 1, 102-06.

64. Ibid.

65. Granada, 132.

66. Muñoz, lib. 1, cap. 20.

67. Esquerda, *Escritos Sacerdotales,* xxiii-xxiv.

68. Granada, 135.

69. Ibid., 136, 134.

70. See Sala and Martín, *OC*, vol. 1, 76.

71. Ibid., 64-66, 71-73.

72. Esquerda, *Escritos Sacerdotales*, xxv-xxvi. The reference to the crucified Christ was repeatedly mentioned in his sermons and is found in most of his writings. In fact, most paintings of the saint portray him gazing at a crucifix.

73. Letter 192 in *San Juan de Ávila, Epistolario: Obras completas*, eds. L. Sala Balust and F. Martín Hernández, vol. 4 (Madrid: Biblioteca de Autores Cristianos, 2003), 641.

74. Sala and Martín, *OC*, vol. 1, 143-44.

75. Granada, 153.

76. Sala and Martín, *OC*, vol. 1, 150-53, 165-66.

77. Ibid., 291.

78. Esquerda, *Escritos Sacerdotales*, xxvii.

79. Muñoz, lib. 1, cap. 27. See Sala and Martín, *OC*, vol. 1, 284-87.

80. Juan Esquerda Bifet, "El doctorado de San Juan de Ávila," *Compartir en Cristo Blog*, June, 2010, http://www.compartirencristo.files.wordpress.com/2010/06/juan-avila-doctorado.doc, 11 (accessed December 6, 2013).

81. Ibid., 14.

82. Granada, 113.

83. Ibid., 116.

84. Muñoz, lib. 2, cap. 3.

85. Granada, 123.

86. Ibid., 125.

87. Ibid., 166.

88. Sala and Martín, *OC*, vol. 1, 298.

89. Granada, 168.

90. Ibid., 171.

91. Muñoz, lib. 3, cap. 25.

92. Esquerda, *Escritos Sacerdotales*, xxxviii.

93. Baldomero Jiménez Duque, *El Maestro Juan de Ávila* (Madrid: Biblioteca de Autores Cristianos, 1988), 220.

94. See Introduction by Manuel Gómez Ríos in Martínez, *Proceso de beatificación*, xii-xiii.

95. "Bien pudiera calificarse de *Doctor de la confianza en el amor de Dios y de la santidad cristiana y sacerdotal.*" Esquerda, "El doctorado de San Juan de Ávila," 21.

96. Granada, 102; Muñoz, lib. 3, cap. 14. This was an age in which contemplative prayer was very much emphasized as can be seen in the lives of St. Teresa of Avila, St. Ignatius of Loyola, and St. John of the Cross. The fact that St. John of Avila never really served as a parish priest gave him the luxury to do this as well.

97.   Granada, 171.

98.   Juan Esquerda Bifet, *Introducción a la doctrina de San Juan de Ávila* (Madrid: Biblioteca de Autores Cristianos, 2000), xiii. From here on, abbreviated as *Introducción a la doctrina.*

99.   The *Biblioteca de Autores Cristianos (BAC)*, a publisher from Spain that since 1944 has offered the best of doctrinal and literary Church sources, has published three different editions of St. John's *Obras completas.* The first one came out in 1952, after Avila was declared the patron of Spanish secular priests; the second one in 1970, after his canonization; and the latest one, between the years 2000 and 2003. The number of volumes varied in the different editions. The latest one, which is the one cited in this work, consists of four volumes: Volume 1 includes the *Audi, filia, Pláticas* (conferences), and *Tratados* (it is dated in 2007 because it is a second printing of the one published in 2000); Volume 2 covers his biblical commentaries, *Tratados de reforma* and *Tratados y escritos menores*; Volume 3 presents his sermons and Volume 4 his letters.

100.   See Sala and Martín, *OC,* vol. 1, 365.

101.   Ibid., 34.

102.   Ibid., 169.

103.   Ibid., 171.

104.   Ibid., vol. 1, 407.

105.   Ibid., 172-76.

106.   Ibid., 185-86. The *Cathalogus* also included some of the works of Luis of Granada.

107.   *John of Avila, Audi, filia—Listen, O Daughter,* trans. J.F. Gormley, The Classics of Western Spirituality (New York: Paulist Press, 2006), 23-24.

108.   Ibid., ix-x.

109.   Rubio and Rubio, 33.

110.   Sala and Martín, *OC,* vol. 1, 64.

111.   See *San Juan de Ávila: Obras completas,* eds. L. Sala Balust and F. Martín Hernández, vol. 2 (Madrid: Biblioteca de Autores Cristianos, 2001), 882. Special mention is made here of M. Bataillon, "the known expert of Spanish literature of the sixteenth century." The translation was commonly attributed to Fra Luis of Granada, but he himself never claimed this. It seems that the assumption arose from a publication in 1555 where the translation, under the title of *Contemptus Mundi,* was attached to other prayers and exercises of piety compiled by the Dominican (See Ibid., 880). Being such a famous work, there were many printings of it attributed to different people. In fact, for a while, even the original Latin text was credited to Juan Gersón, the famous chancellor of the University of Paris (Ibid., 877-78). St. Ignatius of Loyola referred to the book as my "Gersón" or the diminutive "Gersonzito" because of this reason.

112.   Ibid., 888.

113.   Esquerda, *Escritos Sacerdotales,* xxxiii. See *OC,* vol. 2, 1010-1013.

114. Sala and Martín, *OC,* vol. 1, 950.

115. Ibid., 949.

116. *Tratado del amor de Dios* in *OC,* vol. 1, n. 4 (from here on, abbreviated as *TAD*).

117. Ibid., nn. 13-14.

118. *Escritos Sacerdotales,* xxxiv.

119. Esquerda, "El doctorado de San Juan de Ávila," 15.

120. In one of the letters of St. John, there is mention of the notes that he sent to one of his disciples, the Jesuit Francisco Gomez, who had to give some conferences to the priests of Cordoba. This was in 1563, which suggests that the treatise was written during the saint's retirement in Montilla. The composite of those conferences most likely gave shape to the treatise. See Sala and Martín, *OC,* vol. 1, 905; Esquerda, *Escritos Sacerdotales,* 102.

121. Esquerda, *Escritos Sacerdotales,* 5.

122. See Pablo VI, "Homilía del Santo Padre en la Canonización del Beato Juan de Ávila" (May 31, 1970) in *AAS* 62 (1970), 482-487.

123. *Reformación del estado eclesiástico,* in *OC* vol. 2, n. 4 (from here on, abbreviated as *MT1,* which stands for *Memorial para Trento 1*).

124. Ibid., n. 6.

125. Ibid., nn. 19-23.

126. Esquerda, *Escritos Sacerdotales,* 5.

127. Ibid., 6.

128. Esquerda, *Escritos Sacerdotales,* xxviii.

129. See *Advertencias al Concilio de Toledo* and *Algunas advertencias* in *OC,* vol. 2, 645-710; 711-47.

130. Testimony of Fr. Juan de Vargas, "Proceso en Madrid," in Martínez, *Proceso de beatificación,* 26.

131. Sala and Martín, *OC,* vol. 1, 783. The first two talks were taken from the *Tratado del sacerdocio.* He composed the first one for a diocesan synod and sent it to Fr. Francisco Gomez, one of his disciples, in 1563 so that he could preach it. These two were first published together in 1595 and were translated and printed in different languages and multiple editions.

132. Muñoz, lib. 3, cap. 21.

133. Six of St. John's sermons on the Holy Spirit have been translated into English and published in the form of a book. See Blessed John of Avila, *The Holy Ghost,* trans. Ena Dargan (Dublin: Scepter, 1959).

134. See *San Juan de Ávila: Obras completas,* eds. L. Sala Balust and F. Martín Hernández, vol. 3 (Madrid: Biblioteca de Autores Cristianos, 2002), xxiii-xxx. Shortly after St. John of Avila's death, one of his disciples, Fr. Juan Diaz, published many of the sermons of the Apostle of Andalusia. In that 1596 printing, they were actually called "treatises" since the saint was known to preach sometimes up to two hours, thus making it not

unusual for his sermons to be considered as such. Many, in fact, did turn into treatises. After he preached using some brief notes and Scripture passages, some of his disciples would take notes and transcribe them.

135.   Monsignor Esquerda mentions specifically sermons 10, 32, 33, 67, 70, 73, and 81 as being in this category; but they are not the only ones. See Esquerda, *Escritos Sacerdotales*, 178-79, 221-294.

136.   See *Doctrina cristiana* in *OC*, vol. 2, 811-32. The first version came out in 1554, and it was soon translated into Italian. The Jesuit Diego de Guzman, one of his faithful followers, took it with him to Florence where it was used for many years. A one-page sample of it is published in that second volume of St. John's works. See *OC*, vol. 2, 833.

137.   See "Doctrina Cristiana" in *Diccionario de San Juan de Ávila* by Juan Esquerda Bifet (Burgos: Monte Carmelo, 1999), 306 (from here on, abbreviated as *DJA*).

138.   "Hear us all, / for the love of God. / To all fathers / and all mothers / I want to speak / and forewarn, / and to older people / big and small, / the danger and task / in which they are found, / and I say with love / in the name of the Lord: / Please teach / the doctrine of truth / to your little children / since they are babies / and make them come / to know how to serve / our Lord Jesus Christ. . . ." *OC*, vol. 2, 812 (the brackets in the text are the editors'). The flow of the Spanish verse is beautiful. An English translation does no justice to it.

139.   Testimony of Hernando Rodriguez, "Proceso en Montilla," in *Proceso de beatificación*, 604.

140.   Sala and Martín, *OC*, vol. 2, 6.

141.   Ibid., 5.

142.   Muñoz, lib. 1, cap. 9.

143.   Sala and Martín, *OC*, vol. 2, 18.

144.   *Lecciones sobre la Epístola a los Gálatas* in *OC*, vol. 2, 82.

145.   Ibid., 83.

146.   *OC*, vol. 4, xxv-xxvi. This initial collection was entitled *Primera y Segunda parte del Epistolario espiritual para todos estados* (First and Second Part of the Spiritual Epistolary for All States). The disciples planned to organize the letters according to the states of the recipients—religious, clerical, married, single, etc.—but when the process proved to be a lengthy one, they abandoned the idea. The first forty-four letters follow this original design, the *Primera parte*; the rest follow no specific order.

147.   Ibid., xxxiii.

148.   Ibid., xxxvi-xxxvii.

149.   Granada, 59.

150.   Esquerda, *Escritos Sacerdotales*, xxviii.

151.   Ibid., 297.

152.   Ibid., 298.

153.   See Sala and Martín, "Apéndice" in *OC*, vol. 2, 1015.

154. See *OC*, vol. 2, 751-52.
155. Ibid.
156. Ibid., 837.

CHAPTER 1

PRIESTLY OFFICE: CONFIGURATION TO CHRIST, THE HIGH PRIEST

Through the Sacrament of Holy Orders, priests "are signed with a special character and so are configured to Christ the priest in such a way that they are able to act in the person of Christ the head."[1] This is the teaching of the Vatican II bishops in *Presbyterorum Ordinis*, where the priests are acknowledged as collaborators with their bishops, sharing with them "in the authority by which Christ himself builds up and sanctifies and rules his Body."[2] In other words, as bishops and priests, they share in the priestly, prophetic, and kingly office of Christ; and it is in "sanctifying the Body" that they themselves are sanctified.

Though St. John of Avila covers the three different aspects of Christ's office in his writings, it is the priestly role that receives most of his attention. This is not only because the "offering sacrifice" of the priestly ministry acquired increasing centrality in the centuries preceding the life of our saint[3] but because it is precisely that aspect that was being challenged by the Protestant Reformers of his day. St. John saw it as his duty to strengthen the priesthood by sharing his zeal—through his preaching, his writing, and his own example—with all the priests with whom he came into contact. He knew that reform in the Church could happen only through holiness, beginning with the holiness of its leaders.[4]

Called by God

The decadent state of the priesthood—and the Church, in general—in the sixteenth century, according to St. John of Avila, was because too many priests were ordained for the wrong reasons. In the recommendations that he wrote for the Spanish bishops attending the Council of Trent, now commonly known as *Memoriales al Concilio de Trento* (Treatises for the Council of Trent), he writes:

> What has spoiled the clerical state has been that profane people were admitted without knowledge of the high office that is being undertaken and with burning desires for earthly riches; and, once they entered, that they were raised in pernicious freedom, without discipline of knowledge or virtue. . . . Whoever so desires is readily ordained with a brief from Rome to his own detriment, that of the one who ordained him and the whole Church, which is why we find ourselves in the present state.[5]

Since the Council of Trent had several sessions, by the time of St. John's first *Memorial*, some of the earlier decisions of the Council had already been published, mandating different reforms at the diocesan and parochial level. But new laws, he would argue, would mean nothing unless something more profound was done. He had his reasons:

> Some fellows who are raised for the Church, not because they were called by God nor his bishops, but because

when they were born they were destined by their parents for the Church, or, after being born, to titles of churches because of their lineage; or, because to have something to eat they themselves chose the clerical state, these ones, raised in pernicious freedom, without teachers, without a virtuous recollection, with the heat of their age and in the midst of the temptations of the world, without knowing another law than their wicked appetite, how from such a bad state could they suddenly come to be fit for the majestic priestly state . . . ?[6]

The solution, in his opinion, would be that "neither admission should be easy nor the life without rules."[7] Thankfully, this was addressed at the Twenty-Third Session of the Council, and St. John's recommendation to have a seminary in every diocese was mandated for the universal Church, paving the way for the true reform that was needed.[8]

In reality, the recommendation to form seminarians was not new. Relying on his deep knowledge of Church councils, St. John reminded bishops of the decrees of the Council of Toledo—celebrated in the year 527[9]—where it was suggested that young men be taken to monasteries for their training. What *was* new was the idea of having a seminary in every diocese, where the bishop or his delegates could offer this training at the local level. In his usual colorful language, St. John writes:

It seems to me that what the council [of Toledo] says must be practiced in the following way: that in every diocese there must be a college, or at least in those places that have main cities, in which those who are to be ordained priests can be educated first. Just as the best horses are chosen to be taken to the king's stable and are placed under the supervision of a teacher so that, after they are groomed and trained the king can use them without embarrassment, in the same way here, of the virtuous young men that can be found, let them be brought to this recollected place and be entrusted to their rectors and teachers so that, under enclosure and obedience, they can experience fasts and prayers and rules of honest living . . . and let them learn kindness first, and letters afterwards, so that they can be teachers and directors of souls without danger. [10]

The priesthood that our saint envisioned can be seen in this passage. He wanted men who were virtuous, accustomed to experience privations, well acquainted with prayer and the mysteries of God, and ready to serve. Kindness, as he said, had to come before the knowledge that they could offer.

This exalted view of the priesthood explains St. John's response to a young man who was asking him whether or not he should be ordained. In a letter written to him, St. John replies:

Believe me, brother, that it is only the devil who has placed the proud men of these days, in such a broken state, to procure the priesthood so that, having them in such a high place in the temple, he can throw them down. For this is the teaching of Christ, that we must live such a life that deserves dignities but to flee from dignities, and to seek the most holy and safe humility. . . . O if you only knew what a priest should be on earth and the account he must render when he leaves this world . . . !

Brother, why do you want to venture into such a deep sea and be obligated to a strict account on the day of judgement . . . ?[11]

Most likely, he knew something about the recipient of the letter to respond in such a way, for it is unthinkable that he would not be one to promote vocations. The number of men that he formed himself, those he recommended to enter religious life, and even the unlikely women of whom he approved to enter the convent, is a case in point. St. John of Avila had to fight one of his main benefactresses, the Marquise of Priego, in order for her son to enter the Jesuits. The wealthy lady suffered another blow when her daughter-in-law, upon the death of the husband, decided to enter the convent. In both cases, the saint was sought as their spiritual director and as the advocate to appease the woman.[12]

Called to Holiness

During a meeting of bishops and priests held during the Year for Priests in 2010, Pope Benedict XVI spoke of the need for the hermeneutic of continuity in priestly holiness. He stated:

Just as the hermeneutics of continuity are proving ever more urgent for a satisfactory understanding of the Second Vatican Council's texts, likewise a hermeneutic we might describe as "of priestly continuity" appears necessary. This has come down to our day, starting from Jesus of Nazareth, Lord and Christ, and passing through the 2,000 years of the history of greatness and holiness, of culture and devotion which the Priesthood has written in the world. . . .

The men and women of our time ask us only to be truly
priests and nothing more. The lay faithful will find in a
great many other people what they humanly need, but
in the priest alone will they be able to find the word of
God that must always be on his lips (cf. *Presbyterorum
Ordinis*, n. 4); the Mercy of the Father, abundantly and
freely bestowed in the Sacrament of Reconciliation; the
Bread of new Life, "true food given to men" (cf. Hymn
of the Office of the Solemnity of *Corpus Christi* of the
Roman Rite).[13]

"Reductionism," he said, must be avoided. Although in the
decades following Vatican II, priests were seen more like
social workers, their true calling as spiritual leaders could not
be forgotten.[14]

The temptation to be "of the world" is perennial, though
it can take different facets. As mentioned previously, St. John
of Avila was dealing with an age where priests were more
concerned about worldly riches than about serving others and
their personal sanctification. In one of the conferences he
would give to priests (*Pláticas*), he speaks of this needed continuity. He says: "O men of the Church, if you could only see
yourselves in the fire of Christ, your main shepherd and in
those who preceded you: apostles and disciples, bishop martyrs and holy pontiffs!"[15] And making reference to the words
of St. John Chrysostom, he says in another conference:

We are very far, fathers, from that holiness that our
office demands; and if we do not recognize this, we are
blind. We must be clearer and shinier than the rays of the
sun, says St. Chrysostom. *Light of the world and salt of the
earth* Christ calls us (Mt 5:13-14). . . . They are called *salt*

because they are to be transformed in the taste of God:
so much so that, whoever comes into contact with them,
even if they have lost taste for the things of God, they
may recover it and lose taste for bad things.[16]

If all the baptized are called to holiness, as Vatican II reminds
us,[17] then even more so the priest, especially since he is the
means Christ is using to sanctify His body.[18]

Holiness is "the one thing" that must be in the mind of
those that are consecrated to God. Using the example of
King David, St. John of Avila says:

> Here he [David] asks for kindness of heart above all
> things. But, if just as he was king he were a priest, he
> would not be content with saying only, *Lord, give me
> kindness*, but *give me holiness* (cf. Ps 118:66). Because if
> kindness is appropriate for the king, holiness is proper
> to the priest . . . so we must exceed in holiness as in
> dignity, which is not my own invention but a truth of
> the Church.[19]

In saying this, St. John does not imply that a priest's
dignity as a person is greater than that of someone who is
not ordained, but he is merely trying to help the priests of
his day to understand the dignity that is theirs. This is evident
from what he says in that same conference: "O how little
we feel the exalted highness of this dignity! That is why we
are not afraid to go into it or to administer it, nor do we
feel compunction about how short we are of being what we
must be, according to what this dignity requires. This office,
my fathers, was only for people chosen by God who could
exceed others in virtue."[20] Because priests are called to be one
with Christ the Head, quoting Origen, St. John writes: "The

priest . . . is the face of the Church; and just as in the face is reflected the beauty of the entire body, likewise the clergy must be the principal beauty of the Church."[21]

St. John's Recommendation on Celibacy

Keeping in mind what has been just said, it is no surprise then that when the Spanish bishops attending the Council of Trent asked for his opinion on priestly celibacy before the next session of the council, St. John of Avila would recommend the upholding of the discipline. He writes about this in his second *Memorial.* Comparing the priests of the Old Testament with the priesthood instituted by Christ, he says:

> Because in the Old Law the Body of the Lord was not consecrated or handled as it is by today's ministers, it is understandable that they were given permission to give in to their weaknesses, for they were dealing only with figures and lowly things that, compared with the divine body of the Lord, they have no name or being. For this reason, and because novelty, especially in important things, must be seen as suspicious, especially in dangerous days like ours where the safest way to act in order not to err is to follow the ancient ways of the Catholic Church, it would be more convenient, even if it is difficult, to procure legitimate and pure ministers of God in the Church just as she has envisioned them and ordered it instead of giving in to the weaknesses of those who cannot live it, otherwise that would diminish the cleanliness of the celestial ministers and would create a novelty that would only lead to greed and loose living and even greater negligence and carelessness in fulfilling this high office that demands that the man be totally committed and not divided.[22]

Priests are meant to be men "whose destiny and inheritance is the Lord," St. John of Avila would go on to say, to have "contempt for the world and a life accustomed to the cross."[23] If the Council Fathers opted for relaxing the discipline, his recommendation was "that those [who are married] are able to carry out other priestly ministries, but not to say mass."[24] In essence, as we know, this is what the Church decided at Vatican II when the permanent diaconate was reinstituted.

Priestly Consecration

It is no secret that in the years after the Second Vatican Council, there was much turmoil in the priesthood. St. John Paul II speaks of this in his apostolic exhortation *Pastores Dabo Vobis*. It was mainly because of "an erroneous understanding" of the dignity of the priesthood that many left ministry or did not heed the call to enter the seminary.[25] Thanks to the clarifications offered by this Holy Father throughout his pontificate and his own robust priestly witness, the waves of doubt and uncertainty greatly diminished in our own day. In the twentieth century, there was St. John Paul II to restore priestly identity. In the sixteenth century, there was St. John of Avila.

In *Pastores Dabo Vobis*, St. John Paul II reiterated the teaching of the Church that: "The priest finds the full truth of his identity in being a derivation, a specific participation in and continuation of Christ himself, the one high priest of the new and eternal covenant. The priest is a living and transparent image of Christ the priest."[26] He is "called to prolong the presence of Christ, the one high priest, embodying his way of life and making him visible."[27] He does this because of

"the specific ontological bond which unites the priesthood
to Christ the high priest,"[28] the character that he acquires in
being consecrated for service, in being ordained.[29] "There
is an essential aspect of the priest that does not change: the
priest of tomorrow, no less than the priest of today, must
resemble Christ."[30]

For St. John of Avila, this permanent aspect of the priesthood is not just something that he believed and taught, but
something that he lived. Fra Louis of Granada speaks repeatedly of the "immutability" he saw in St. John over the years
that he was in contact with him.[31] In one of his sermons, St.
John explains why he tried to live his life that way. He says:

> It is written, *Homo sensatus in sapientia permanet sicut sol;
> stultus autem sicut luna mutatur* (cf. Sir 27:12), and there is
> no one who does not know of this change, because some
> are sometimes in grace and at times in sin; others, even
> if there are always in the state of grace, are sometimes
> lukewarm, sometimes devout; they love more, or less;
> they increase, they decrease. But our *Just one . . . permanet
> fixus sicut sol*; because he does not increase or decrease,
> he always had that same fervor that was full and alive to
> love in the measure that could be loved, and he had this
> same love for men when he walked and when he rested,
> when he ate and when he fasted; and he did not love
> men more when he was dying for love of them on the
> cross than when he was eating or sleeping. With so much
> love he would take a step for them just as he gave his life
> for them.[32]

Therefore, if the priest "represents the person of Jesus Christ our Lord in the priestly office,"[33] he must also live like the Lord, the High Priest.

The representation of Christ by the priest, according to the teachings of St. John, must be so real that "the priest must be transformed into Christ."[34] He must be "totally consecrated to the Lord."[35] Needless to say, the priest's humanity remains; but, as the Magisterium of the Church reminds us, the grace that we receive in the Sacraments helps us to live this out in our daily lives. In *Pastores Dabo Vobis*, St. John Paul II states: "By this grace the priest . . . is able the better to pursue the perfection of Christ, whose place he takes. The human weakness of his flesh is remedied by the holiness of him who became for us a high priest 'holy, innocent, undefiled, separated from sinners' (Heb 7:26)."[36]

Naturally, spiritual perfection does not happen automatically. The person must be willing to make a conscious response to God's love and strive to strip himself of selfish desires that get in the way. St. John of Avila speaks of this in a beautiful letter that he wrote to an unnamed disciple, who was also a priest. He writes: "This is part of what the Lord told us when he commanded us to take up our cross if we want to be his disciples. I say partly because the cross consists mainly of the death of one's opinion, self-will and the rational passions; this is the old man who must die just as Christ died on the cross." And he goes on: "This is explained very well by [St. Paul] in Corinthians 6 (cf. 2 Cor 6:4ff) where he includes corporal works like fasts and vigils among the things in which ministers must apply themselves, so that the whole man may be on the cross."[37]

Such recommendations are also seen in current documents of the Church to help priests live out their consecration. In the *Directory on the Ministry and Life of Priests* published by the Congregation for the Clergy, we read: "Priests are not to fail from following those ascetical norms proven by the experience of the Church and required even more so in present day circumstances."[38] And again, quoting the words of Pope Benedict XVI, the document continues:

> Indeed, the priest no longer belongs to himself but, because of the sacramental seal he has received (cf. *Catechism of the Catholic Church*, nn. 1563, 1582), is the "property" of God. The priest's "belonging to Another," must become recognisable to all, through a transparent witness. . . . In the way of thinking, speaking, and judging events of the world, of serving and loving, of relating to people, also in his habits, the priest must draw prophetic power from his sacramental belonging.[39]

Contemplative Prayer

In the film *The Lion King*, there is a scene where Simba, the young heir to the crown, runs away from home and things fall apart in his absence because the wrong person has assumed the leadership that belonged to him. In a moment of solitude in the jungle, he hears the voice of his father, who tells him in a deep, authoritative voice: "Remember who you are!"

Such things happen not only in animated movies, but also in real life. Although the priest is called to lead people in prayer and to intercede for them, as will be discussed shortly, there is this aspect of his own private prayer that is essential to his identity as a priest of Jesus Christ. Without it, it is very easy to get caught up in activism or to divert one's energy into things that other people in the community could be doing. What is worse, as in the case of Simba, a person not called by God can assume the spiritual leadership that belongs only to the priest. It is in that contemplative gaze, as it was in the case of Moses,[40] that the priest, the man of God receives the insights and instructions that God's people need to hear. It is also there that the priest finds his own identity, that he "remembers who he is."

This is precisely the advice that St. John of Avila gives Pedro Guerrero, one of his classmates who had been just appointed bishop. In a letter St. John wrote to Guerrero, St. John tells him:

> The first thing [that I recommend], is that you turn your heart completely to God, frequenting the exercise of prayer, commending to God's mercy the good of your flock and asking for the help of heaven so that you may have something to offer them, because, if it does not come from there [heaven], what will you be able to give them other than things that do not nourish them or give them life? For we read about Moses that whenever he was in doubt he would go before the tabernacle of the Lord, and from there he would come out knowing what to do and with the strength he needed to carry it out.[41]

It is not by chance that St. John offers this as "the first thing" he recommends. It shows the importance that he himself placed on prayer, as is attested by his biographers.[42]

In his "Treatise on the Priesthood" St. John speaks of this important relationship that must exist between the Lord and His representative. He writes:

> The Lord says, I have called you friends, because I have declared to you the things that I heard from my Father (Jn 15:15). And just as the priest will be asked about God's Law because he is his messenger, as Malachi says (cf. Mal 2:7), he will also be asked about God's will in this or that since he has a special friendship and relationship with the Lord, for it is believed that the Lord will not fail to reveal to him what must be known for the good of the people.[43]

When this is missing, there is no "holiness of life" or "the strength of prayer," St. John says in one of his conferences.[44] For "those who want to help themselves by carefully doing works pleasing to God, but do not try to pray, are swimming or fighting with only one hand and are walking with only one foot."[45] When it comes to a priest, he would warn, there is the added risk that "he may give as God's counsel what is really just his own opinion."[46]

This perennial wisdom of the Church was reiterated at Vatican II when the formation of priests was addressed. The Council Fathers said that: "Those who are to take on the likeness of Christ the priest by sacred ordination should form the habit of drawing close to him as friends in every detail of their lives. . . . They should be taught to seek Christ in faithful meditation on the Word of God and in active participation in the sacred mysteries of the Church, especially the Eucharist and the Divine Office."[47] And in a more recent pronouncement, we read: "*Doing* serves no purpose if there is no *being with Christ*. Here lies the horizon of the identity, life, ministry and ongoing formation of the priest: a task of immense work that is open, courageous, enlightened by the faith, sustained by hope and rooted in charity."[48]

St. John of Avila was certain that being called by God only leads "to the conclusion that [priests] must be exemplary . . . because, if the king were to raise a captain, a soldier would not be enough."[49] Therefore, he would exhort them: "if you are a priest, you must live, speak, treat and converse in such a way that you lead others to serve God."[50]

The Eucharist as the Heart of the Church

The Church has always taught that the Eucharist is "the summit toward which all the activity of the Church is directed" and "the fount from which all her power flows."[51] These words from the Second Vatican Council are almost identical with those used by St. John of Avila in one of his sermons. The sacramental Body of Jesus, he says, is "the end and consummation of the other sacraments."[52] It is the sacrament *par excellence* since it brings us into full union with Jesus.

It is no surprise, therefore, that in *Presbyterorum Ordinis*, we are told that it is to the Eucharist that the ministry of priests is directed:

> For their ministration, which begins with the announcement of the Gospel, draws its force and power from the sacrifice of Christ and tends to this, that "the whole redeemed city, that is, the whole assembly and community of the saints should be offered as a universal sacrifice to God through the High Priest who offered himself in his passion for us that we might be the body of so great a Head."[53]

Similar words can be found in the magisterium of St. John Paul II. In his second apostolic letter, *Dominicae Cenae,* he states: "The Eucharist is the principal and central *raison d'être* of the sacrament of the priesthood, which effectively came into being at the moment of the institution of the Eucharist, and together with it."[54] At an *Ad Limina* visit with U.S. bishops, he also said: "The spirituality of all diocesan and religious priests is linked to the Eucharist. Here they obtain the strength to make the offering of their lives together with Jesus, High Priest and Victim of salvation. . . . From his Cross the Lord Jesus speaks to all his priests, inviting them to be, with him, signs of contradiction before the world."[55]

St. John Paul II did say that the spirituality of the priest is "linked" to the Eucharist, but he did not say that it is the *only* thing that determines it. That the Council fathers wanted to emphasize the preaching of the Word in *Presbyterorum Ordinis* by saying, "which begins with the announcement of the Gospel," in the passage quoted above when mentioning the Eucharist is also significant. The threefold office of the priest, in which he must find his sanctification, cannot be properly lived out if he focuses only on one aspect of his ministry. That would also be a "reductionism," as Pope Benedict had said. St. John Paul II will later clarify this issue in *Pastores Dabo Vobis.* Nevertheless, the centrality of the Eucharist can never be forgotten.

The Celebration of the Eucharist as a Means to Sanctification

The connection between the Eucharist and the holiness that is needed from its ministers is a constant theme in the writings of St. John of Avila. In the "Treatise on the Priesthood," he recalls those holy men from of old who would take the office out of obedience because they were mindful of their unworthiness. Yet, once ordained, "they would order their lives to be what they ought, seeking purity and true sanctity; and, even when they had it in abundance, they felt they were lacking in it, for they realized the high dignity that it required and that no sanctity can truly be its equal or deserve it."[56] As St. John explains, to handle the Eucharist, true purity and holiness is required since it is "the holiest of all things."[57]

In the Gospel, Jesus speaks of how the altar in the temple would make the gift presented holy because of the consecration.[58] Expanding on a similar idea, the Apostle of Andalusia writes:

> St. Jerome says that the virgin dedicated to God is God's sacrifice and it must be evident; that, since the sacrifice sanctifies what it touches, whoever speaks, hears or looks at her must be edified. How much more is this asked from the priest! If he is what he must be . . . everything about him can declare that he is an ark of the testament of God, a reliquary of God; may he be so full of Him that, whoever looks at, hears or sees him, even if it is a worldly or distracted person, may experience something of that divine strength that is present in the priest.[59]

When the priest is mindful of what he is doing and who he represents, even the vestments can be reminders of the virtues that he must always be seeking, St. John would say. If he only pretends to have these virtues, "when people go look for Jesus in him it will happen as in the holy sepulcher, that they only find the linen and shroud in which he was vested for the burial."[60]

In the celebration of the Mass, the rite itself reminds the priest of what he can do to seek purity of soul and intention. In another passage of his Treatise, St. John exhorts:

> Since the priest has many clear reasons to see if he is well dressed in order to be pleasant and beautiful before the eyes of God, let him not go in with his eyes closed so that he does not hear the terrible sentence: *Amice, quomodo huc intrasti non habens vestem nuptialen?* (Mt 22:12); and, with tied hands and feet, be thrown into the darkness outside, since he loved the inner darkness without wanting to see the light to declare his sins and fulfill his obligations. . . . To warn their priests of this purification, even of very small things, the Church ordered that before proceeding to the consecration of the most holy Body of Christ, they should wash the tips of their fingers.[61]

This led St. John to conclude: "Blessed are we if we can know and take advantage of the great honor and price that God has for us. And woe, woe, woe to us, if being so precious in His eyes we do not appreciate ourselves or Him!"[62]

The Letter to the Hebrews gives in Jesus the model of the perfect priest. He is the one who not only offers the sacrifice but offers His very self, His own body and blood.[63] It has already been mentioned how St. John of Avila mentions this in disputing the claims of Martin Luther that a "presbyter" could preach the Word of God without major personal sacrifices or a commitment to celibacy and that any Christian could offer sacrifice.[64] In his "Treatise on the Priesthood," he spells out what being a priest of God entails:

> The priest . . . represents the Lord in his passion and death, so he must also represent him in the meekness

with which he suffered, in the obedience that led him to
the cross, in the purity of chastity, in the deep humility,
in the fire of charity that would make the priest pray
for everyone with visceral groans and to offer himself
to suffering and death for their remedy if the Lord so
desires. Therefore, the representation must be so real
that the priest must be transformed into Christ and, as
St. Dionysius writes, *in likeness of one*; being so conformed
to each other that they are no longer two, but that what
St. Paul says can be fulfilled: *Qui adhaeret Deo, unus spiritus
est* (1 Cor 6, 17). This is the representation of the sacred
passion that is done at mass, and this is what it means
when the priest has his arms in form of a cross, when
he raises them and lowers them, his vestments and
everything else.[65]

Therefore, "this is the priestly mirror on which the priest
must see himself," our saint would say, "to offer himself,
house and honor, and his very life, for himself and the
whole world."[66]

Intercessory Prayer

The prayer of the priest is a continuation of the prayer
of Christ the High Priest, the one who "lives forever to make
intercession for them" (Heb 7:25). In addition to presiding
at the Eucharist, the priest constantly stands in the presence
of God, praying for others and for their needs. He is *padre de
todos* (father of all people), as St. John of Avila would say.[67]

The responsibility of praying for others is a serious one.
St. John would emphasize this in the conferences he gave
to priests:

> These words, fathers, scare me very much, for they ask
> for great strong prayer as to benefit the whole world,
> for [St. John Chrysostom] says that the confidence
> that Moses and Elijah had was little, and one of them
> obtained pardon for that great army that was going
> through the desert (cf. Ex 32:10-14; Nm 14:13ff), and
> the other one would close the sky whenever he wanted
> so that it would not rain, and would open it, and with his
> prayer he would bring fire from heaven to kill others, and
> also with his prayer he would give life to the dead (cf. 1
> Kgs 17:18). Woe to me, if the confidence of these ones is
> not enough compared to the prayer that the priest must
> offer for the whole world.[68]

With St. Basil, then, St. John of Avila would say, "we must
represent and imitate the groans and prayers of Jesus that the
priestly office demands."[69]

The importance attached to this prayer of intercession is
unfathomable.[70] The words of our saint on the subject in that
conference for priests are worth quoting at length:

> This, fathers, is not my invention; it is the word of
> God, of that God who has honored us in making us his
> ministers which he will take into account and will charge
> us for this responsibility, for he tells us: *You did not take
> the opposite side, nor did you put yourself as a wall in favor of the
> house of Israel, to be standing at war on the day of the Lord* (cf.
> Ez 13:5). And somewhere else he says: *I looked among them
> for a man who could act as a fence and oppose me in favor of the
> earth so that I would not destroy it, and I did not find him; and I
> poured out my wrath against them, and I consumed them with the
> fire of my anger* (cf. Ez 22:30-31).[71]

While this concern makes sense, it is somewhat surprising the way in which St. John suggests that priests carry out this intercession. They must "cry" for the sins of others because priests are "the eyes of the Church whose role is to cry for all the evils that come to the body."[72] And that is how they need to be tested before ordination, he says in one of his sermons. Rather than seeing if they know how to sing or even read, they must be tested on their charity "and on prayer, to see if they know how to pray well and stand before God to intercede for others . . . to be a bridge between God and men, to feel the ills of others and to cry for them."[73] Priests are to have "motherly hearts" who "bitterly cry when they see their spiritual children dead."[74]

When we recall that Jesus "wept" over Jerusalem[75] because He desired to gather her children "as a hen gathers her brood under her wings" (Lk 13:34)[76], we realize that, once again, the role of the priest is to be one with the Lord, to assume the heart and sentiments of the Good Shepherd as He makes intercession for others.

The Sacrament of Reconciliation

From biblical times, it has been the function of priests to reconcile people to the community.[77] If the priest is to "cry" for the sins of others, as St. John of Avila would say, in the Sacrament of Penance, he embodies the compassion of Christ as he absolves the penitents[78] and reconciles them with God and with others.

Even though our saint spent most of his time and energy as a professor, it is common knowledge that he spent part of his retirement hearing confessions in the local parish in Montilla. People would also seek him for confession and spiritual

guidance in his home. As he trained priests, he would emphasize how they could help people to make good confessions,[79]
and he also left among his writings a "dialogue" between pen-
itent and confessor.[80] He was mindful that "the ignorance of
confessors" and their "wicked life" was the source of many
problems,[81] which is why the Council of Trent mandated
bishops to be more attentive to those they commissioned as
ministers of the Sacrament.

The Church has always taught that "while it is possible
to God's grace to carry out the work of salvation through
unworthy ministers, yet God ordinarily prefers to show his
wonders through those men who are more submissive to the
impulse and guidance of the Holy Spirit,"[82] through those
who seek holiness of life. In the case of the Apostle of
Andalusia, it has already been stated how that young lady for
whom he wrote the *Audi, filia* changed her life after she went
to confession to him.

The opposite, though, can also be true. In hearing confessions, priests come into contact with many people who are
more advanced than they in the virtue of charity and in the
spiritual life in general. There is no doubt that this ministry
of reconciliation can also have a saving effect on the priest
and assist him in his own spiritual growth.

Conclusion

A priest is chosen by Christ to sanctify all the members
of His body. "It was not you who chose me, but I who chose
you" (Jn 15:16), Jesus tells His first priests in the Upper Room
as He entrusts the continuation of His mission to them.
Having told them to "[remain] in me" (Jn 15:5) as branches
on the vine in order to have life, the priests' incorporation

into the Mystery of Christ—as well as its constant renewal through their priestly prayer—assures not only their own physical and spiritual survival, but also their ability to communicate Christ's life to their spiritual children. In Baptism, priests are incorporated into the Body of Christ; in receiving the Sacrament of Holy Orders, they become His instruments to incorporate others into that spiritual reality.

The Eucharist is the Sacrament *par excellence* where all the members become one with Christ, their head. In presiding at the Eucharist and at the other sacraments, the priest himself is transformed. If "the fragrance always remains in the hand that gives the rose," as Heda Bejar pointed out, the priest who offers God's love to others is himself touched by it. The more a priest is mindful of his unmerited yet awesome dignity as Christ's minister and the more open he is to the work of the Spirit in his life, St. John of Avila would teach, the more he will be able to see the hand of God in each of his duties and his encounters with others.

But his priestly office is only one aspect in which these beautiful realities come to fruition. The ministerial priesthood calls the recipient to be priest, prophet, and king in service to the People of God. The following chapters unfold the rest of these realities and demonstrate how, in the faithfully carrying out of those responsibilities, the diocesan priest can discover his own spirituality.

NOTES

1. Vatican II, *Presbyterorum Ordinis* (1965), sec. 2.
2. Ibid.
3. See David Bohr, *The Diocesan Priest: Consecrated and Sent* (Collegeville, MN: Liturgical Press, 2009), 52.
4. Interestingly enough, four centuries later, the Church would express the same concept at Vatican II. The decree *Optatam Totius* begins with the words: "The Council is fully aware that the desired renewal of the whole Church depends in great part upon a priestly ministry animated by the spirit of Christ. . . ." (from here on, abbreviated as *OT*).
5. *Memorial primero al Concilio de Trento* (from here on, abbreviated as T1) in *Obras Completas* (from here on, abbreviated as OC), vol. 2, n. 6.
6. Ibid., n. 10. See also *Tratado del amor de Dios* (from here on, abbreviated as TSS), n. 33.
7. Ibid., n. 6.
8. Chapter eighteen of that twenty-third session mandated the seminaries. See *The Canons and Decrees of the Council of Trent*, trans. by Rev. H.J. Schroeder, O.P. (Rockford: Tan Books and Publishers, 1978).
9. See Francisco Martín Fernández and José Carlos Martín de la Hoz, *La formación sacerdotal: Historia y vida* (Madrid: San Pablo, 2014), 28.
10. *Memorial primero al Concilio de Trento* (from here on, abbreviated as *MT1*) in *OC*, vol. 2, n. 12. St. John refers to canon 24 of the Fourth Council of Toledo. See note 10 by Sala and Martín on that same page of the *Memorial* (491).
11. Letter 7 in *OC*, vol. 4, 46-47.
12. Both Antonio de Córdoba and the Countess of Feria (later known as "Sor Ana de la Cruz"), persevered in religious life and were famous for their holiness. See Sala and Martín, *OC*, vol. 1, 125-27; 139-40.
13. "Address to Participants in the Conference Organized by the Congregation for the Clergy" (March 12, 2010), in *Acta Apostolicae Sedis* (from here on, abbreviated as *AAS*) 102 (2010), 240-242. See also Nicolás Álvarez de las Asturias, "Hermenéutica de la santidad sacerdotal" in *Entre todos, Juan de Ávila: Elogio al Santo Maestro en el entorno de su proclamación como Doctor de la Iglesia Universal* (Madrid: Biblioteca de Autores Cristianos, 2011), 31. See Ignacio Oñatibia Audela: "No ha habido en la historia de la Iglesia ninguna época en que no se le haya recordado al presbítero su obligación de vivir en santidad de acuerdo con las exigencias de su alta función." Oñatibia said this at a conference on the spirituality of the diocesan priest in Spain. It was published as "La espiritualidad presbiteral en su evolución histórica" in *La espiritualidad del presbítero diocesano secular* (Madrid: EDICE, 1987), 25.
14. Ibid.

15. *Pláticas* 7 in *OC*, vol. 1, n. 6.

16. *Pláticas* 1 in *OC*, vol. 1, n. 8. The saint's reference to St. John Chrysostom's is *De sacerdotio*, 1.6, 4: PG 48, 681. For a more complete list of St. John of Avila's reference to the Church Fathers, see *TSS* n. 18 in *OC* vol. 1, 923-26. In addition to St. John Chrysostom, St. John of Avila also quotes St. Augustine, St. Ambrose, St. Jerome, and St. Gregory the Great.

17. "All in the Church, whether they belong to the hierarchy or are cared by it, are called to holiness." Vatican II, *Lumen Gentium* (1964), sec. 39.

18. The indispensable aspect of the priesthood is explained through the concept of *In persona Christi*. See Santiago del Cura Elena, "In Persona Christi-In Persona Ecclesiae" in *Diccionario del sacerdocio*, 354.

19. *Pláticas* 2 in *OC*, vol. 1, n. 4. The translation for the Latin is: "The priests of the Lord offer bread and incense to God, therefore they are holy."

20. Ibid.

21. *TSS* in *OC*, vol. 1, n. 11 (the citation from Origen is *In Lev. homil.* 5,3,4: PG 12, 452-454). In *Lumen Gentium*, the call to holiness for bishops and priests is not forgotten: "The forms and tasks of life are many but holiness is one . . . Each one, however, according to his own gifts and duties must steadfastly advance along the way of a living faith, which arouses hope and works through love.

In the first place, the shepherds of Christ's flock, in the image of the high and eternal priest, shepherd and bishop of our souls, should carry out their ministry with holiness and eagerness, with humility and fortitude . . . They should not be afraid to lay down their life for their sheep and, being a model to their flock (See 1 Pt 5:3), they must foster a growing holiness in the Church, also by their own example.

Priests, who resemble the episcopal rank . . . , should grow in the love of God and of their neighbor by the daily exercise of their duty, should keep the bond of priestly fellowship, should abound in every spiritual good and bear a living witness of God to all, imitating those priests who, in the course of the centuries, left behind them an outstanding example of holiness, often in a humble and hidden service" (sec. 41).

22. *Memorial segundo al Concilio de Trento* (from here on, abbreviated as *MT2*) in *OC*, vol. 2, n. 91.

23. Ibid.

24. Ibid.

25. See John Paul II, *Pastores Dabo Vobis* (from here on, abbreviated as *PDV*), sec. 11.

26. Ibid., sec. 12. The magisterium of previous popes on the priesthood was clearly presented when the council fathers spoke of the means of sanctification for priests in *Presbyterorum Ordinis*. See sec. 12, note 7. The Synod of Bishops in 1971 also focused on "The Ministerial

Priesthood" to address the confusion felt by some in the Church those years after the Council.

27. Ibid., sec. 15.

28. Ibid., sec. 11.

29. For an excellent work on priestly character, See Monsignor David Toup's *Reclaiming Our Priestly Character* (Omaha: IPF Publications, 2008). It is an abridged copy of his doctoral dissertation. The latest edition of the *Directory on the Ministry and the Life of Priests* also states that "In this his specific Christological identity the priest must be aware that his life is a mystery totally grafted onto the mystery of Christ and of the Church in a new way, and that this engages him totally in the pastoral ministry and gives sense to his life. . . . This awareness—founded on the ontological bond with Christ—maintains due distance from 'task performance' notions that have sought to look upon the priest as nothing more than a social worker or administrator of sacred rites 'at the risk of betraying Christ's Priesthood itself' and reduce the life of the priest to the mere expedition of duties" (Vatican City: Libreria Editrice Vaticana, 2013), nn. 6-7 (from here on abbreviated as *Directory*).

30. *PDV*, sec. 5.

31. See Luis de Granada, O.P., *Vida del padre maestro Juan de Avila* 2nd edition (Madrid: Edibesa, 2010), 104, 107 and 170-71.

32. Sermon 33 in *OC*, vol. 3, n. 3.

33. *Pláticas* 2 in *OC*, vol. 1, n. 9.

34. *TSS* in *OC*, vol. 1, n. 26.

35. 35   *Pláticas* 1 in *OC*, vol. 1, n. 4.

36. 36   *PDV*, sec. 20.

37. 37   Letter 161 in *OC*, vol. 4, 552-53.

38. 38   *Directory*, n. 82.

39. 39   Ibid., n. 61, (the quote is of the Pope's "Address to the Participants at the Theological Conference Organized by the Congregation for the Clergy" of March 12, 2010).

40. See Exodus 19:3.

41. Letter 177 in *OC*, vol. 4, 588.

42. Granada writes that Father Avila would spend two hours in prayer in the morning and two hours in the evening. See *Vida del padre maestro Juan de Avila*, 102. See also Sala and Martín in *OC*, vol. 1, 219-23. The context in which these long hours of prayer took place, however, must be kept in mind. St. John lived in sixteenth century Spain where long periods of contemplative prayer were customary, thanks to figures like St. Teresa of Avila. Granada also is not precise as to the period of the saint's life to which he is referring. It is possible that he writes about St. John's retirement, when he had less responsibilities as a priest. The example of the saints, as always, must be adapted to one's time and circumstances. It is said, for example, that St. Benedict prescribed two hours of *lectio divina* for

his monks in the Rule he wrote for them. Today, most Benedictine monasteries dedicate from thirty to forty-five minutes to that important exercise.

43. *TSS* in *OC*, vol. 1, n. 9.

44. *Pláticas* 2 in *OC*, vol. 1, n. 16. Pope Benedict XVI spoke of this during an audience he granted to the priests of the Spanish College studying in Rome shortly after he announced that he would be declaring St. John of Avila a Doctor of the Church. He said: "the priest renews his life and draws strength for his ministry from contemplation of the Divine Word and intense dialogue with the Lord. He is aware that he will be unable to take Christ to his brethren or to meet him in the poor and the sick, if he does not first discover him in fervent and constant prayer. It is necessary to nourish a personal relationship with the One, whom one then proclaims, celebrates and communicates. Herein lies the foundation of priestly spirituality, until one becomes a transparent sign and living witness of the Good Shepherd." "Address to the Pontifical Spanish College of St. Joseph in Rome" (May 10, 2012), http://w2.vatican.va/content/benedict-xvi/en/speeches/2012/may/documents/hf_ben-xvi_spe_20120510_collegio-spagnolo.html (accessed January 15, 2016).

45. *Audi, filia*, ch. 70 (Gormley's translation, 208).

46. Sermon 5 [2] in *OC*, vol. 3, n. 22.

47. *OT*, sec. 8.

48. *Directory*, 154 (italics in the original. The number here indicates a page number, not paragraph. The quote is taken from the Conclusion of the document).

49. *Pláticas* 6 in *OC*, vol. 1, n. 5.

50. Ibid. Following *OT* sec. 8, Pope Benedict XVI emphasized contemplative prayer and the importance of the spiritual life—what he sometimes called "friendship with Jesus"— in his meetings with priests and seminarians throughout his papacy. This is especially significant given that he is one of the most intellectual popes we have had in recent decades. See "Meeting with the Clergy in Warsaw" (May 25, 2006) in *AAS* 98 (2006), 465-468; "Address at the Beginning of the Academic Year of the Pontifical Roman Universities" (October 23, 2006) in *AAS* 98 (2006), 817-819; "Meeting with the Clergy of the Dioceses of Belluno-Feltre and Treviso" (July 24, 2007) in *AAS* 99 (2007), 710-730. Noteworthy is also the fact that in *Pastores Dabo Vobis*, St. John Paul II dedicates a full chapter to spirituality (ch. 3) before he addresses the four pillars of formation in the latter part of the document (ch. 5). A similar format is followed in the *Directory* where "Primacy of the Spiritual Life" (in ch. 2) is also addressed.

51. Vatican II, *Sacrosanctum Concilium* (1963), sec. 10 (from here on, abbreviated as *SC*).

52. Sermon 34 in *OC*, vol. 3, n. 29. The Spanish bishops point out how, for St. John of Avila, the Eucharist was "the oven" in which his heart would burn with apostolic zeal and how his personal seal had a

Eucharistic motif. Both point to the centrality of the Eucharist in his life. St. John also promoted frequent reception of Holy Communion for those who were properly disposed. See Conferencia Episcopal Española, "San Juan de Ávila, maestro de evangelizadores: Mensaje al pueblo de Dios en el V centenario del nacimiento de San Juan de Ávila" (November, 1999), in *OC*, 365, 368 (Appendix IV).

53.   *PO*, sec. 2.

54.   John Paul II, *Dominicae Cenae* (1980) in *AAS* 72 (1980), 113-148, n. 2. The Pope repeated this statement in his last encyclical, *Ecclesia de Eucharistia* (2003) in *AAS* 95 (2003), 433-475, English translation (Washington, D.C.: United States Conference of Catholic Bishops, 2003), n. 31.

55.   "Address to a Group of Bishops from the United States of America on Their 'Ad Limina Apostolorum' Visit" (September 9, 1983) in *AAS* 76 (1984), 106-110, English translation, (Vatican City: Libreria Editrice Vaticana, 1984), n. 6.

56.   *TSS* in *OC*, vol. 1, n. 25.

57.   Ibid., n. 12.

58.   See Matthew 23:19.

59.   *TSS* in *OC.*, n. 13. The reference to St. Jerome is Pseudo-Jerome, *Epist.* 12, *Virginitatis laus*, 16: *Patrologia Latina* 30, 181. See also *Pláticas* 1 in *OC*, vol. 1, n. 4.

60.   Ibid.

61.   Ibid., n. 23.

62.   *Pláticas* 1 in *OC*, vol. 1, n. 6.

63.   See Hebrews 9:11-14.

64.   See *Lecc 1SJ[I]* in *OC*, vol. 2, Lesson 16, 249. Along with St. Thomas Aquinas and other scholars of the time, St. John of Avila assumed that the Letter to the Hebrews was written by St. Paul.

65.   *TSS* in *OC*, vol. 1, n. 26 (the reference to St. Dionysius is actually Pseudo-Dionysius, *De eccles. hierarch.* c.3, 5: PG 3, 444).

66.   Ibid., n. 10. The priest/victim aspect of the priesthood has continued throughout the centuries in the Magisterium, theologians, and spiritual masters. See Fulton J. Sheen, *Those Mysterious Priests* (New York: Double Day, 1974), especially chapters 2 and 11, and *PDV*, sec. 21.

67.   *Pláticas* 2 in *OC*, vol. 1, n. 5.

68.   Ibid., n. 6.

69.   Ibid., n. 9 (the reference to St. Basil is from *Moral.* reg.56 c.5: PG 31, 786ff).

70.   Pope Francis has emphasized this intercessory aspect of the priesthood. From the beginning, and with every chance he has, he reminds priests to be mediators between God and others, not mere intermediaries who grant favors to others. See "Homily for Chrism Mass" (March 28, 2013), http://w2.vatican.va/content/francesco/en/homilies/2013/documents/papa-francesco_20130328_messa-crismale.html (accessed

March 30, 2013); "Discorso per Convegnio 'Una vocazione, una formazione, una missione'" (November 20, 2015), http://w2.vatican. va/content/francesco/it/ speeches/2015/november/documents/papa-francesco_20151120_formazione-sacerdoti. html (accessed February 20, 2016.).

71. *Pláticas* 2 in *OC*, vol. 1, n. 18.
72. Ibid., n. 19.
73. Sermon 10 in *OC*, vol. 3, n. 10.
74. *Pláticas* 2 in *OC*, vol. 1, n. 16.
75. See Luke 19:41.
76. See Matthew 23:37.
77. See Luke 5:14 and 17:14.
78. Sermon 43 in *OC*, vol. 3, n. 9.
79. See *Pláticas* 5 in *OC*, vol. 1.
80. *Dialogus inter confessarium et paenitentem* in *OC*, vol. 2, 769-97.
81. *Tratado sobre el sacerdocio* in *OC*, vol. 1, n. 44.
82. *PO*, sec. 12.

CHAPTER 2

PROPHETIC OFFICE: APOSTOLIC LIFE IN THE PRIESTHOOD

In the Gospel of Mark, we read that Jesus appointed the Twelve Apostles "that they might be with him and he might send them forth to preach and to have authority to drive out demons" (3:14-15). In the previous chapter, we saw how priests continue "to be with him" in personal prayer and as His representatives—*in persona Christi*—as they preside at the different sacraments. The following pages explore the way in which priests are also "sent forth" to preach and carry out other priestly duties.

Being Sent Forth

There is no doubt that St. John of Avila saw himself and the priesthood as a continuation of the ministry of the Apostles. In one of his sermons, he says this much:

> O happy sheep who were alive at the time of the Great Shepherd, and happy will be the ones that fall in the hands of the prelate who imitates that zeal! He ordered it that way: the Pope took his place, the prelates succeed the apostles, and the priests the seventy two disciples,

> as St. Jerome says; these are intrinsic to the nature of
> the Church; and the religious are added to help prelates
> and priests.[1]

Therefore, priests must always be ready to do what is asked
of them and to go where they are needed.

Although being a missionary is a vocation within itself,
the mission of the Church belongs to all the baptized. That
being the case, bishops and priests have a special responsibility in preaching the good news. The Decree on the Church's
Missionary Activity from Vatican II, *Ad Gentes*, issues a strong
reminder about this point. It says:

> All bishops, as members of the body of bishops which
> succeeds the college of the apostles, are consecrated
> not for one diocese alone, but for the salvation of the
> whole world. The command of Christ to preach the
> Gospel to every creature (Mk 16:15) applies primarily and
> immediately to them—with Peter, and subject to Peter.
> From this arises that communion and cooperation of
> the churches which is so necessary today for the work of
> evangelization. . . .

> Since the need for workers in the vineyard of the
> Lord grows from day to day, and since diocesan
> priests themselves wish to play a greater part in the
> evangelization of the world, this sacred Synod desires
> that bishops, being conscious of the very grave shortage
> of priests which impedes the evangelization of many
> regions, would, after a proper training, send to those
> dioceses which lack clergy some of their best priests who
> offer themselves for mission work, where at least for a

time they would exercise the missionary ministry in a spirit of service.[2]

The Apostle of Andalusia intuited this solution centuries before the Council. As soon as he was ordained, he made his way over to Seville where he hoped to board a ship that would take him to the New World to preach the Gospel there. It is well known that, given the needs that the Spanish kingdom was facing with the advances of the Reformers, it was decided that his preaching skills could be better used in his home country.[3] But even there, the life he led did not cease to be apostolic. His simple habits and his constant movement throughout the different cities of Andalusia that earned him the title of "Apostle" from his biographers and the Church were well attested. This "thirst for souls," St. John would say, is what drove Jesus to leave everything. The priest also should follow in his footsteps:

> O happy shepherds who could share in this hunger and thirst for the salvation of souls that the Lord had, for, given the great need that is there, if there is no zeal and care, they will not be able to carry out what is needed! The Lord died on the cross for souls; he left inheritance, honor, fame and even his own mother to care for them; therefore, whoever does not mortify his interests, honor, gifts, love of family, and does not take on the mortification of the cross, even if he has good wishes in his heart, could probably carry his children to labor, but he will not be able to give birth to them (cf. Is 37:3).[4]

The *"Priestly School"* of *St. John of Avila*

Before the Council of Trent, the office of bishop did not provide the structure that we are used to today in the Church. Bishops were constantly absent from their dioceses, and priests were committed only to churches from which they were receiving benefices.[5] In his writings, St. John would criticize these "worldly lords" (*señores mundanos*) who had huge and wealthy residences in which poor people were afraid to set foot.[6] Although he hoped that the Church would correct this situation—which, in fact, it did by introducing many reforms through the Council—he felt that he could make his own contribution by forming a constellation of priests who would go throughout the different cities of Andalusia to preach the Gospel and administer the Sacraments. This is what eventually came to be known as the *escuela sacerdotal* of St. John of Avila.

It was not a school per se, but a group of priests who gathered around St. John to receive his teaching and be spiritually led by him.[7] They were so inspired by his testimony that they wanted to live with him, and some even promised him obedience.[8] While it is true that at one point, he dreamed of creating a congregation of priests, he gave up on this idea when he discovered that St. Ignatius of Loyola was doing something very similar with the founding of the Jesuits.[9] Instead, St. John saw his role as helping people discern their vocation and encouraging them to participate actively in the mission of the Church, whatever their calling might be.

Luis Sala Balust gives us a pointed summary of the life of these apostolic men who followed St. John of Avila. He writes:

Their dress was very modest: cassock and a moderate cape, and at home, clothes of a grayish wool material. Rejecting honors and riches, they consecrated their energies to the religious formation of youth, according to the rules that they received from Avila. They would read scholastic and positive theology. They would preach in the city at all major feasts and they were directors of souls. If they were needed, they would go out giving missions through the different villages.[10]

With the help of these priests—up to twenty-four in the city of Cordoba alone—St. John of Avila founded different colleges, since he realized that children were the future of society. This agglomeration of priests, at times, acted as seminaries where candidates would prepare for ministry. It was precisely how the University of Baeza was born in 1538. St. John of Avila founded it to form the future professors that would, in turn, form other priests. Not surprisingly, he was appointed as its first rector. In 1543, Pope Paul III granted the university the right to confer even doctoral degrees.[11]

It is very significant that no one would graduate from the University of Baeza without going out on missions throughout different cities.[12] This is because that is precisely why the candidates were in that university: to prepare themselves to be preachers and directors of souls. The pastoral component could not be divorced from the education the men were receiving.[13] This is a sign that, in the mind of the Apostle of Andalusia, a priest was called to be *with* and *for* the people.

The temptation to get wrapped up in oneself or in spiritual delights has always been there. The way in which St. John of Avila responds to this temptation in his own time is very admirable. Living at a time when the effects of the *devotio moderna* and the mystical desire to look only for the "way of love"[14] can still be felt, he advises a balanced approach between love of God and love of neighbor. This can be seen, for instance, in a letter he writes to one of his priest disciples. After giving some recommendations for the priest's prayers and his personal study, he tells the priest:

> Spend the evening serving your neighbor in the following way: know what sick people are in danger of death and go visit and encourage them, do your best to be present when they die, because it will be good for you and it would be of great benefit to them; other times go to the hospital and console the sick; others, if you know of people who are at odds with others and you feel you can help, go talk to them; and I would like you ordinarily to read in public, if there are some young people inclined for this, something on good manners, something like Tulio, etc., or something by Plato, or similar things without going into the mysteries of Christianity, because this is the foundation that is needed in order to be a disciple.[15]

The fact St. John says that "it would be good for you" to visit people who are close to dying is a reminder that the ministry of the priest helps his own spirituality. In this particular case, visiting these parishioners could help the priest be mindful of his own death and reflect on how he wants to serve God until that moment comes.[16]

The balanced suggestions of St. John of Avila were so effective that they were followed in similar ways in France with what became known as the "French School" and in Italy, with St. Charles Borromeo.[17] Although the reform that was enacted in these countries had its own set of challenges, most major spiritual figures mention the Apostle of Andalusia as a precursor.[18]

The Priest as Preacher and Teacher

St. John of Avila has been known as "the Apostolic Preacher" throughout the ages. All his biographers and early editions of his works refer to him with titles that revolve around this aspect of his priesthood.[19] Fra Louis of Granada, in first writing the life of St. John, sees St. John's person as being inseparable from his preaching. This is evident in the title Fra Louis chose for his work: *Vida del Padre Maestro Juan de Ávila y las partes que ha de tener un predicador del Evangelio.* Indeed, as *Presbyterorum Ordinis* states, preaching is "the first task" of the priest since no one can be saved unless they come to believe as a result of hearing God's Word.[20]

The Council of Trent declared that preaching is a bishop's main responsibility.[21] This follows what Jesus Himself said about His own mission in the Gospel of Mark, that preaching was the purpose for which He had come into the world.[22] As one of those who continues the mission of the apostles, the bishop has an understandable responsibility to preach the Good News. And since priests are collaborators of the bishop, preaching is also, therefore, their main task, as *Presbyterorum Ordinis* declares.[23] Always mindful of Church councils and what was needed for the good of people, the Apostle of Andalusia speaks of this preaching duty in his writings on reform.[24]

The love that St. John had for preaching God's word is palpable in his sermons and in his writings. The priest, he believed, was the voice of Jesus. He explains this in one of his sermons, which is worth quoting at length:

> Poor me and others like me, for we have the office of St. John [the Baptist] and we do not have his holiness! *Labia sacerdotis custodiunt scientiam et legem requirunt ex ore eius* (cf. Mal 2:7). The priest, the preacher, angel; *quia ángelus significat nuntius*, for the preacher is God's messenger and God speaks through his mouth. We are God's messengers, royal priests, and I am not sure if because we do not know how to represent this office or why, our hearers only look at us with earthly eyes and only see the exterior. If the preacher first cried because of his unworthiness of having such an office and prayed that people would come to the sermons saying, "I am going to hear God," and they prepared themselves to hear the word of God, that, even if it is preached by a sinful and miserable man like me, they are the words of God and not the preacher's, for in the name of God he tells them to you, as if a letter from the emperor came to this village, you would hear the words as coming from him, and so you obey them, even if the one who reads them is not the emperor, but a messenger; if you came to hear sermons in this way and with this faith, you would believe what is said in them in a different way and they would be of more benefit to you. I am not St. John the Baptist, but, because I am a preacher, I have his office, and I tell you, in the name of God and on his behalf to prepare your souls. God wants to come and dwell in each one of you who are here.[25]

When St. John had an opportunity to suggest to the bishops meeting at Trent ways in which they could renew the

Church, the office of preaching also found a prime spot in his *Memoriales*. Besides recommending formation for confessors and pastors, colleges—or seminaries, as they will later be known—had to place special emphasis on preparing preachers, "whose office is really forgotten in the clergy."[26] It was essential that bishops formed good priests for this ministry so that "beneficial nourishment [could] be offered to the sheep." Otherwise, the experienced St. John said, these preachers could even "contradict those who offer the true teaching,"[27] as it happened when he was denounced to the Inquisition.

What made the preaching of St. John so popular and effective that people would even "get up early to find a seat in church"[28] whenever they knew he would be giving the sermon? Thankfully, it is not a secret. We do know the way in which he prepared himself and which those aspiring to touch the hearts of others and aid in their conversion can imitate.

Prayer and Study

According to St. John of Avila, the most important step in preparing to preach was personal prayer.[29] Whenever his disciples would come to him to present their plan of life, he would often recommend taking time away from studying and dedicating it to prayer.[30] It was not a matter of "reading and then [going] to vomit what has been read."[31] Those who knew him could testify that "he would study the sermons he preached on his knees at prayer."[32] Fra Louis of Granada tells us that he heard him say that "the night before the sermon was enough" for the immediate preparation.[33] Five or six lines written on a single page was all he needed to preach up to two hours.[34] But yes, as Granada writes, when the sermon had to be brief, St. John would have to study more, "not to find what to say, but to shorten what he had to say," since the fountain of his knowledge and spiritual insights was abundant.[35] In his own recommendations, St. John of Avila tells priests to "study the sermon three or four days at leisure, and the day before the sermon to employ it in delighting himself in what he ought to say," but always making sure "not to preach without study nor without that day of personal recollection."[36] In other words, prayer and study must always go hand in hand.

Clear Objectives

Louis of Granada was actually the recipient of Letter I in St. John of Avila's epistolary. Scholars place the letter in 1544 since St. John speaks of the "new calling" that Granada had received, and it was in that year that he was appointed as *Predicador general* (an itinerant preacher) in the provincial chapter of Osuna which took place that year.[37] It is interesting that the friar gives such an importance to the saint's recommendations when it comes to preaching since Dominicans have preaching as the order's main charism. The reason seems to be because the saint focused not so much on methods, but on the motives and ultimate goal of the preaching. These recommendations seem to have provided additional insights to the friar beyond those he had received in his formation in the Order of Preachers.

Spiritual Fatherhood

The Apostle of Andalusia was certain that it is through the office of preaching that one begets spiritual children. Ever the interpreter of St. Paul, he reads a passage from the Apostle in this context. In that letter to Granada, St. John says:

Christ the man was the first one on whom that full and life-giving spirit came to dwell, begetting children of God through the word and dying for them, and for this he deserved to be called *Pater futuri saeculi* (Is 9:6). . . . [Jesus] wanted to put this spirit and this tongue in some so that, for his glory, they can also enjoy the title of spiritual fathers, as He is called, according to what St. Paul so daringly affirms: *Per Evangelium ego vos genui* (1 Cor 4:15).[38]

This spiritual fatherhood born of preaching is also mentioned when St. John of Avila writes to the bishops at Trent in his first *Memorial.*[39] But what does he mean by that expression? Besides the fact that the preacher must first have "the spirit of a good son of God, the common Father,"[40] St. John explains to Granada:

Having in our inner being reverence, trust and pure love for God, as a faithful son has for his father, it remains to ask him for the spirit of fatherhood for the children that we beget. Because it is not enough for a good father to beget and then pass on the burden of educating them to another; but, with persevering love, he suffers all the hardships that must be endured in raising them, until they are placed in the hands of God, taking them out of this dangerous place as the father has great care for the wellbeing of his daughter until he sees her married.[41]

The love that God places in the heart of the priest could also be seen as that of a mother, as witnessed in the Sacred Scriptures. The Apostle of Andalusia makes this assertion in one of his sermons: "It is as when a mother loves her son very much and spends her life clinging to him; if she wants health it is in order that her son have health, she has no joy except her son's, no contentment except that of her son, as the Apostle would say to those from Thessalonica: *Nunc vivimus, si vos statis in Domino* (1 Thes 3:8)."[42] Therefore, "the children that we beget through the word ought not to be children of voice but of tears,"[43] St. John says.

As a true father himself, St. John of Avila could tell Granada that "if they [these spiritual children] die, believe me, father, that there is no pain that could be equal to this."[44] This is the case because clergy are dealing with eternal souls, not just with bodies who are temporarily in this world:

> This pain does not go away with any earthly consolation; not with seeing that, if some die, others are born; not with saying what is enough with all other evils: *The Lord gave, the Lord has taken away; blessed be the name of the Lord* (Jb 1:21). Because if we are dealing with the soul, and the loss of a soul that belonged to God, and this leads to his dishonor and the increase of the reign of our sinful adversary, there is no one who can console so understandable and such numerous pains.[45]

Preaching and the Desire to Convert Souls

From what has been said, we can see how the priest's spiritual fatherhood leads to the desire to work for the salvation of souls. St. John of Avila would recommend preachers go to the pulpit *templados*—that is, with hunger for souls. Granada has an excellent description of this when he speaks of St. John of Avila. He writes:

> From this same love and desire [to save his spiritual children] would come also the great fervor and fire with which he preached. Because he would say that, when

he had to preach, his primary concern was to go to the pulpit "templado." With this word he meant that, those who hunt with birds try that the hawk or the falcon with which they hunt be "tempered" [templado], that is, that it be hungry, because this would make it go more eagerly for the prey, so in the same way he would make sure to go up to the pulpit not only with actual devotion, but with this great hunger and desire to win a soul for Christ; this would make him preach with greater zeal and fervor of spirit.[46]

St. John of Avila's efforts were not without results. It was precisely in hearing him preach that the future saints John of God[47] and Francis Borgia[48] were converted. From the moment of their conversion, these great apostles of Christ considered John of Avila their spiritual father. To him they would return time and again to consult him on different things regarding their calling or the details of their ministry.[49]

PREACHING AND GOD'S LOVE

Pope Francis has emphasized God's mercy from the beginning of his pontificate. In the bull instituting the Extraordinary Jubilee of Mercy, he writes: "The Church is called above all to be a credible witness to mercy, professing it and living it as the core of the revelation of Jesus Christ."[50] Mercy, charity, and love are different names of the same patient and generous reality of our God who, although He is just, He "responds with the fullness of mercy. Mercy will always be greater than any sin, and no one can place limits on the love of God who is ever ready to forgive."[51] Since charity is "the core of the revelation of Jesus Christ,"[52] this was not a new concept to St. John of Avila. In fact, one of his treatises deals precisely with this point, his *Tratado del amor de Dios*.[53] Though he emphasized the concept of sin and the need for conversion because of the times in which he was living, he always came back to this reality of God's love. His preaching was imbued with this call to return to the love of the Father.

Granada mentions that, upon being asked by a virtuous theologian what recommendations he would give for good preaching, St. John simply responded: "loving Our Lord very much."[54] And, of course, as the great commandment[55] declares, from the love of God is derived love for neighbor. That was also a natural consequence in our saint, as Granada relates:

> Being this bait of love a very efficacious way of catching souls, it is not surprising that this would not be lacking in our great hunter and great imitator of the Apostle. And what I can say as a summary is that I will never know for sure with what he won more souls for Christ, if with the words of his teaching or with the greatness of his charity and love—accompanied by good works—that he would show everyone. Because in loving them he would adjust himself to the needs of others, as if he were everyone's father, making himself, as the Apostle says, *all things to all people to help everyone* (1 Cor 9:22). He would console the sad ones, strengthen the weak, encourage the strong, help the tempted, teach the ignorant, awake the slothful, he would try to raise the fallen ones, but never with harsh words, but with loving ones; not with anger, but *with a meek spirit*, as the Apostle advises (cf. 1 Cor 4:21).[56]

St. John's second biographer concurs. According to him, the words of the Apostle of Andalusia, "even though they were of correction, were wrapped in love, charity and zeal for the benefit of their souls, and because of that people would listen with noticeable affection."[57] And as a result, when the sermon was over, "they would all walk with their heads down, silent and remorseful."[58]

PRAISE OF GOD, NOT THE PREACHER

A common temptation for some priests is to want to draw people to themselves rather than to God. Although this is understandable given a person's human need to be loved and appreciated, when the priest is not aware of this tempation or does not keep it in check, it can affect the way he preaches or relates to others. St. John of Avila addresses this situation. In the letter that he sent to Louis of Granada at the beginning of his preaching ministry, he writes:

> For the office for which you have been called, your reverence must see that your filial spirit for God, our common Father, is not diminished, nor the one of spiritual father for those that God gives you as children. Regarding the former, that most high Majesty must be especially reverenced, adoring it with very deep humility, not minding yourself but rather losing yourself in the great abyss of his being and being faithful to him, seeking in everything and above all his glory, renouncing and adjuring *ex toto corde* one's own, saying like Joseph: *Everything that belongs to my Lord he put in my hands, except you, his wife* (cf. Gn 39:8f). The glory of God must be given to God, for they belong to each other; if we want to give it to another, is there a worse marriage or a greater adultery that the glory of the Creator be given to the creature? The wife that we must seek should be the souls that we

work with, and Christ must be honored in them and we must be forgotten; they must remember him more, except where he sees it necessary that through our memory and esteem they love him and acknowledge him.[59]

This reminder is so necessary that he repeats it again and again to the different priests with which he worked. In another letter, he says:

Let us look only for the glory of God, seek it and preach it; whoever looks for his own is similar to the one who went to tell a young lady that the son of the king wanted to marry her if she agreed and the messenger ends up keeping for himself the one that he was sent to seek for the son. We are sent so that they can love Christ, for He loves them; let us be careful not to seek our own interests, for that would be a great treason. . . .

Many times, father, it happens that in this office we are honored and despised; but the servant of God must be deaf to one and the other, although he must be happier with being despised than in being honored, for that conforms him more to Christ who was dishonored for seeking the Father's honor.[60]

St. John knew what he was saying. When the preacher seeks his own glory and tries to please his listeners, he ends up "editing the Gospel and giving it contradictory meanings or he will teach a doctrine contrary to the will of God: he will make God say what He did not mean."[61]

Preaching with One's Life

The Church has always recognized the importance of personal testimony in the preaching of the Gospel. In *Presbyterorum Ordinis*, for example, we read:

> Priests then owe it to everybody to share with them the truth of the Gospel in which they rejoice in the Lord. Therefore, whether *by their exemplary behavior* they lead people to glorify God; or by their preaching proclaim the mystery of Christ to unbelievers; or teach the Christian message or explain the Church's doctrine; or endeavor to treat contemporary problems in the light of Christ's teaching—in every case their role is to teach not their own wisdom but the Word of God and to issue a pressing invitation to all men [and women] to conversion and to holiness.[62]

It is not by accident that "exemplary behavior" is mentioned before the actual actions of preaching and teaching. As a common Spanish proverb says, "*las palabras llaman la atención, pero el ejemplo arrastra*" (words catch others' attention, but witness actually drags the person). When those listening see a contradiction between the person's words and his actions, the actions carry more weight. This is why St. Charles Borromeo told his priests in a beautiful excerpt that we find in the Office of Readings for his feast: "Be sure that you first preach by the way you live. If you do not . . . , your words will bring only cynical laughter and a derisive shake of the head."[63]

St. John of Avila felt that he had to remind bishops of this truth in his day since preaching was their "principal responsibility."[64] In that list of recommendations that he wrote for the Spanish bishops that were going to be meeting in the Synod of Toledo, he says very strongly:

> In ancient times prelates had poor tables, their guests were pilgrims and people in need, the music at their gatherings was the reading of sacred Scriptures; this is all according to what the councils prescribe for them. Their servants were people that came to their houses as disciples of virtue, for they saw them as true teachers who professed it. This was the case of Clement with St. Peter, and Mark, Luke and Timothy with St. Paul, and Lawrence with Sixtus, and many others.

> Their beds, far from comfort, were full of severity to be mindful of others. Their curtains, the upholstery of their homes, were either bare walls or adorned with paintings or pictures that moved others to greater devotion; this way they were interiorly full of heavenly treasures and they were revered more than the emperors.

> Now, I am afraid to say that, because of our sins, what the pontiff and martyr Boniface said about priests applies to some of the bishops of our day: '*Quondam sacerdotes aurei, ligneis calicibus utebantur; nunc lignei sacerdotes, aureis calicibus utuntur.*'[65]

This reality was so important to him that he would mention it to individual bishops whenever he had the opportunity. He would say things like: "Bed of silk is not fitting, nor courtly dresses. *Episcopus vilem suppellectilem, et tamen eam pauperem habeat; et auctoritatem dignitatis suae fide et vitae meritis tueatur,* says a council."[66] And to another: "Do not think, your excellency, that you will persuade others to reform if you yourself do not go reformed."[67]

To priests, he would speak along the same lines. In a sermon he preached on Holy Thursday, St. John of Avila says:

> *Ponit vestimenta sua*; to serve others he took off what he licitly could have, and this way he gives an example that the greater ones, for the sake of others, should not make use of some things that they could licitly have. . . . Christ did not look at *licet*, but to *expedit*, and *aedificat*, *ut Paulus: Omnia mihi licent, sed non omnia aedificant, non quaerens quod mihi utile est* (cf. 1 Cor 10:23). When serving, it is convenient to take off that which is ornate because many times the pomp of the superior gets in the way of edifying his subjects.[68]

And because St. John knew that priests could fall into making justifications like all other human beings when they try to come up with ways to look for a comfortable life, he addressed this tendency in one of his priestly conferences. There, he tells the priests:

> Each one of you could say that you are giving a good example in the way that you are now living. The greatest difficulty in each particular case is to apply universal rules to the individual circumstances; it is here that we can have different opinions, because *omnis scientia est de universalibus*, and no one is able to prescribe individual cases in all circumstances. And so we say that the married person must dress a certain way and the clergyman in a different one, but which one is appropriate is difficult to say; because each person will say that what he is wearing is decent and, this way, by dressing up themselves in the

profanity of the world, they say that it is appropriate for their state of life. So how can we come to the truth? St. Thomas, 1-2: *Quod, sicut se habet principium, in speculativis respectu conclusionum, ita finis in practicis respectu mediorum*, etc., therefore, if the end, for those of you who are clerics, is to win souls for God, let us see with what kind of dress and instruments you will be able to do this; the end will give you the answer. . . . The apostles and the disciples lived very differently from what we see today.[69]

In preaching to others then, actions speak louder than words,[70] and "when a preacher speaks from what he practices, he does a great favor to the people."[71]

Prophetic Voice

At times, the priest will find circumstances in which he needs to say something outside of preaching in order to correct situations not in line with the Gospel. Since St. John of Avila lived at a time when reform was badly needed in the Church, he had to do much correcting. His recommendations for the Spanish bishops at the synod in Toledo are full of such passages. But in concrete cases, too, he did not hesitate to speak the truth.

A witness in his canonization process mentions how he corrected a bishop for having too many animals of different kinds in his farm. According to the saint, this was scandalizing to the underprivileged people who had to go see the bishop. Likewise, to one who had a very "worldly" picture in his quarters, he also pointed it out, telling him that it was not helpful in bringing people to greater devotion. The bishops "were so edified by the correction that from then on they would consult him about some of the serious and difficult issues that came up in their administration."[72]

St. John was not afraid of making recommendations— even for the Pope. This can be seen in his second *Memorial* for the Council of Trent. The reform that the Church needed had to be at every level. Since the Pope was "the supreme shepherd," the "principal watchtower," he also needed to be on board with these changes. It is worth looking at some brief excerpts of what the saint suggests for him:

> Who will not follow the vicar of Christ when they see that he follows Christ? Who among the clergy will dare to live the way he wants to when they see their prince living a life of penance for the good of the Church? Then the barking of the heretics will stop, for they do use as an excuse the bad example that they say they have seen in the Apostolic See; with the good odor that now could come from it, the bad one from former times will go away and can witness even to those who are outside the Church; it can be so strong as to overcome them or invite them back to the Church, for they do say that is the reason why they left.[73]

He goes on to say that since the Pope presides over all the churches, he needs to oversee bishops to make sure they are fulfilling their duties as shepherds so that the council can be fully implemented. Since St. John speaks "not as a Luther or a Savonarola, but rather as St. Bernard or as St. Catherine of Siena did when they had to speak in similar terms"[74] for the good of the Church, his words were welcomed and heeded.[75]

The Apostle of Andalusia follows the example of the Old Testament prophets who spoke on behalf of the poor. He writes to kings to encourage them not to allow their citizens to fall into poverty since "from poverty come many sins and evils against God and neighbor."[76] Likewise, he reminds bishops of their responsibility to care for widows and the poor and the fact that the rents they received for the properties of their dioceses, after providing the essentials for their personal needs, had to be given to the poor as it was mandated by the Church.[77] Yet, in writing to priests, he warns them of the temptation to get caught up in those works that can actually impede them from carrying out their true ministry. He says:

> Do not get involved in remedying corporal needs
> except in ordering in general how this is to be done,
> as in ordering a group or similar things, and let that be
> sufficient; your [spiritual] children must know that they
> must not come to you hoping for any temporal favor,
> because if they do, it will be a stumbling block for what
> you actually need to do. And this is mandated in the
> Fourth Carthaginian Council [c. 117], where it says [c. 20]:
> "Let the bishop not care himself for the widows, orphans
> and pilgrims, but through the archdeacon or assistants,"
> and it also said: "May he only tend to lecturing, prayer
> and the preaching of the word. . . .[78]" Flee from all these
> temporal things, remembering how the Lord would throw
> it on people's faces, saying: *You look for me, not because of the
> signs you have seen, but because you ate and were full* (Jn 6:26).

"This rule has an exception," St. John continues: "If you know of a special corporal need from which depends something for the soul, then you can respond to it; but this truly happens a few times, even though the person who needs it says that it is frequent."[79]

St. John of Avila could discern what Vatican II would proclaim later about the laity being responsible for worldly realities.[80] He was well founded on this since it was there in Sacred Scripture from the beginning when the Apostles declared: "It is not right for us to neglect the word of God to serve at table" (Acts 6:2).

Teaching as an Extension of Preaching the Good News

When Jesus sent forth His disciples to preach the good news, He told them: "Go, therefore, and make disciples of all nations, baptizing them in the name of the Father, and of the Son, and of the holy Spirit, *teaching them* to observe all that I have commanded you" (Mt 28:19-20, emphasis added). In the ministry of preaching, as St. John of Avila would say, spiritual children are born. But they also need formation in order to grow and mature into active disciples of the Lord.

The concern is not absent from the recommendations of the Apostle of Andalusia nor from his own ministry. In his second *Memorial* for the Council of Trent, he writes to the bishops of the need for catechesis and good books for children. This, he says, would keep Christians "firm on true doctrine," so that "drinking from it, they could keep themselves from the falsehood of heresies."[81] We can sense the sadness that this true pastor felt when catechesis was lacking:

> Because of our sins we can see in our days the great damage that has come to the Church because this [doctrine] has been missing or because it has been done as a joke. One of the causes—and not a minor one— for which many Christians have lost their faith is that they were so slimly formed and founded on it without appreciating the Christian mysteries, and they have been

easily persuaded by any error against the faith as people who are not firmly attached to the truth. . . . With great sorrow we have experienced, and can see fulfilled, what the prophet Isaiah said: *Therefore my people will be deported, for lack of knowledge* (Is 5:13), etc.[82]

This is precisely why St. John would spend his evenings teaching others; and wherever his disciples from his "priestly school" went, they also had directives from him to make the instruction of catechism a priority.[83] He even composed prayers and lessons in the form of song so that it would be easy for children to learn and share with others.[84] And besides his own efforts, he also encouraged the bishops at Trent to compose a catechism for children,[85] one for adults in the vernacular,[86] and one for priests in Latin, making it mandatory for all of them to have a copy so that "pastors and preachers . . . could read effectively from it."[87]

Prophetic Living and the Evangelical Counsels

Because those who enter religious life in the Church make a public vow to follow the evangelical counsels, sometimes people get the impression that religious are the only ones who are called to live them. This is not biblical nor is it the teaching of the Church. The Gospel of Luke tells us that when Jesus called people to set aside their family and to "renounce all [their] possessions" (14:33), he was not just talking to the Twelve or to a small group of disciples. Jesus addressed this call to the "great crowds [that] were traveling with him" (Lk 14:25). He intended for every disciple of His to have an undivided devotion to Him and to the Father's will.

The Church spells out the living of the counsels in *Lumen Gentium*. Speaking of the holiness that each baptized person is called to embrace in imitation of the holiness of Christ, the dogmatic constitution says: "This holiness . . . is expressed in many ways by the individuals who, *each in his own state of life*, tend to the perfection of love, thus helping others to grow in holiness; it appears in a manner peculiar to itself in the practice of the counsels which have been usually called 'evangelical.'"[88] The constitution then goes on to specify how each vocation can put this into practice.[89]

There is no question, therefore, that diocesan priests are called to live out the radical spirituality of the evangelical counsels.[90] The Decree on the Training of Priests, *Optatam Totius*, makes this clear: "With special care they should be so trained in priestly *obedience, poverty and a spirit of self-denial*, that they may accustom themselves to living in conformity with the crucified Christ and to giving up willingly even those things which are lawful, but not expedient."[91] Since the directives in this decree "are immediately concerned with the diocesan clergy,"[92] no one can deny that the spirit of the counsels applies to them as well. St. John Paul II reminds us of this in *Pastores Dabo Vobis* when he speaks of "priestly life and the radicalism of the Gospel."[93] The evangelical counsels are a great aid in being a prophetic witness in the life of the Church, in living in imitation of the first apostles who followed the Lord. Consequently, they are indispensable for the spirituality of the diocesan priest.

POVERTY

St. John of Avila was certainly familiar with the evangelical counsels. They were the vows traditionally made in the Church by those entering religious life. He speaks of them in his correspondence with those seeking to enter that state.[94]

But he also saw them as the response of "every good Christian"[95] to the love shown to them by Christ. If Christ tells His disciples to follow Him, St. John reasons, "Would not the Christian be embarrassed and pained to see Christ poor when he himself is rich, to see Christ tired when he is rested, to see Christ carrying a cross and barefoot, with blood dripping from his body, and him without any discomfort?"[96] "Just as the worldly person wishes to receive gifts, honor and riches, the Christian must wish to be dishonored, to be poor and to experience difficulties."[97]

St. John had a great love for poverty. In one of his sermons, he explains why:

> What a heavy burden it was to be poor before Christ came into the world; it was to be despised, to be rejected! But the Rich One came down from heaven and chose a poor mother, a poor guardian, and is born under a poor portal, he takes a manger for his cradle, and was wrapped in poor swaddling clothes (cf. Mt 8:20), and later, when he was an adult, he so loved poverty that he did not have a place to lay his head, and, finally, he was such a lover of poverty that there is no longer a Christian, if he is a true Christian, who does not value more being poor than rich. Thus, after he came in such poverty, many left their inheritances in order to become poor, wanting more to be poor with Christ than rich with the world.[98]

As always, the saint is speaking here not just with words, but with actions. He, too, was one of those who gave away his inheritance in order to follow the Lord.[99]

In regard to priests, St. John speaks of imitating the hunger for souls that was found in Jesus, whose food was "to do

the will of the [Father] and to finish his work" (Jn 4:34). In a
sermon preached on a feast of an evangelist, St. John lays out
what Jesus envisioned for His "helpers."[100] Since "what they
do is commonly done by the people,"[101] that is, they follow
the example they see in them, it was important that they "not
be loaded with temporal subsidies because, busy with these,
they will not tend well to the care of souls, which asks for the
whole man."[102] "The spiritual alms," he continues, "that are
due to souls, are better than the corporal ones."[103] So once
again, the priest must remember that he is a spiritual father,
not an earthly one who is called to provide for the material
needs of the faithful.

Since people do tend to imitate what they see in their
pastors, St. John was careful to live a very simple lifestyle. As
Monsignor Esquerda tells us:

> All the biographers of Master Avila underline his life of
> evangelical poverty. . . . During his first years of ministry
> in Seville, he already distinguished himself for his life
> of poverty and his closeness to the poor. During his
> later apostolic journeys, he would stay in poor homes,
> declining the invitation to live in palaces. For example, in
> Zafra (1546) he did not want to live in the house of his
> friends, the Count and Countess of Feria.[104]

This is true. Even in his retirement in Montilla, he chose
to live in a small house that his friends had for their servants
rather than in the main house with the wealthy benefactors.[105]
He would also eat very simply,[106] and when people insisted on
replacing his shoes or his hat, he would respond: "When I go
up on the pulpit to denounce vices and exhort others to live a
life of poverty and mortification and they see me with a nice

cassock and a good hat, what will my listeners say?"[107] Even
the benefice that he had accepted in order to incardinate
into the diocese of Cordoba was designated to pay for the
studies of poor students from the schools he founded with
his disciples.[108]

This action of giving his stipend to pay for the education
of children was more than a gesture of kindness. The Apostle
of Andalusia explains this in *Plática* 8, where he challenges
one of his beloved professors on the subject of Church rents.
Domingo de Soto had just published an important work
entitled *De iusticia et iure* where he basically said that clergy
could do whatever they wanted with their income. In this
conference given to priest, St. John turns to the authority of
Church Fathers like St. Jerome and St. John Chrysostom and
that of St. Paul to say that, "if the Gospel gives [the priest]
enough to support himself, everything that remains must be
used in works of charity."[109] In the teachings of Vatican II,
similar words can be found: "Priests as men whose 'portion
and inheritance' (Nm 18:20) is the Lord ought to use temporal goods only for those purposes to which the teaching
of Christ and the direction of the Church allow them to be
devoted."[110] The following words from *Presbyterorum Ordinis*
are ones with which St. John of Avila would agree:

> In fact priests are invited to embrace voluntary poverty.
> By it they become more clearly conformed to Christ and
> more ready to devote themselves to their sacred ministry.
> For Christ being rich became poor for our sakes, that
> through his poverty we might be rich. The apostles by
> their example gave testimony that the free gift of God
> was to be given freely.

Guided then by the Spirit of the Lord, who anointed the Saviour and sent him to preach the Gospel to the poor, priests and bishops alike are to avoid everything that might in any way antagonize the poor. More than the rest of Christ's disciples they are to put aside all appearance of vanity in their surroundings. They are to arrange their house in such a way that it never appears unapproachable to anyone and that nobody, even the humblest, is ever afraid to visit it.[111]

We priests of the twenty-first century would do well to reflect on these words and the example of saints like John of Avila for, as a prominent theologian and evangelizer has observed: "The lack of evangelical poverty—along with the lack of humility and charity—has always been the main cause of divisions in ecclesial communities and also among their own members."[112]

CHASTITY

Just as there is an interconnection between the different moral virtues,[113] St. John of Avila sees an intrinsic connection between the different evangelical counsels. One cannot be chaste unless he is used to experiencing privations and simplicity of life. He explains this in a sermon he preached during Lent:

Do you think that relaxing and sleeping and having a full belly helps you in reaching chastity? No, brother, Christ rests on clean linen corporals; just as cotton, in order to become linen has to first undergo so many processes, in the same manner the one who wants to be chaste must punish his body with fasts. Whoever flees from fasts and discipline and gives himself to relax, to eat, and to give comforts to the body, is unable to remain chaste. Whoever wants chastity without abstinence, as St. Jerome says, can say good-bye to it.[114]

St. John also makes similar assertions in his treatise *Audi, filia*. Although the work was written specifically for a lay woman, his teaching here could also be of benefit to priests. He writes:

> Saint Paul, a "vessel of election" (cf. Acts 9:15) did not trust his flesh. He says that he chastises it and brings it into subjection lest, while he preaches to others about living virtuous lives, he might himself become wicked (1 Cor 9:27) by falling into some sin. How can we, who have less virtue and greater causes for fear than Saint Paul, think that we can be chaste without disciplining the body? It is very hard to preserve humility in the midst of honors, temperance in the midst of abundance, and chastity in the midst of pleasures. Anyone who sought to quench the fire burning up his house by throwing dry wood on it would be worthy of scorn. Much more worthy of scorn are those who, on the one hand, desire chastity, and on the other hand, satiate their flesh with delicacies and pleasures and give themselves to idleness. These things not only do not quench the fire that is already burning, but they suffice to rekindle it where it has been practically quenched.[115]

It has already been said how St. John recommended against changing the Church's discipline on celibacy. This sacred office calls for "the whole man, not one who is divided,"[116] he would say. Since a priest is the one who represents Jesus in the community, "the most pure body of Jesus

Christ" must be handled "by a priest with a pure body."[117] Therefore, St. John writes, chastity is the "proper virtue, the very and most proper virtue of the apostolic priest."[118]

Because chastity is such an important virtue, our saint also would take precautions not to put himself in situations that would compromise it. He would never allow a woman to come into his house—not even his benefactress, who owned it. If a woman wanted to speak with him and to go to confession, he would see her only in a church.[119] In his letters, he also warns other priests about similar imprudent but dangerous practices in regard to confession and spiritual counsel.[120]

OBEDIENCE

In regard to obedience, the obedience of Jesus is the point of reference for St. John of Avila.[121] Even before Jesus was born, John says, Jesus was giving us lessons on obedience: "Cesar [*sic*] ordered that each one should go to his home town to register and to pay some sort of tribute, and God obeys. Should I not be embarrassed of not being obedient?"[122] In *Audi, filia*, he recommends this "humble obedience" for everyone:

> You can be certain that even if you search much, you will not find any other path as certain and safe for finding God's will as this one of humble obedience, so much advised by all the saints and so well practiced by many of them. The lives of the holy fathers bear witness to this. Among them, being subject to one's elder was regarded as a very great sign that one had arrived at perfection.[123]

This is the reason why, beginning with St. John himself, spiritual direction has always been discussed and commended by all spiritual masters. St. Francis de Sales certainly mentions the Apostle of Andalusia when he makes reference to this practice.[124]

In the life of the priest, since he promises obedience to his bishop,[125] he must also imitate the obedience of Christ, who humbles Himself to come to the altar when the words of the priest are spoken. The words pronounced by St. John of Avila in one of his priestly conferences are worth pondering:

> What a great lesson for us! What an admirable example! He can certainly say to us: *"Si ego Dominus et magister* (cf. Jn 13:14), being glorious, and being served by saints in angels in heaven (as he is); if I humble myself to obey so promptly and willingly, should it not be right for you to obey me and everyone else because of me?" Who does not remain astonished and with profound humility after having consecrated as to say like St. Peter and St. John the Baptist: *You*, Lord, *are coming to me?* (cf. Lk 5:8; Mt 3:14). What priest, upon deeply pondering this admirable obedience that Christ has for him, the greater one to the lesser one, the King to the subject, God to creature, would have the heart not to obey our Lord in his holy commandments and to lose his life, even on a cross, before losing his obedience?[126]

St. John Paul II concurs in *Pastores Dabo Vobis*. The humility and self-emptying of Jesus are "the model and source of the virtues of obedience, chastity and poverty which the priest is called to live out as an expression of his pastoral charity for his brothers and sisters."[127] It is to this pastoral charity and the spirituality of the Good Shepherd that we now turn in the next chapter.

Conclusion

St. John of Avila is known as the Apostle of Andalusia because of his extensive preaching ministry in that southern region of Spain. As he traveled through different cities, he elicited many conversions, including those of two men who later would be known as St. John of God and St. Francis Borgia. His preaching method was so effective that it won him many "spiritual children," as he would say. Much of a biography written of the saint by the Dominican Louis of Granada is dedicated to his effective preaching ministry. The reason it was powerful, he and others would agree, was because, besides his obvious love for the Lord and for his listeners, he preached with his example.

The fact that preaching is "the first task" of diocesan priests, as the Church states, is a call and an obligation for the priest to be conformed to Christ and to His holy word. As the priest prays and prepares to preach, he must allow God's word to scrutinize his thoughts and his way of life so that he can be a clearer and more powerful sign of Christ's presence in the midst of the community. There is no question that the priest's preaching ministry can assist him in his own spirituality.

Teaching is an extension of the prophetic office of bishops and priests. Again, as is the case with parents and with catechists in general, the teacher's example is the best way in which the Christian faith can be passed on from generation to generation. Thus, a spiritual observance of the evangelical counsels can be a helpful tool in becoming effective teachers and preachers of the Gospel. Following the example of Christ, the poor, chaste, and obedient Son of God, a diocesan priest, along with all Christians, can also preach with his own witness, as was the case of the humble Fr. Avila.

NOTES

1. Sala and Martín in *San Juan de Ávila: Obras Completas*, eds. L. Sala Balust and F. Martín Hernández, (Madrid: Biblioteca de Autores Cristianos, 2000-07), (from here on, abbreviated as *OC*). Sermon 81 in *OC*, vol. 3, n. 5 (the reference to St. Jerome is *Ep.* 78 mans.6: *Patrologia Latina* (from here on, abbreviated as *PL*) 22, 704. Religious are not an afterthought; they are also part of the Church. St. John expresses this in sermon 18 where he calls them the "heart" of the Mystical Body of Christ. See n. 19 and also "Religiosos" in *Diccionario de San Juan de Ávila* (from here on, abbreviated as *DJA*), 797-801.

2. Vatican II, *Ad Gentes* (1965), sec. 38 (from here on, abbreviated as *AG*). The universal aspect of the priest's ministry appears in several other Church documents. See *Presbyterorum Ordinis* (1965), sec. 10 (from here on, abbreviated as *PO*); *Lumen Gentium* (1964), sec. 28 (from here on, abbreviated as *LG*); John Paul II, *Pastores Dabo Vobis* (1992), sec. 32 (from here on, abbreviated as *PDV*).

3. Some authors speculate whether or not the saint remained in Spain because of his Jewish ancestry. Although it is not ever mentioned by him or his biographers, it is possible. The Spanish crown did decree an edict on June 15, 1510 barring all converts, their children, and grandchildren from going to the New World; this also included clergy. See *OC*, vol. 1, 32 (footnote 10).

4. Sermon 81 in *OC*, vol. 3, n. 5. It would be interesting to explore the relationship between the diocesan priest and his own family of origin. In *Pastores Dabo Vobis*, St. John Paul II does mention the importance of family in the life of the seminarian (see sec. 68) and in the on-going formation of the priest (see sec. 79). Unless priests are incardinated in a different diocese, they will spend most of their lives close to their families. Some even request assignments that would allow them to care for elderly parents. While the relationship will necessarily be different than that of a religious or a missionary, in the case of the diocesan priest, the call to "leave everything to follow the Lord" seems to suggest that he should have a certain amount of freedom to carry out his ministry. For St. John of Avila, this was no longer an issue since he was an only child and his parents had already died before he was ordained. *PDV*, however, does mention the need of forming candidates the way Jesus formed His apostles (see sec. 60) so that they can follow Him in the same way (see sec. 42). Louis Bouyer has an important insight in regard to ministry and family. He writes: "In renouncing family life (and many other things), the monk has no other purpose than that of freeing himself from the world in order to belong wholly to Christ. But the priest frees himself from belonging to

a particular family in order to be 'all things to all people,' according to the word of St. Paul (See 1 Cor 9:22)." *Introduction to the Spiritual Life*, 161.

5.   See Aidan Nichols, O.P., *Holy Order: Apostolic Priesthood from the New Testament to the Second Vatican Council* (Dublin: Veritas Publications, 1990), 104.

6.   See *Advertencias al Concilio de Toledo* in *OC*, vol. 2, n. 4 (from here on, abbreviated as *Advertencias*).

7.   See Baldomero Jiménez Duque, "La escuela sacerdotal de Ávila y San Juan de Ávila," in *El Maestro Ávila: Actas del Congreso Internacional*, Madrid 27-30 noviembre 2000, Junta Episcopal 'Pro Doctorado de San Juan de Ávila' (Madrid: Conferencia Episcopal Española, 2002), 893. On this "priestly school," see also Luis Sala Balust, "La escuela sacerdotal del Beato Maestro Padre Ávila," in *Semana Avilista* (Madrid, 1952), 183-197.

8.   See Letter 225 in in *OC*, vol. 4, 724-26, where St. John responds to one of these disciples who asks for some recommendations for his spiritual growth. It is very telling that St. John constantly says "it seems to me" as he gives his recommendations (*me parece*). He does not want his disciples to be conditioned, but to follow the guidance of the Spirit in what they feel called to do.

9.   See Sala Balust, "La escuela sacerdotal," 191.

10.   Ibid., 189.

11.   Ibid., 188-90.

12.   Luis Muñoz, *Vida y virtudes del venerable varón el P. Maestro Juan de Avila, predicador apostolico; con algunos elogios de las virtudes y vidas de algunos de sus mas principales discípulos. 1635*. In *Vidas del padre maestro Juan de Avila*. Edited by Luis Sala Balust. Reprint, Barcelona: Flors, 1964, 1.1, c. 20. Biblioteca Virtual Miguel de Cervantes, https:/2/bib.cervantes-virtual.com/ servlet/SirveObras/78038402103470573565679/index.htm (accessed March 15, 2014).

13.   See Sala and Martín, *OC*, vol. 1, 103.

14.   Ibid., 68.

15.   Letter 5 in *OC*, vol. 4, 36-37. In other letters, St. John of Avila addresses the dangers of spiritual delights in more detail. Letter 247 talks about "fleeing from the desire to have revelations and things of the sort" and Letter 184 speaks at length of those who look only for consolations, tears, and delights. The latter is written as a warning to some of his disciples who were treading on dangerous grounds because they were not following his balanced recommendations. Sadly, they were processed and burned by the Inquisition after St. John of Avila's death since they did not heed his warning (See *OC*, vol. 1, 280). From all the disciples who saw themselves as being part of St. John's "school," about thirty of them entered the Society of Jesus, some became Discalced Carmelites or hermits, and others continued serving the Church as professors or authors (See *OC*, vol. 1, 275-76; 305ff).

16.   See Ibid., 33-34. See also Letter 1, 13.

17.   See Juan Esquerda Bifet, ed., *Escritos sacerdotales* (Madrid: Biblioteca de Autores Cristianos, 2012), xxxvi.

18.   Besides the fact that St. Francis de Sales cites John of Avila extensively in his works, it is well-known the admiration that Cardinal Berulle, one of the main figures of the French School, had for our saint. See *OC*, vol. 1, 267, footnote 368.

19.   See Sala and Martín, *OC*, vol. 1, 245.

20.   *PO*, sec. 4.

21.   See Council of Trent, Session 5, ch. 2 and session 24, ch. 4.

22.   See Mark 1:38.

23.   See *PO*: "The People of God is formed into one in the first place by the Word of the living God, which is quite rightly sought from the mouth of priests. For since nobody can be saved who has not first believed, it is the first task of priests as co-workers of the bishop to preach the Gospel of God to all men [and women]. In this way they carry out the Lord's command 'Go into all the world and preach the Gospel to every creature (Mk 16:15) and thus set up and increase the People of God" (sec. 4). See also *PDV*, sec. 26.

24.   In his *Advertencias al concilio de Toledo*, he reminds bishops of this primary responsibility of theirs (See n. 17) and instructs them to secure good preachers for their parishes, both diocesan and religious. These were essential, he thought, to assist pastors and parish priests whose "familiarity with the people sometimes got in the way of the good doctrine they could offer" (*como son caseros y tienen con ellos gran familiaridad, no reciben tan de veras su doctrina, aunque ella sea muy buena*), n. 34. This also explains why he formed his "priestly school," this group of qualified preachers.

25.   Sermon 2 in *OC*, vol. 3, n. 2.

26.   *Memorial primero al Concilio de Trento* (from here on, abbreviated as *MT1*) in *OC*, vol. 2, n. 14.

27.   *Memorial Segundo al Concilio de Trento* (from here on, abbreviated as *MT2*) in *OC*, vol. 2, n. 69.

28.   See Sala and Martín, *OC*, vol. 1, 245.

29.   *PDV* also states: "[The priest] needs to approach the word with a docile and prayerful heart so that it may deeply penetrate his thoughts and feelings and bring about a new outlook in him, 'the mind of Christ' (1 Cor 2:16). . . . Only if he 'abides' in the word will the priest become a perfect disciple of the Lord," sec. 26.

30.   See Sala and Martín, *OC*, vol. 1, 247.

31.   Sermon 49 in *OC*, vol. 3, n. 8.

32.   *OC*, vol. 1, 247 (stated by a witness from his canonization process in the city of Granada).

33.   Muñoz, *Vida*, 57.

34.   Sala and Martín, *OC*, vol. 1, 248.

35.　Muñoz, *Vida*, 58.
36.　Letter 5 in *OC*, vol. 4, 39-40.
37.　See Sala and Martín, Introduction to Letter 1 in *OC*, vol. 4, 5.
38.　Ibid., 5-6.
39.　See *MT1*, n. 14.
40.　Letter 1 in *OC*, vol. 4, 6.
41.　Ibid.
42.　Sermon 49 in *OC*, vol. 3, n. 8.
43.　Letter 1 in *OC*, vol. 4, 7. He goes on to give the example of St. Monica and how God listened to her after the many tears she shed for her son.
44.　Ibid., 8.
45.　Ibid.
46.　Ibid., 42. Perhaps this is the great wisdom of the Church in the Eucharistic fast that applies to both the faithful and the priest. Those of us that have had many celebrations on a given feast or a Sunday when we have been unable to observe it can testify to the lack of energy that one experiences during the celebration. If the body is digesting the food, this physiological reaction does have an effect in the overall energy of the person, in this case, the preacher.
47.　The dramatic conversion of John of God took place in Granada on the feast of St. Sebastian (January 20) in 1537. See Sala and Martín, *OC*, vol. 1, 64-66.
48.　The Duke of Gandia, as Francis Borgia was known, heard St. John of Avila preached in Granada during the funeral of the Spanish empress. It was on May 16, 1539. After hearing him, Borgia was resolved "never to serve a master who would die." See Sala and Martín, *OC*, vol. 1, 71-72.
49.　Another noteworthy conversion was the one of a prominent university professor, Bernardino Carleval. It is said that when he heard of the preaching of St. John of Avila, he said, "let us go listen to this idiot to see what and how he preaches." However, after hearing him, Carleval was captivated by the man's simplicity and spiritual depth. He became one of his main collaborators in the founding of the University of Baeza. Ibid., 68-69.
50.　*Misericordiae Vultus: Bull of Indiction of the Extraordinary Jubilee of Mercy* (Vatican City: Libreria Editrice Vaticana, 2015), n. 25.
51.　Ibid., n. 3.
52.　We are reminded that Pope Benedict XVI chose *Deus Caritas Est* as the title for his very first encyclical, which was published on Christmas day, 2005. See *Acta Apostolicae Sedis* (from here on, abbreviated as *AAS*) 98 (2006), 217-252, English translation (Vatican City: Libreria Editrice Vaticana, 2006).
53.　See *OC*, vol. 1, 951-74.

54.   Luis de Granada, O.P., *Vida del padre maestro Juan de Avila*, 2nd edition (Madrid: Edibesa, 2010), 39.

55.   See Matthew 22:34-40.

56.   Ibid., 50-51.

57.   Muñoz, lib. 1, c. 22.

58.   Ibid., lib. 1, c. 11. The loving, respectful correction of St. John of Avila extended to brother priests. In his canonization process, one of the witnesses shared how the saint corrected a priest when he was celebrating Mass irreverently. St. John pretended to fix a candle on the altar as he drew close to the priest and whispered to his ear and said: "treat him well; he is a Son of a good Father." The priest was moved to tears and afterwards, they spoke in the sacristy where they embraced. See Sala and Martín, *OC*, vol. 1, 225 (Montilla process).

59.   Letter 1 in *OC*, vol. 4, 6.

60.   Letter 4 in *OC*, vol. 4, 29-30. St. John speaks from experience here about being despised for the Gospel. In his early days in Andalusia, a priest slapped him in public out of jealousy. See Sala and Martín, *OC*, vol. 1, 35.

61.   *Lecciones sobre la Epístola a los Gálatas* in *OC*, vol. 2, n. 8. A Catholic journalist has produced a thought-provoking analysis of what happens in a society when the Gospel is only partially preached and not as Jesus intended it. See Ross Douthat, *Bad Religion: How We Became a Nation of Heretics* (New York: Free Press, 2012).

62.   *PO*, sec. 4 (emphasis added).

63.   *Acta Ecclesiae Mediolanensis*, Medionali 1599, 1177-78, quoted in *The Liturgy of the Hours*, vol. 4 (New York: Catholic Publishing Book, 1975), 1545 (November 4th).

64.   See *Advertencias* in *OC*, vol. 2, n. 17.

65.   Ibid., n. 2. The translation of this Latin phrase is: "In ancient times golden priests used wooden chalices; now wooden priests use golden chalices."

66.   Letter 177 in *OC*, vol. 4, 589. The translation is: "The bishop must have simple and poor dress so that his authority is manifested in his faith and not in the way he dresses." The passage is taken from the Council of Cartagena IV c.15 (See note 7 on p. 589).

67.   Letter 182 in *OC*, vol. 4, 603.

68.   Sermon 33 in *OC*, vol. 3, n. 21.

69.   *Pláticas* 6 in *OC*, vol. 1, n. 6.

70.   See Sermon 33 in *OC*, vol. 3, n. 20.

71.   Sermon 18 in *OC*, vol. 3, n. 1.

72.   Testimony of Diego de las Casas, *Proceso en Córdoba* in *Proceso de beatificación del Maestro Juan de Ávila*, ed. Jose Luis Martinez (Madrid: Biblioteca de Autores Cristianos, 2004), 203. See also Sala and Martín, *OC*, vol. 1, 62 and 253, where the incident is mentioned.

73. *MT2* in *OC,* vol. 2, nn. 41-42.
74. Sala and Martín, *OC,* vol. 1, 274.
75. See Ibid., 362.
76. *Advertencias necesarias para los reyes* in *OC,* vol. 2, n. 13.
77. See *Advertencias* in *OC,* vol. 2, nn. 24-25.
78. Letter 1 in OC, vol. 4, 10.
79. Ibid. In his recommendation to the Spanish bishops, St. John suggests the formation of groups (*cofradías*) to minister to the poor and to beg for alms if necessary. Those in prison also could not be neglected. See *Advertencias* in *OC,* vol. 2, nn. 27-28.
80. See *LG,* sec. 33.
81. *OC,* vol. 2, n. 53.
82. Ibid. The timelessness of St. John's recommendation can be appreciated in current authors who tell us of the challenges the Church is experiencing today in keeping Catholics from going into Evangelical communities or drifting into unbelief. See Sherry A. Weddell, *Forming Intentional Disciples: The Path to Knowing and Following Jesus* (Huntington: Our Sunday Visitor, 2012).
83. See Granada, 41.
84. This was his *Doctrina cristiana* that was translated into other languages and accompanied missionaries to the New World and other countries where they were sent. See *OC,* vol. 2, 811-833 (the last page features one of his compositions in Italian and dates from a Jesuit manuscript in the city of Messina in 1556). The martyrdom of St. Paul Miki and other Jesuit companions in Japan mentions the sung catechetic lessons they would teach children. It is possible that these were the compositions of St. John of Avila, taken there by the Spanish Jesuits. See *Acta Sanctorum* Febr. 1,769, cap. 14, 109-110 in *The Liturgy of the Hours,* vol. 3 (New York: Catholic Book Publishing, 1975), 1368 (February 6th).
85. *MT2* in *OC,* vol. 2, n. 57.
86. Ibid., n. 62.
87. Ibid., n. 63.
88. *LG,* sec. 39 (italics added).
89. See Ibid., n. 41.
90. For a thorough study of the evangelical counsels and the priesthood, See Rev. Andrew H. Cozzens, "*Imago Vivens Iesu Christi Sponsi Ecclesiae:* The Priest as a Living Image of Jesus Christ the Bridegroom of the Church through the Evangelical Counsels," STD diss., Pontificia Studiorum Universitas A S. Thoma Aq. in Urbe, (Rome, 2008).
91. Vatican II, *Optatum Totius* (1965), sec. 9 (emphasis added).
92. This is written in the "Introduction" of the actual document before paragraph numbers are given (See Flannery edition, 707).
93. See *PDV,* sec. 27-30.
94. See Letter 224 in *OC,* vol. 4, 715-23.

95. *Lecciones sobre 1 San Juan [I]* (from here on, abbreviated as *Lecc 1SJ[I]*) in *OC*, vol. 2, Lección 14, 230.

96. Ibid., 231.

97. Ibid.

98. Sermon 3 in *OC*, vol. 3, n. 11.

99. See Granada, 107.

100. Sermon 81 in *OC*, vol. 3, n. 4.

101. Ibid., n. 8.

102. Ibid., n. 9.

103. Ibid.

104. "Pobreza" in *Diccionario de San Juan de Avila* (from here on, abbreviated as *DJA*), 746.

105. See Sala and Martín, *OC*, vol. 1, 200.

106. Ibid., 208, 258.

107. Ibid., 229.

108. See Esquerda, *Introducción a la doctrina*, 506 (footnote 69).

109. *Pláticas* 8 in *OC*, vol. 1, n. 2.

110. *PO*, sec. 17.

111. Ibid. Almost fifty years later, the same teaching appears in the *Directory*: "The priest, whose inheritance is the Lord (See Nm 18:20), knows that his mission, like that of the Church, takes place in the midst of the world and that created goods are necessary for the personal development of man. Nonetheless, he will use such goods with a sense of responsibility, moderation, upright intention and detachment proper to him who has his treasure in heaven and knows that everything is to be used for the edification of the Kingdom of God (Lk 10:7; Mt 10:9-10; 1 Cor 9:14; Gal 6:6). He will therefore abstain from those lucrative activities that are not consonant with his ministry. Moreover, the priest must avoid offering grounds for even the slightest insinuation that he may conceive his ministry also as an opportunity for obtaining benefits, favouring friends and relatives or seeking positions of privilege. Quite on the contrary, he must be in the midst of all in order to serve others unreservedly, following the example of Christ, the Good Shepherd (See Jn 10:10). Moreover, recalling that the gift he has received is gratuitous, he is to be disposed to give in like manner (Mt 10:8; Acts 8:18-25) and use what he receives for the exercise of his office for the good of the Church and works of charity, after having provided for his honest sustenance and the fulfilment of all the duties of his state.

Lastly, even though the priest does not make a public promise of poverty, it is incumbent upon him to lead a simple life and abstain from whatever may smack of worldliness, thereby embracing voluntary poverty in order to follow Christ more closely. In all aspects (living quarters, means of transportation, vacation, etc.) the priest is to eliminate any kind of affectation and luxury. In this sense the priest must battle every day in order not to lapse into consumerism and the easy life that pervade society in many parts of the world. A serious examination of conscience will help him to assess his tenor of life, his readiness to attend to the faithful and perform his duties; to ask himself if the means and things he uses respond to true need or if he may not be seeking convenience and comfort, taking flight from sacrifice. Precisely at stake in the consistency between what he says and what he does, especially with respect to poverty, are the priest's credibility and apostolic effectiveness" (n. 83).

112.   Juan Esquerda, "Intuiciones de San Juan de Ávila para una teología y espiritualidad del sacerdote ministro en el presbiterio de la iglesia particular," *Compartir en Cristo Blog*, June, 2010, https://compartirencristo. wordpress.com/sacerdocio/articulos-sacerdocio/avila-intuiciones-sac-minis.doc, 41, (accessed October 15, 2014).

113.   See St. Thomas Aquinas, *Summa Theologica*, trans. Fathers of the English Dominican Province, vol. 2 (1948; repr., Notre Dame: Christian Classics, 1981), I.II. q.65 (from here on, abbreviated as *Summa*).

114.   Sermon 11 in *OC*, vol. 3, n. 24. The reference to St. Jerome is *Ep.* 54, 8-9: PL 22, 554.

115.   Ch. 5, 51-52 (Gormley's translation).

116.   *MT2* in *OC*, vol. 2, n. 91.

117.   *Tratado sobre el sacerdocio* (from here on, abbreviated as *TSS*) in *OC*, vol. 1, n. 15.

118.   Ibid.

119.   See Sala and Martín, *OC*, vol. 1, 201, 212.

120.   See Letters 4 and 5. Obviously, these practices must be brought up to date in the context of our own culture. But the warning is valid. There is a reason why most parishes have installed windows in office doors and even in confessionals.

121.   The obedience of Jesus as the model for all believers is the constant tradition of the Church. See Cardinal Joseph Ratzinger: "The sublime Christological obedience, which reverses the disobedience of Adam, finds concrete form in *ecclesiastical obedience*, and for the priest, ecclesiastical obedience in turn is, in a quite practical fashion, obedience to his bishop. The Council could probably have more strongly emphasized that there must first of all be a *common obedience of all to the Word of God and to the way it is presented to us in the living tradition of the Church*. This shared obligation is also a freedom that all share; it protects us from arbitrary actions and decisions and ensures that ecclesiastical obedience has a truly Christological character. Ecclesial obedience is not positivistic in type; it is not just the same as response to formal authority. It is obedience to some-one who is himself obedient and who embodies the obedient Christ. . . . To that extent, in the priest's obedience to the bishop there is always an element of transcending the local Church—this is a Catholic obedience: the bishop is being obeyed because locally he represents the Church as

a whole. . . . Obeying Christ means obeying his body, obeying him in his body. . . . That is why obedience, correctly understood, has to be rehabilitated and be made effective in the heart of Christian and priestly spirituality." "Ministry and Life of Priests," in *Pilgrim Fellowship of Faith: The Church as Communion*, trans. Henry Taylor (San Francisco: Ignatius Press, 2005), 166-68 (emphasis in the original). The same article appears in *Priesthood: A Greater Love*, published by the Congregation for the Clergy, International Symposium on the Thirtieth Anniversary of the Promulgation of the Conciliar Decree *Presbyterorum Ordinis* (Philadelphia: Edizioni San Paolo, 1996), 115-130. In the latter, however, the article is mistakenly titled "Life and Ministry of Priests."

122. Sermon 5 in *OC*, vol. 3, n. 16.

123. Ch. 55, 170 (Gormley's translation).

124. "Et pour cela, choisissez-en un entre mille, dit Avila; et moi je dis: entre dix mille, car il s'en trouve moins que Ton ne saurait diré, qui soient capables de cet office." *Introduction à la vie dévote* (*Oeuvres*, ed. Migne), vol. 3., p. I, chap. 4, as cited in *OC*, vol. 1, 401.

125. *MT2* in *OC*, vol. 2, n. 71.

126. *Pláticas* 1 in *OC*, vol. 1, n. 2.

127. *PDV*, sec. 30.

Chapter 3

Kingly Office: The Spirituality of the Good Shepherd

In the Gospel of Matthew, Jesus is introduced as "king," "ruler," and "shepherd" (Mt 2:1-6). Throughout His ministry, He presents Himself as the Good Shepherd who comes to establish the Kingdom of God, a kingdom that is ruled very differently from earthly powers. When His disciples want to imitate those earthly leaders, He rebukes them. He gives them clear examples that He is among them as one who serves[1] and gives His life to make His teaching concrete, but not before praying to the Father that "they may all be one" (Jn 17:21). As Jesus' representative, the priest has the same function: he must work to establish the Kingdom of God and to bring unity to the community. And, as we shall see, this, too, contributes to the priest's own spirituality and sanctification.

Pastoral Charity

Priests are to be "true shepherds of souls after the example of our Lord Jesus Christ, teacher, priest and shepherd."[2] Since priests, however, are human beings, the way in which they live out their priesthood will look different in each individual case. This is so because of their own personality, gifts, and the pastoral setting in which they are involved. In the case of St. John of Avila, the shepherding aspect of his ministry is not obvious because he was never the pastor of a parish community. He was a renowned preacher and a theologian; he spent most of his life traveling through different cities and setting up schools for the formation of children and future priests. This was the life that he chose for himself since the office of preaching and teaching was "very much neglected in the clergy," as he told the bishops at Trent.[3] Being a man of the Church, however, his writings reveal that he was not unaware of parish life and this shepherding aspect that all priests must live in one way or another.

The term "pastoral charity" seems to have originated at Vatican II. In *Presbyterorum Ordinis*, the Council Fathers write: "Priests will achieve the unity of their lives by joining themselves with Christ in the recognition of the Father's will and in the gift of themselves to the flock entrusted to them. In this way, by adopting the role of the good shepherd they will find in the practice of pastoral charity itself the bond of priestly perfection which will reduce to unity their life and activity."[4] By the time St. John Paul II wrote *Pastores Dabo Vobis*, the use of the phrase "pastoral charity" was common, and the phrase appears profusely in the exhortation. The Pope, there, spells out what is meant by that phrase. He says:

> Jesus presents himself as "the good shepherd" (Jn 10:11, 14), not only of Israel but of all humanity (cf. Jn 10:16). His whole life is a continual manifestation of his "pastoral charity," or rather, a daily enactment of it. He feels compassion for the crowds because they were harassed

and helpless, like sheep without a shepherd (cf. Mt 9:35-36). He goes in search of the straying and scattered sheep (cf. Mt 18:12-14) and joyfully celebrates their return. He gathers and protects them. He knows them and calls each one by name (cf. Jn 10:3). He leads them to green pastures and still waters (cf. Ps 22-23) and spreads a table for them, nourishing them with his own life.[5]

St. John of Avila speaks of the concept when he says that pastors "must intercede for [their faithful] before God with the affection that fathers and mothers have for their children," for they are, indeed, called "father" by them.[6] In a long letter that he writes to a layman involved in government, he also tells him that whoever is a leader must be "the father of many in his love and their slave in his work."[7] Leadership involves only service, he says, "and whoever is not rich in love must quit this battle, for it is not for him."[8] A servant's life should be about "the pleasing of God and the common good"[9] because just as the virtue of charity "is the main virtue for the salvation of a Christian, it is as well for the good performance of public service."[10] One who serves must forget about his own interests[11] and follow the example of the Lord who humbled Himself to come among us as one who serves.[12]

Since the life of St. John of Avila was one of service, the call to serve comes out constantly in his preaching. In a sermon that he preached for a religious community, for example, he gives a summary of his own life modeled after that of Jesus. If St. John came to serve and to give His life as a ransom for the many, he asks: "how can a little worm be so full of pride and command?"[13] He was convinced that "the

Son of the Virgin *did not come to be served, but to serve,*" that "he came to serve so that we can learn how to serve, so that [we] can be on fire with love every time that [we] see Jesus Christ serving for [us], pouring his blood for [us]."[14]

Although this is obvious from Scripture, modern scholars continue to reflect on how Jesus saw power and authority as an act of service. Father Nicholas Cachia, for example, in sharing the results of his doctoral research, says:

> The verb *poimainein,* to shepherd, continues to have—as in the OT—the connotation of governing, ruling. This is perceived, however, in the light of how Jesus understood authority: service. The authority over all the flock which is delegated to Peter in John 21 is enveloped within his love for Jesus. This is complemented by the command of Jesus to follow him, understood by John to be a reference to his death. Thus, the commission Peter receives is seen as one of service, love and self-sacrifice to the end in the manner of Jesus himself.[15]

Thus, to follow Jesus as an ordained minister who continues the ministry of Peter and the Apostles is really a call to have the heart of a shepherd, to be filled with love for God and His people.

Having a Shepherd's Heart

The image of the Good Shepherd has been a constant source of inspiration for bishops and priests from the very beginnings of the Church. The writings of St. Augustine and St. Gregory the Great on the subject are constantly coming up in the Office of Readings. This is no accident. As Father

Cachia explains, Jesus is the ultimate model for all those who have the responsibility of caring for souls:

> The unifying criterion of the shepherd image as it emerges from this Johannine chapter [Chapter 10] is, what may be called, the pastoral love or charity of the shepherd. He is presented as the shepherd essentially *for others*. There is no action of his which does not have a relation to the sheep entrusted to him. . . . His life is one of complete service, dedication, and constant reaching out towards the sheep, notwithstanding the consequences this might have on him. All this springs from his love: a love which he receives from the Father and which he transmits to all those who were given to him.[16]

God promised to give shepherds after His own heart[17]; He is true to His word and continues to appoint those shepherds in every generation. In St. John of Avila, that promise was once again fulfilled.[18]

THE SENTIMENTS OF JESUS

The mystery of Christ is the basis for all of John of Avila's theology. That mystery, though, is intrinsically connected to the priesthood of Jesus, as Pope Benedict XVI acknowledged of St. John. Speaking to a group of Spanish priests, the Holy Father said: "The main teaching of the Apostle of Andalusia is the mystery of Christ, Priest and Good Shepherd, lived in harmony with the Lord's sentiments, in imitation of St Paul (cf. Phil 2:5)."[19] Having already announced that he was going to declare St. John of Avila a Doctor of the universal Church, Pope Benedict XVI could see in St. John "a reflection of Jesus the Good Shepherd," as had been previously said of our saint, who "in intimacy with the Lord . . . filled himself with his 'love' (cf. *PDV* 70) and his pastoral charity."[20]

In his "Treatise on the Love of God," St. John of Avila captures the love that Jesus had in His heart. Everything the Lord underwent as He faced His Passion, St. John says, was an expression of His love for those the Father gave Him:

> If what he was asked to do for the salvation of all he had to do for each one of them, he would do it. And if, just as he was suffering on the cross for three hours, he had to be there until the day of judgment, there was enough love for that if it were necessary. In this manner he loved much more than what he suffered; the love that was contained in his heart was much greater than what he showed externally with his wounds.[21]

The word translated here as "heart" is actually *entrañas* (entrails) in the original Spanish of St. John of Avila. He speaks of what is the primary concern of Jesus, what is at the core of His being. Pope Francis refers to this love in our Lord in *Misericordiae Vultus*: "It is hardly an exaggeration to say that this is a 'visceral' love. It gushes forth from the depths naturally, full of tenderness and compassion, indulgence and mercy."[22] Nicholas Cachia concurs:

> Both Evangelists [Matthew (cf. 9:36) and Mark (cf. 6:34)] describe Jesus' reaction to the people's religious and spiritual needs through the use of the important verb *splanchnizomai* (to be moved, to pity in one's inward parts [*splanchna*, the seat of feelings], feel compassion). This verb says more than just his emotive reaction: 'Jesus is theologically characterized . . . as the Messiah in whom

divine mercy is present.' In Jesus, the compassion of God for humankind is proclaimed.[23]

This explains why St. John of Avila was fond of meditating on the Passion of Christ and would recommend this practice to everyone. It was not that he was fixated on suffering or that he did not see importance of other Christian mysteries. For him, the Cross was the ultimate expression of Christ's love for us, a great grace for which we need to be grateful and in which we must rejoice. He speaks of this in his "Treatise." In the form of a prayerful reflection, he writes:

> What else did you mean, Lord, with those words when you said: *I must be baptized with a baptism; how do I live in anguish!* (Lk 12:50)? Until the hour arrives, Lord, you live in anguish; your desire to see yourself bathed in blood for us was so great that every hour that this was delayed seemed to you like a thousand years because of the greatness of your love. And from here was born that glorious feast of Palms [Palm Sunday] that you wanted for us to observe when you were going to suffer, to show the world the joy in your heart, for you wanted to go to the wood of the cross surrounded by roses and flowers. It does not seem, Lord, that you were going to the cross, but rather to a wedding, for such is the celebration that you want along the way.[24]

According to St. John, then, because of the configuration of the priest to Christ, as was mentioned earlier, [25] shepherds ought to have the same kind of love: "In the heart of the cleric, there must burn the fire of the love of God and zeal for souls. *Bonus pastor animam dat pro ovibus suis* (cf. Jn 10:11), as Christ did."[26] When this "fire of love" is missing, St. John says, the consequences can be serious:

> But woe, woe to the lukewarm spirit of our day, very far from living a heavenly life . . . ! *Woe to the world because of scandals!* (Mt 18:7), said the Lord; and being lukewarm is not the least stumbling block on the path of virtue. . . . *Woe to the world because of the scandal* of being lukewarm into which so many fall!; but *woe to him through which the scandal comes!* (cf. Mt 18:7). If simple people live tepidly, this is bad; but this evil has a remedy and they only hurt themselves; but if their teachers are lukewarm, then the Lord's *woe to the world* because of its lukewarm spirit is fulfilled as is the *woe* that threatens the lukewarm teachers, for they join their tepidness to the others' and even extinguish their fervor.[27]

Priests "must be entirely on fire with the love of God, as a holocaust."[28] Thus, St. John could tell one of his disciples that, "remembering how the Lord offered himself on the cross for the whole world," he should "ask for a little bit of that burning charity so that the minister can conform himself to the Lord."[29]

The Apostle of Andalusia often preached about this overwhelming charity in Christ's heart.[30] Since, in the words of the Lord, "from the fullness of the heart the mouth speaks" (Mt 12:34), it is obvious that St. John himself practiced this.

The Venerable Fulton Sheen wrote once:

> I believe that when we priests die the Lord will show us His Scars as He promised to do to all mankind at His second coming. He will look at our hands to see if they have been scarred from giving, our feet to see the

calluses from travel to preach His Gospel, and our side to see if we have loved to a point of sacrifice. Woe to us who come down from Calvary with hands unscarred and white.[31]

Along the same lines, St. John of Avila said to his brother priests: "If there is no kindness, what good is knowledge, or good work, or prophecy, or even performing miracles? Even if [a priest] has everything, if he has no charity, the source of goodness for a person, St. Paul daringly utters: *Nihil sumus* (cf. 1 Cor 13:2)."[32]

SOLICITUDE FOR THE FLOCK

In the Gospel, after our Blessed Mother receives the news that she has been chosen as the mother of the Messiah, she is quick to go out to visit her cousin Elizabeth.[33] The Church sees in this a model for all Christians to follow; it is the natural process of going from being a grateful receiver to becoming a generous giver, the journey from contemplation to action. It is not out of place to speak of Mary in a study on priests, for as Monsignor Esquerda writes, "Configuration to Christ, under the action of the Holy Spirit, is a process of virtues and gifts . . . that looks to Mary as a model and a Mother."[34] In *Lumen Gentium*, we also read: "In her life the Virgin has been a model of that motherly love with which all who join in the Church's apostolic mission for the regeneration of mankind should be animated."[35] It has been stated how St. John of Avila believed that priests must have motherly hearts.[36] In fact, in his Treatise on the Priesthood, he repeats three times that they must have fatherly and motherly affection.[37] In this, we can see that, truly, "the priestly ministries are the actualization of the Church's maternity."[38]

Besides the motherly affection, sometimes in the Church, we hear of the "spousal character" of the priesthood. St. John Paul II, for example, writes:

> The priest is called to be the living image of Jesus Christ, the spouse of the Church. . . . Therefore, the priest's life ought to radiate this spousal character, which demands that he be a witness to Christ's spousal love and thus be capable of loving people with a heart which is new, generous and pure—with genuine self-detachment, with full, constant and faithful dedication and at the same time with a kind of 'divine jealousy' (cf. 2 Cor 11:2) and even with a kind of maternal tenderness, capable of bearing 'the pangs of birth' until 'Christ be formed' in the faithful (cf. Gal 4:19).[39]

But however we describe the love that is present in the heart of the minister, the point, St. John of Avila reminds us, is that "religious and priests, since they are dedicated to God, must try to love with tenderness, to have the same sentiments that were in the work of our Redeemer."[40] Because "the purpose of his incarnation, his life, his work and his death was the good of souls,"[41] those who take his place now must also have this as their aim.

Nicholas Cachia says this of the Good Shepherd: "The love of Jesus for the sheep is manifested in a particular way in his personal, intimate knowledge of the sheep. He knows each one by name and calls each one to follow him. The sheep hear his voice; they recognize and follow him. There is full communion of life, based on reciprocal knowledge, between the shepherd and the sheep."[42] And he goes on as he speaks of the commission St. Peter receives from our Lord to "tend his sheep":

> In his *De Sacerdotio*, St. John Chrysostom writes: "What greater advantage could there be, than to be obviously doing what Christ himself declared was proof of love for Christ?" He continues, referring to John 21: "He did not want to prove then how much Peter loved him . . . but he wanted Peter and all of us to learn how much he loves his own Church, in order that we might show great concern for the same thing."[43]

Being very familiar both with the Scriptures and the writings of St. John Chrysostom, the Apostle of Andalusia would remind the religious leaders of his day of their obligation to personally care for the sheep. Making reference to 2 Samuel 6, where God struck Uzzah because he laid the ark of God on a cart pulled by animals, St. John of Avila would say: "Let prelates, pastors and those with benefices fear, and with much reason, because it is mandated that they themselves carry the ark of God on their shoulders, that is, their faithful, caring for them, teaching them, suffering their burdens and struggles, making their work easier and fulfilling personally their office and residence."[44] And to the Spanish bishops, he would write: "Let bishops be reminded that they were not chosen . . . except to be pastors and caretakers of the flock . . . carrying them on their shoulders, even if this means not sleeping at night, not taking their siesta; even if it means spilling their blood and giving their life, as Christ did."[45] And to Bishop Cristobal de Rojas y Sandoval, the one entrusted with the task of leading the Synod of Toledo, he would say:

Raise your eyes, your Excellency, to see the Son of God placed on the cross, stripped and crucified, and try to strip yourself of the world, the flesh, status, greed, honor and self so that this way you can be entirely like Jesus Christ and so that your undertaking can be efficient and fruitful. Die to everything and you will live for God, and this will also help others to live well, because if you do not do this, you may lose yourself and lose others, for the word of Christ our Lord cannot fail: *Nisi granum frumenti*, etc. (Jn 12:24).[46]

He had reason to issue these reminders. He had already written to those at the Council of Trent of the "sad state" of the episcopacy: "they are more concerned about lording and commanding than in administering and having fatherly hearts and deeds. Satisfied with that, they left the care of souls in the hands of others, of preachers and confessors, many of which do not have enough knowledge, or holiness of life, or zeal for souls, or even simple prudence . . . this is why the Church is in such a sad state."[47] Therefore, he had to say again: "How different it is to see Christ nailed on the yoke of the cross, pouring his blood for his sheep and to see [the bishops] sitting in their parlors full of gifts and vanity while they drink the blood of their sheep . . . mindless of the many entrusted to them because they are focusing on their own pleasures!"[48]

Priests, however, are called to be "builders of souls;"[49] along with pontiffs and bishops, they are "guards of the vineyard,"[50] and they must "keep watch over their flock so that they can say like the Lord: *No one will take them from me* (cf. Jn 10:30)."[51] Our love for God must be shown in the love that we have for those entrusted to our care. This is what St. John writes to a brother priest in one of his letters:

One cannot but say and cry with Saint Augustine: *Sero te cognovi, pulchritudo tam antiqua; sero te cognovi, pulchritudo tam nova!* . . . Even though he cried because he had not known God by faith since he was wrapped in his errors, if we are content with merely knowing God by faith and we do not know him in the experiential way that is born of love, along with the human junctures that come our way, we too have reason to cry and to say like him: oh the days when I did not love you![52]

By now, the famous homily of Pope Francis at his first Chrism Mass in the Petrine ministry is well known. There, he begged priests to "be shepherds, with the 'odour of the sheep', make it real, as shepherds among your flock."[53] The sacrifices that pastors make for the sake of their people do not go unnoticed. St. John of Avila would point that out:

New Christians . . . seeing a good example, that [priests] only seek the good of souls, usually convert more than just by listening to the preaching; for that charity that Christ left burning in the hearts of his ministers is so strong that it overcomes everything. Because who would resist a heart that wants the good of the other—especially his eternal good—and is willing to die for him? They tell me that in Japan what most moves gentiles to conversion is to see that those in the Society [of Jesus] have gone so many miles of land and sea to selflessly seek their salvation with great trials and deathly dangers.[54]

This would lead him to conclude that "if [people] fell into the hands of ministers who knew how to spiritually care for souls and had zeal for their salvation, certainly the Christian people would be very different from what we now see."[55]

Looking for the Lost Sheep: Evangelization

The image of the shepherd would not be complete without establishing its relationship with the "lost sheep." Jesus, in fact, understood His mission as being sent to "the lost sheep of the house of Israel" (Mt 15:24). Origen has a pointed reflection on what this entails for those entrusted with the care of souls. Nicholas Cachia gives us his words:

> A special emphasis should be made on the duty of the shepherd with regard to those who stray away from the flock. Origen addresses the sensitivity of the pastors and encourages them to imitate the example of the Good Shepherd, saying: "You are the shepherd; you see the little sheep of the Lord, unaware of the danger, being carried along the precipices and hanging from the cliffs! And do you not run to them? Do you not call them back? Do you not even restrain them by your voice and deter them by the cry of your rebuke? Are you so forgetful of the mysteries of the Lord, how he left ninety-nine in the heavens and for only one little sheep which strayed, came down on earth, found it, and carried it back on his shoulders to the heavens? And we, are we absolutely not to follow the example of the master shepherd in caring for the little sheep?"[56]

Sermon 19 of St. John of Avila is dedicated to this parable of the lost sheep.[57] From the words of St. John, we can see that, in a way, things have not changed much in the Church, that we have always had similar challenges. He states: "St. [John] Chrysostom says the greatest difficulty that the apostles had as they preached the Gospel in the world was to make people believe such *good news* about the mercy of

God."[58] Can it be true that God cares about us? Does it really matter whether or not we respond to Him with love? The Apostle of Andalusia has a very tender explanation that if people heard it and reflected on it, perhaps they would think twice about living faithless lives. In this sermon, he says:

> A father has three or four children and one of them, the little one, does not know how to speak, and even though the older ones say something in a very reasonable and wise way, the parents are not necessarily excited; but, when the little one who does not speak says *taita*, then there is rejoicing in the father, mother and the whole house.—Why? Did not the others say better things?—Yes; but they rejoice because they see that the child that did not speak said *taita*. And just in the same way, when God sees that the sinner, who was mute, speaks in confession, crying for his sins, God rejoices and heaven with him. And it seems to me that the reason why there is great rejoicing in heaven is that merits of Jesus Christ are applied to the conversion of a sinner.[59]

Priests have been given this wonderful ministry of reconciliation. St. John realized that "the burning heart of Jesus with zeal for God's honor and the salvation of souls brought him into the world"[60] and that the Lord himself said: "As the Father has sent me, so I send you" (Jn 20:21). Therefore, priests are called to be those "prudent stewards" who distribute God's graces to His children and help them, in turn, to be reconciled to the Father and to honor Him.[61] When one is mindful of the awesomeness of this ministry, St. John would write to a brother priest, this, indeed, drives us to seek those who are lost:

O father, if we only had burning in our hearts the zeal for the house of God! If we only had stuck in our hearts these jewels that the Lord had in his, since for them he went to the cross! . . .

They dishonor Him and lose themselves! I think that, if we were what we ought, we would not give *sleep to our eyes* nor rest to our heads until we found *a dwelling for the Lord* (Ps 131:4f).[62]

St. John Paul II constantly made appeals during his papacy for a "new evangelization."[63] The call for it really began with St. Paul VI when he wrote his Apostolic Exhortation *Evangelii Nuntiandi*. There, he said that it was "a service rendered to the Christian community" but also "to the whole of humanity,"[64] since the Good Shepherd did say, in fact: "I have other sheep that do not belong to this fold" (Jn 10:16). St. Paul VI also said that it was a task that needed to be accomplished "with ever increasing love, zeal and joy."[65] St. John of Avila would agree. Toward the end of his sermon on the lost sheep, he has a beautiful passage where he makes reference to the Song of Songs:

> Lord, since we see you carrying the little lost sheep on your shoulders, what do you say to it so that it can go with you, or what do you give it so that it falls in love with you? Our Lord does with the soul what a good husband would do with his wife when she has gone with another but he still loves her and wants her to come back to him. What would this one do? He would go where he knew he would find her and would say to himself: "Maybe she will stand at the window and see me, and by seeing me she will remember that I am her husband, and that the one

that she is with is a ruffian, and she will remember the love that I had for her and what I did for her, and she will be moved to love me again and will come out and come back to me."[66]

In other words, we ought to act with patience and love. As Pope Francis has reminded us with his new emphasis on evangelization, "We are told quite clearly: 'do so with gentleness and reverence' (1 *Pt* 3:15) and . . . overcome 'evil with good' (*Rom* 12:21)."[67] Indeed, it has been our common experience that "goodness always tends to spread."[68]

It could be argued that today, the Church faces a similar challenge in trust and confidence as the Catholic world faced in the days of the Reformation—though hopefully, to a much lesser degree. If that is the case, these words of the Apostle of Andalusia to the priests of his day could also serve us well:

> If the head and members unite under God, we will be so powerful that we will overcome the devil in our lives and we will free the people from their sins; because, just as the sinfulness of the clergy is a very efficient cause of the sinfulness of the laity, God made the clerical state so powerful that, if it is as God envisioned it, it influences the people in every kind of virtue, just as heaven influences the earth. And this way we will recover the esteem that we have lost among the people because of our negligence; we will be *repaid for the years* that were lost, the ones that *the locust* of our negligence *has eaten* (cf. Jl 2:25).[69]

Virtues of a Good Shepherd

St. John of Avila was convinced of the influence that bishops and priests can have on the faithful. A virtuous life in them will necessarily translate into a faithful flock. He writes about this in his treatises of reform: "the sheep would not be afraid to walk the path where they see that their pastor is ahead of everyone, full of virtues and determined even to die, if necessary, for the good of their sheep, as the Son of God did. . . . "[70] Therefore, they have "a greater obligation to give good example to their parishioners."[71]

In his Treatise on the Priesthood, St. John of Avila lists a series of virtues that all pastors and confessors must have. Making reference to the Fathers, he states why possessing these qualities is of upmost importance:

> Besides this obligation that he has of being a good priest and guarding his own conscience, he has the responsibility of helping and teaching the souls of parishioners, something that, as St. Gregory says, requires no less sanctity than for offering the holy sacrifice of the altar. And St. [John] Chrysostom, upon pondering this, says that, in assuming the care of souls, he is entrusted with the mystical Body of Jesus Christ so that he can heal it, strengthen it and make it beautiful with all kinds of virtues so that it can be worthy of being called body of such a head, as is Jesus Christ.[72]

St. John also begins by reiterating a life of prayer and holiness because without living a good life, whatever "wisdom" a leader possesses will actually lead him to many errors.[73] In his brief treatment of the virtues, then, he mentions specifically prudence, patience, and fortitude.[74]

PRUDENCE

The first virtue that St. John of Avila mentions specifically for pastors is prudence. Making reference to St. Gregory the Great who said that "the care of souls is the greatest of all arts," St. John says: "Much prudence is necessary to lead so many different people and to give each one the medicine that is good for them."[75] Likewise, for those hearing confessions, even when they are not pastors, they need "much prudence, charity, chastity, careful speech and fervent prayer."[76] As can be seen, prudence is listed first here as well.

Monsignor Juan Esquerda states, "One who governs a human community needs the virtue of prudence to know the objectives that are being sought as well as the necessary or opportune means that can be followed."[77] Since this is the case for any leader, our saint also recommends prudence to the man involved in government mentioned earlier. His words to him on prudently seeking the advice of others are worth reading. He tells him:

> Just as counsel must be sought with those who have "human" prudence in order to know what we must do, to govern according to "divine" prudence it is convenient to consult those who have it. Because even though . . . the one who leads must have some insight so as to not depend completely on another, this should not make him think that he has wisdom to deal with all his responsibilities without asking others. For there is nothing more opposed to the wisdom that comes from heaven than pride and trusting in one's own judgment; humility is a sure sign that one actually has it, for it is written: *Ubi humilitas, ibi et sapientia* (Prv 11:2). A ruler then, high or lowly, wise or unwise, must be a friend of seeking counsel

and open to receiving it; because one of the conditions that James the Apostle mentions in order for heavenly wisdom to descend is that it not be stubborn or hard-headed, *but peaceful and persuadable* (Jas 3:17). We have an example of this in David who, even though he had the spirit of the Lord and was very close to him, had the prophet Gad with him (cf. 1 Sm 22:5), and afterwards the prophet Nathan (cf. 2 Sm 7:2ff), and he administered his own affairs and duties according to what they told him.[78]

The Church values counsel so much that nowadays, pastoral councils are recommended at every parish and bishops have set up offices and departments in chanceries to assist pastors in carrying out their ministry. As we read in Sacred Scripture, "For lack of guidance a people falls; security lies in many counselors" (Prv 11:14).

PATIENCE

Priests also need the virtue of patience, St. John of Avila says, "to suffer the importune requests of the sheep, both wise and unwise."[79] Whatever challenges we experience in ministry can actually be means of purification for ourselves and opportunities to demonstrate our love for God. St. John speaks of this in one of his letters. He writes: "The Father loved his Son very much, and He handed him over to face many sorrows. The Son also loves you much and sends you these ones: carry them with patience, as the Son endured his, and you will be loved by Him."[80] For, as St. Paul would remind us, "in [our] flesh [we are] filling up what is lacking in the afflictions of Christ on behalf of his body, which is the church" (Col 1:24).

If every Christian is in need of strength, St. John of Avila observes, shepherds need it even more "so that they are not overcome by threats and mean actions of those who do not want to be taken out of the sins or reprimanded."[81] His recommendation to them is this: "It is convenient to be as the prophet says: *Repletus sum fortitudine Domini, ut annuntiem Iacob scelus suum* (Mi 3:8); this virtue is so necessary as rare in those who have public offices because there are few who are not affected by wanting to please friends and by being afraid of displeasing their enemies."[82]

Shepherding at the Service of Unity in the Church

Jesus came to restore the relationship of love and unity that humanity enjoyed with God before the fall. As the Good Shepherd, He saw it as his role to establish the "one flock" God had intended (Jn 10:16). He expressed this in His priestly prayer on the night before He died for us: "I pray . . . that they may all be one, as you, Father, are in me and I in you, that they also may be in us. . . . that they may be one, as we are one" (Jn 17:20-22). And, as Nicholas Cachia tells us, Jesus Himself becomes the source of unity, which is the great novelty that marks the difference between the Old and the New Testament, the time of preparation from the time of fulfillment:

> In the prophets, God brings back the people to the promised land; in 1 Peter, the people are brought back "to the Shepherd and Guardian of our souls": "For you were straying like sheep, but have now been brought back to the Shepherd and Guardian of our souls" (1 Pt 2:25). Thus, now the people are not brought to a land but

to a person. Through his passion and death Christ, the humble and obedient Servant of YHWH, became the focal point of the whole salvific process. The people, who before were "straying like sheep" are now conducted to this unifying reality, the Shepherd. In these words we may hear what Jesus himself says in John's Gospel: "And I, when I am lifted up from the earth, will draw all men to myself" (Jn 12:32).[83]

Divisions, St. John of Avila reminds us, do not come from God.[84] It is the teaching of the Church that, "the universal Church is seen to be 'a people brought into unity from the unity of the Father, the Son and the Holy Spirit.'"[85] And, thus:

in order to establish a relationship of peace and communion with himself, and in order to bring about brotherly union among men, and they sinners, God decided to enter into the history of mankind in a new and definite manner, by sending his own Son in human flesh, so that through him he might snatch men from the power of darkness and of Satan (cf. Col 1:13; Acts 10:38) and to him reconcile the world to himself.[86]

Priests have always been seen as sharers in Christ's ministry of becoming "the 'pontifex' . . . who unites man to God."[87] Already in the second century, we have the words of St. Ignatius of Antioch that testify to priests sharing in such ministry. In writing to a group of faithful, the bishop said:

You must be made holy in all things by being united in perfect obedience, in submission to the bishop and the presbyters. . . . It is fitting, therefore, that you should be in agreement with the mind of the bishop as in fact you are. Your excellent presbyters, who are a credit to God, are as suited to the bishop as strings to a harp. So in your harmony of mind and heart the song you sing is Jesus Christ. Every one of you should form a choir, so that, in harmony of sound through harmony of hearts, and in unity taking the note from God, you may sing with one voice through Jesus Christ to the Father. If you do this, he will listen to you and see from your good works that you are members of his Son. It is then an advantage to you to live in perfect unity, so that at all times you may share in God.[88]

And in *Presbyterorum Ordinis*, we read: "Priests exercise the function of Christ as Pastor and Head in proportion to their share of authority. In the name of the bishop they gather the family of God as a brotherhood endowed with the spirit of unity and lead it in Christ through the Spirit to God the Father."[89]

The Apostle of Andalusia speaks of this regal aspect of the cleric's ministry in one of his priestly conferences. Priests, he says, begin by ruling over their own passions and then go on to rule others, "giving them greater benefits and exercising things of greater power than those that earthly kings have over their subjects."[90]

Hierarchical Structure of the Church

The whole world is arranged in a hierarchical manner. The examples given by St. Athanasius in the Office of Readings should be familiar to us. There, we read:

Think of a musician tuning his lyre. By his skill he adjusts high notes to low and intermediate notes to the

rest, and produces a series of harmonies. So too the
wisdom of God holds the world like a lyre and joins
things in the air to those on earth, and things in heaven
to those in the air, and brings each part into harmony
with the whole. By his decree and will he regulates them
all to produce the beauty and harmony of a single, well-
ordered universe. . . .

To illustrate this profound mystery, let us take the
example of a choir of many singers. A choir is composed
of a variety of men, women and children, of both old
and young. Under the direction of one conductor, each
sings in the way that is natural for him: men with men's
voices, boys with boys' voices, old people with old
voices, young people with young voices. Yet all of them
produce a single harmony. Or consider the example of
our soul. It moves our senses according to their several
functions so that in the presence of a single object they
all act simultaneously: the eye sees, the ear hears, the hand
touches, the nose smells, the tongue tastes, and often the
other parts of the body act as well as, for example, the
feet may walk.

Although this is only a poor comparison, it gives some
idea of how the whole universe is governed.[91]

Likewise, the Church, thanks to the action of the Holy
Spirit, is composed of different members in a hierarchical
fashion. In *Lumen Gentium*, we read: "Guiding the Church
in the way of all truth (cf. Jn 16:13) and unifying her in
communion and in the works of ministry, [the Holy Spirit]
bestows upon her varied hierarchic and charismatic gifts, and
in this way directs her; and he adorns her with his fruits (cf.

Eph 4:11-12; 1 Cor 12:4; Gal 5:22)."[92] And, as then-Cardinal Ratzinger pointed out, "the sacrament that most significantly goes by the name of *ordo* is the ultimate and only enduring and obligatory structure that constitutes, so to speak, the predetermined set form of organization in the Church and that makes her an 'institution.'"[93] Indeed, the Sacrament of Holy Orders is there to give order to the whole household of God, the Church, as the Vatican II Fathers stated: "For the exercise of this ministry, as for the rest of the priests' functions, a spiritual power is given them, a power whose purpose is to build up."[94] Of this power, the Church prays in the Liturgy of the Hours: "May our faith prove we are not slaves, but sons, not so much subjected to your law as sharing your power."[95] Just as in a body, the different living cells share in the exchange of life and nutrients, in the household of God, all the different members also share in the power and authority needed in order for the entire body of Christ to function properly: parents with their children, teachers with their pupils, and so forth.

St. John of Avila speaks of this organic structure of the Church in his sermons. "This—he would say—is the sign of the Church in which God dwells: that it has a head, which is the Pope, who everyone else must follow and obey."[96] It was the will of the Chief Shepherd, he would utter in another one, "that the Pope stayed in his place, and that prelates succeed the apostles, and pastors the seventy-two disciples."[97] In the sad case of those who separated themselves from the Church during the days of the Reformation, "the knife of heresy cut them off from the union and obedience to the pope, the head of the Church and vicar of Christ, and they lost the life of grace."[98] The same is true for those Catholics, even today, who refuse to eat "the nourishment of obedience to the mandates of the Church."[99]

The Priest as Servant of All the Charisms

The Second Vatican Council has been described by many as a "new Pentecost." Under the action of the Holy Spirit, the Church reconnected once again with its charismatic dimension to complement its hierarchical structure. In this, it found "the freshness of youth," as *Lumen Gentium* puts it.[100] St. John Paul II spoke of this special grace that was "rediscovered" in the Church:

> Whenever the Spirit intervenes, he leaves people astonished. He brings about events of amazing newness; he radically changes persons and history. This was the unforgettable experience of the Second Vatican Ecumenical Council during which, under the guidance of the same Spirit, the Church rediscovered the charismatic dimension as one of her constitutive elements: "It is not only through the sacraments and the ministrations of the Church that the Holy Spirit makes holy the people, leads them and enriches them with his virtues. Allotting his gifts according as he wills (cf. 1 Cor 12:11), he also distributes special graces among the faithful of every rank . . . He makes them fit and ready to undertake various tasks and offices for the renewal and building up of the Church" (*Lumen gentium*, n. 12).

The institutional and charismatic aspects are co-essential as it were to the Church's constitution. They contribute, although differently, to the life, renewal and sanctification of God's people. It is from this providential rediscovery of the Church's charismatic dimension that, before and after the Council, a remarkable pattern of growth has been established for ecclesial movements and new communities.[101]

In his very first encyclical, *Redemptor Hominis*, St. John Paul II also wrote of the "singular, unique and unrepeatable grace by which each Christian in the community of the People of God builds up the Body of Christ."[102] Having been present himself at the Council, he was imbued with its "truly catholic"[103] theology of *communio*, which said that:

> Since Christians have different gifts (cf. Rom 12:6) they should collaborate in the work of the Gospel, each according to his opportunity, ability, charism and ministry (cf. 1 Cor 3:10); all who sow and reap (cf. Jn 4:37), plant and water, should be one (cf. 1 Cor 3:8) so that "working together for the same end in a free and orderly manner" they might together devote their powers to the building up of the Church.[104]

In the mind of the Church, "it is the priests' part as instructors of the people in the faith to see to it either personally or through others that each member of the faithful shall be led in the Holy Spirit to the full development of his own vocation . . . , to reach Christian maturity."[105] While it is true that we also have the duty to discern whether or not individual gifts come from the Holy Spirit, the Council says that priests "must discover with faith, recognize with joy, and foster with diligence the many and varied charismatic gifts of the laity, whether these be of a humble or more exalted kind."[106]

Unfortunately, as some authors point out, "the novelty of the council was not conceived of, on a popular level, as a new

Pentecost."[107] In his Apostolic Exhortation *Catechesi Tradendae*, St. John Paul II acknowledges that many times, baptized people remain with only the "capacity" to receive the gifts of the Spirit without ever developing them or embracing them because they are not catechized or evangelized.[108] At times, sad to say, baptized Catholics who feel a need to be spiritually nourished or who want to develop their gifts leave the Church to find assistance in another Christian community.[109]

Priests are not necessarily free of fault for this present state of the Church. As Pope Francis points out, "Frequently, we act as arbiters of grace rather than its facilitators."[110] What leads us to act this way? There is room for personal reflection here. In the 2015 movie *Jurassic World*, there is a scene where the two main characters speak of the need to protect people from the huge dinosaurs that have escaped from their cages. When the woman goes to the main park keeper to ask for help, since he is the only one that can control them, he helps her understand that it is not a matter of "control" but of relationship, of mutual respect.[111] Perhaps there is a lesson here for us, too. Whether we feel threatened by others, insecure of our own gifts, or, God forbid, that we lack faith in what God can do in, through, and for the Church, or whatever other reason, we cannot shy away from our responsibility. The religious leaders in the times of Jesus made that mistake. As Father Cachia reminds us, "As a result of their obstinacy before Jesus, the Pharisees lose their acquired right to lead the people of Israel."[112] And, as another author points out, "it was the inability of the Pharisees to rejoice in Jesus' 'charism' that prompted him to warn of an unforgivable sin against the Holy Spirit (Mark 3:29)."[113]

Indeed, "Prophets like Samuel always need priests like Eli to teach them to hear the Lord."[114] And, when they find them, we may have more Francisis or Catherines of Siena who help us to renew the Church—and our own lives—with their sanctity.[115]

Father Timothy Hepburn says that, "when Jesus raised up his 'joyful shout,' rejoicing in the Holy Spirit as he witnessed the charismatic signs that indicated the shifting of kingdoms, he demonstrated the proper attitude toward receiving charisms with rejoicing (êggalliasato, Luke 10:21)."[116] St. John of Avila would concur. In one of his priestly conferences, he says, while making reference to St. John Chrysostom: "all clerics are shepherds, gardeners and soldiers and farmers; which means: they must seek the good of souls in the office which each holds according to the talent given by God."[117] Monsignor Esquerda also says of the Apostle of Andalusia, after about fifty years of studying his works:

> From Master Avila I learned that this is one of the characteristics of the spirituality of the diocesan priest: from the radical following of the gospel (as the apostles did), to appreciate and foster all charisms and vocations, offering the priestly service in communion with the particular and universal Church. It is then that the richness of the consecrated and lay vocations can be valued, as are also the new charisms that the Holy Spirit communicates to the Church in every age.[118]

Vocations to the Priesthood

If the priest is to encourage and foster all the different charisms and vocations, it should almost go without saying that he is to be especially attentive to those who can serve among his own ranks. While it is true that "the duty of fostering vocations falls on the whole Christian community,"[119] the Church believes that "this duty *belongs to the very nature of the priestly mission* which makes the priest share in the anxiety of the whole Church lest laborers should ever be wanting to the People of God here on earth."[120] It is "a necessary requirement of [his] pastoral charity toward [his] own particular church"[121] to find someone to take his place. Because of this:

> each priest will devote special dedication to vocational activity, never failing to encourage prayers for vocations, sparing no pains in catechesis, attending to the formation of altar servers and fostering suitable endeavors through a personal relationship helping to discover talents and being able to discover God's will for a courageous choice in the following of Christ.[122]

Pastores Dabo Vobis puts the main responsibility for priestly vocations on the shoulders of the bishop.[123] St. John of Avila agrees with this position, acknowledging that the bishop also is in need of help in this important task. In writing to the bishops that would be gathering for the Synod of Toledo, he says:

> It is essential that bishops have in every city people they can trust who may look for the candidates, inquiring with school teachers since they are the ones that form them, so that from them they can receive information on those whom they see with those gifts and inclination. And if the bishops at the synod say that no such candidates can be found, let them know that it is a great mistake to think that our Lord would not provide worthy persons in

his Church who can be his true ministers. God himself, who asks for such ministers and shed his blood so that they could exist, has placed his divine Spirit in many; if it seems that there are not any it is because prelates do not look for them, but this is their responsibility since they are ministers of the Lord.[124]

It is evident from his writings and his life that he considered himself one of these assistants to the bishops. While he encouraged all vocations—he would say: "you are not all to walk the same path; for not everyone should be married, not everyone priests, friars or nuns"[125]—when he saw someone that could be a good priest, he would make himself available to guide the candidate and, if there was a need, he would even help pay for his studies.[126]

Jesus, the One Shepherd

The Church teaches that "Christ is always present" in and to His people, that "he is present in the sacraments so that when anybody baptizes it is really Christ himself who baptizes."[127] This is true not only of his priestly role, but of the entirety of his being, for, as we read in *Lumen Gentium*: "The Church is . . . also a flock, of which God foretold that he would himself be the shepherd (cf. Is 40:11; Ex 34:11 f.), and whose sheep, although watched over by human shepherds, are nevertheless at all times led and brought to pasture by Christ himself, the Good Shepherd and prince of shepherds (cf. Jn 10:11; 1 Pt 5:4)."[128] The awareness of Christ's sacramental presence was already recognized by the early Church Fathers, as Nicholas Cachia states: "The leaders of the community are shepherds in so far as they are shepherds in Christ, the Good and Chief Shepherd of the flock. He is the source, the center

and the end of their ministry. The Fathers believed that
Christ is present in their actions and words; in actual fact, it is
Jesus himself who is shepherding the flock through them."[129]
Indeed, a sermon from St. Augustine confirms this. He says:

> All good shepherds are one in the one good shepherd;
> they form a unity. If only they feed the sheep, Christ is
> feeding the sheep. The friends of the bridegroom do
> not speak with their own voice, but they take great joy
> in listening to the bridegroom's voice. Christ himself is
> the shepherd when they act as shepherds. "I feed them,"
> he says, because his voice is in their voice, his love in
> their love.[130]

And so, St. John Paul II wrote to priests in one of his
annual Holy Thursday letters:

> *Jesus Christ* is among us, and tells us: "I am the Good
> Shepherd" (Jn 10:11, 14) . . . It is He who goes about all
> the cities and villages (see Matt 9:35), *wherever we are sent*
> to carry out our priestly and pastoral service. It is He,
> Jesus Christ, who teaches . . . , preaches the Gospel of
> the Kingdom and heals every disease and every infirmity
> of man, *wherever we are sent for the service of the Gospel and
> the administration of the sacraments.* It is really He, Jesus
> Christ, who continually feels compassion for the crowds
> and for every man who is tired and exhausted, as "sheep
> without shepherd."[131]

Continuing Education of the Priest

If Christ is the "Chief Shepherd," this means that His
representatives are totally dependent on him.[132] "The ecclesial
minister is called to be, first and foremost, a disciple of Jesus,

one who follows and serves Jesus wherever he is (Jn 12:26). This intimate and personal relationship becomes an essential prerequisite for him to be a good shepherd of the flock in union with Jesus and under Jesus, the Good Shepherd."[133] As it has already been mentioned, St. John of Avila believed in the need of this important connection. In his Treatise on the Priesthood, he writes: "there must be between Christ and the priest a very deep interior friendship, similarity of customs, a love and hatred of the same things, and a love that is so endearing to the point that, from two, there can remain only one."[134]

This intimacy begins with personal prayer, but if the priest is to truly have "similarity of customs" and "a love and hatred of the same things" as Jesus, the Good Shepherd, then it cannot stop there. If he is to put on the mind of Christ, this will necessarily entail continuing education, or better yet, permanent formation, since there cannot be a moment when he can claim to have perfectly reached that point. Father Cachia alerts us to this when he speaks of the "good" shepherd. He says: "Worthy of note is the adjective used in John 10:11: 'I am the good shepherd.' In Greek: '*egô eimi ho poimên ho kalos*.' How are we to understand this adjective *kalos*? According to Grundmann, 'when speaking of *kalos*, the Greek had in view the total state of soundness, health, wholeness and order, whether in external appearance or internal disposition.'"[135] As the Lord Himself put it, "no one is good but God alone" (Mk 10:18). Therefore, the tradition of the Church has rightly acknowledged that "the priest—like every other member of the Church—ought to grow in awareness that he himself is continually in need of being evangelized."[136]

The figure of a shepherd, in itself, is a reminder that priests must try to stay ahead of the people, to set a good example for them. Once again, we can turn to Cachia:

> The image [of the shepherd] includes the idea of moving, walking ahead (see Jn 10:4). This indicates the necessity of dynamism, which alludes to the need of pastoral and communal discernment in the Holy Spirit following the signs of the time. Thus, it calls for openness to new methods and new ways of answering Jesus' call to follow him, who is the Good Shepherd and who is always present and leading.[137]

This is the reason why the Apostle of Andalusia spent his whole life working with priests and pointing out the need for permanent, continuous formation. As another personality said of him:

> St. John of Avila has taught us, in his life and in his writings, that the priest is not only formed to be ordained, but to be faithful to the vocation received and to the continuous mission to which God continues to call while in ministry, for in fact "God continues to call and send forth, revealing his saving plan in the historical development of the priest's life and the life of the Church and of society."[138]

The more a priest is able to continue growing and expanding his horizons, the more he will be able to do for those entrusted to his care.[139]

The Priest, Leader and Brother

The Church has always professed the two perfect natures of Jesus: He is truly man and truly God.[140] The fact that He became one with us at the Incarnation does not mean that He stopped being God. He came as God's only Son, but in coming to dwell among us, He also became our brother. In the same way, one who is called to represent Jesus in the Church community does not cease to be a member of that group; he remains a brother. In *Presbyterorum Ordinis*, we read: "Priests, in common with all who have been reborn in the font of baptism, are brothers among brothers as members of the same Body of Christ."[141] Cachia also explains:

> The shepherd image thus serves to bring out the two essential dimensions of the spiritual life of the priest. The first is the vertical dimension, his relation to each person of the Trinity, and particularly to Jesus Christ. The minister always remains a disciple of the Lord and as such he answers God's call to serve him in the people whom he redeemed by his own blood. The second is the horizontal dimension, his relation to the communion of believers, of which the minister forms part, and to which he is sent to serve with the same attitude of the Good Shepherd, an attitude of service, of total self-dedication and of love to the end.[142]

This teaching is expounded in *Pastores Dabo Vobis*, where the love and self-dedication of the minister—although a brother— is spoken of as "spousal love," another way of expressing the pastoral charity that must be exercised. There, we read:

> The priest is called to be the living image of Jesus Christ, the spouse of the Church. Of course, he will always remain a member of the community as a believer alongside his other brothers and sisters who have been

called by the Spirit, but in virtue of his configuration to Christ, the head and shepherd, the priest stands in this spousal relationship with regard to the community. "In as much as he represents Christ . . . , the priest is placed not only in the Church but also in the forefront of the Church."[143]

The priest is one of them and does not serve "from above," that is with superiority, but as one who is sharing in their struggles, "a believer alongside his other brothers and sisters."[144] This is an area where the Catholic "both/and" can be seen beautifully. Two different realities are brought together and are now inseparable, just as the two natures of Jesus, just as the wine and water during the Mass.

Being a member of the community helps the priest to serve the people better.[145] St. John of Avila was conscious of this. In a letter he wrote to a brother priest, he says: "God . . . himself became man so that, being in the flesh, He could communicate with humanity. It is a great dignity to have the same office that God himself exercised."[146] And, we would add, to do it in the way Christ Himself did it!

Jesus came to do the will of the Father. He told the Apostles that His very food was "to do the will of the one who sent [him]" (Jn 4:34). According to St. John of Avila, it was not the good that was found in humanity that led Jesus to do everything he did for us—since we were actually unde-serving—but the desire to carry out God's will.[147] Likewise, *Presbyterorum Ordinis* tells us, "among the virtues especially demanded by the ministry of priests must be reckoned that disposition of mind by which they are always prepared to seek not their own will but the will of him who has sent them."[148] The asceticism or self-denial that the priest can practice is "to discover and carry out that will in the course of his daily routine by humbly placing himself at the service of all those who are entrusted to his care by God in the office that has been committed to him and the variety of events that make up his life."[149] Here again, we can also find in our saint the inspiration to continue doing this ourselves in our priesthood. In the conclusion of St. John's biography, Fra Louis of Granada writes:

> The Christian reader will find in this *Life* that we have written many things that will rightly edify him and make him marvel at, especially the fervor and unquenchable thirst that this man of God had for the salvation of souls. He procured it in so many ways, preaching, writing letters, organizing curriculums and colleges, supporting poor people and responding to all those who came to ask for his advice at every hour of the day.[150]

But, as St. John himself reminds us, it is precisely because of all those occupations that the priest must pursue his own holiness, so that he can continue to be the "good shepherd" God is asking him to be for those entrusted to his care.[151]

The strength required to exercise one's ministry will obviously be obtained through prayer and our inner disposition to see God in all the different events of the day and the people we encounter. Speaking specifically of those who have the care of souls, St. John of Avila writes:

> If he sees how many and how diverse are the occupations required by his office, it will be evident how handy and part of his nature it must be to have recourse to holy prayer, for it is not easy to have prayer and devotion in

the midst of many occupations even when they are good. Therefore, it is necessary that his holiness be very firm, because there are many occasions to lose it in ministry, as common sense and experience show us and as St. John Chrysostom ponders; St. Augustine also marvels much at those who have virtue as the foundation of this office.[152]

This need for prayer points once again to the interconnectedness of the different aspects of a priest's ministry. As he shepherds the people, he must also return to prayer and find in his own preaching and presiding the spiritual nourishment that he needs as a fellow disciple in order to continue being faithful to his own calling.

The desire to be a "good shepherd" for God's flock—a shepherd that is healthy, that is holy, that is generous with his time—is the actual energy that drives the priest to strive for his own sanctification. We could say that, in general, the "spirituality of the good shepherd" is what defines the spirituality of the diocesan priest. This is what Father Nicholas Cachia suggests: "The shepherd image thus serves as an excellent synthesis of the spirituality of those called to be leaders of the community. Through our reference to this image the three functions of preaching, of cult and of government become in Jesus the expression of the love of a shepherd from whom they take their inspiration."[153] And yet, in his own study, Father Cachia also says: "Although the shepherd image is a very rich one, it should not, as should no other image, be made an absolute. It has to remain an image. It cannot by itself represent the whole symbolized reality, whether this symbolized reality be Jesus Christ himself or the one who ministers as leader in the Church."[154] Therefore, while we could speak of the spirituality of the good shepherd, as he suggests, we must remember that there is more to the spirituality of the diocesan priest than just his shepherding role. His configuration to Christ calls him to be priest, prophet, *and* king—all three, in one ontological reality. This is explicitly expressed in Church documents and confirmed by several reputable theologians.[155] And by being faithful to his own vocation, the priest will also help the faithful in living out their own baptismal call to exercise those same roles in their common priesthood.

Conclusion

Although St. John of Avila was never a parish priest, the active life he led founding colleges and guiding others spiritually point to his abilities as a shepherd. He busied himself in caring for God's flock and in bringing unity and holiness of life to the Church. Many of his suggestions for reform were actually implemented at the Council of Trent, beginning to turn the tide that would lead to a holier and more committed priesthood, as can be attested by the reforms carried out in France by the French School of spirituality and in Italy, through great leaders like St. Pius V and St. Charles Borromeo. Truly, the desire to lead others to holiness can be a priest's own motivation for reaching that holiness himself. As mentioned in the previous chapter, teaching is much more effective when it is accompanied by personal testimony.

Beginning at Vatican II, the Church has spoken of pastoral charity as the one unifying element of a priest's spirituality, especially those who are responsible for the care of souls— that is, diocesan priests. As the priest aspires to be a humble leader—to make present the one Shepherd who is Jesus

Christ—he is at the service of all the baptized, helping them to grow spiritually and to develop the charisms that the Holy Spirit has bestowed upon them. In doing this, he himself is challenged to continue growing so that he can be an effective minister, a worthy representative not only of his bishop, with whom he has to be in communion, but of Christ. In faithfully living out his vocation, then, the diocesan priest works to make present the kingdom of God on earth, finding this way his own sanctification. Like Jesus the Master, his food, too, is to do the will of the Father,[156] to carry out his priestly duties in humble obedience.

NOTES

1. See John 13:1-17.
2. John Paul II, *Pastores Dabo Vobis* (1992) (from here on, abbreviated as *PDV*), sec. 57.
3. *Memorial primero al Concilio de Trento* (from here on, abbreviated as *MT1*) in *Obras completas* (from here on, abbreviated as *OC*), vol. 2, n. 14. St. John saw the need for two different sets of priests for the reform the Church needed in his day. One was pastors and confessors, and the other one was preachers. Since he had the gift of preaching, his ministry mainly focused on the latter. See Ibid., n. 13.
4. Vatican II, *Presbyterorum Ordinis* (1965) (from here on, abbreviated as *PO*), sec. 14.
5. *PDV*, sec. 22. An entire doctoral thesis has been written on the relationship between pastoral charity and the spirituality of the diocesan priest. See Thomas Cheruparambil, "Pastoral Charity: The Underlying Principle of the Spirituality of Diocesan Priests, A Study on *Pastores Dabo Vobis*," STD diss., Pontificia Studiorum Universitas a S. Thoma Aq. in Urbe (Rome, 2002).
6. *Tratado sobre el sacerdocio* (from here on, abbreviated as *TSS*) in *OC*, vol. 1, n. 36.
7. Letter 11 in *OC*, vol. 4, 61.
8. Ibid.
9. Ibid.
10. Ibid., 63.
11. Ibid., 60.
12. Ibid., 65.
13. Sermon 80 in *OC*, vol. 3, n. 13.
14. Ibid.
15. Nicholas Cachia, "The Good Shepherd: Living Christ's Own Pastoral Authority," in *Good Shepherd: Living Christ's Own Pastoral Authority*, edited by Edward G. Mathews, Jr., Fifth Annual Symposium on the Spirituality and Identity of the Diocesan Priest (Omaha: The Institute for Priestly Formation, 2006), 16. Father Cachia wrote his doctoral dissertation on this subject and defended it at the Gregorian University in 1997.
16. Ibid., 13. See *Pastores Dabo Vobis*: "Formation . . . aims at giving oneself generously and freely. . . . 'When we speak of forming future priests in the spirituality of the heart of the Lord, we mean they should lead lives that are a response to the love and affection of Christ the priest and good shepherd: to his love for the Father in the Holy Spirit, and to his love toward men that was so great as to lead him to give his life in sacrifice for them'" (sec. 49).
17. See Jeremiah 3:15.

18.   The "heart of Christ" in the writings of St. John of Avila was the topic of a doctoral thesis at the Gregorian University. See Bum Sik Min, "Il 'Cuore di Cristo' come centro della spiritualitá sacerdotale in San Giovanni d'Avila," STD diss., Pontificiae Universitatis Gregorianae (Rome, 2012). Msgr. Juan Esquerda also sees the doctrine of St. John as an obvious link in the development of the devotion to the Sacred Heart. See "Corazón de Cristo" in *Diccionario de San Juan de Avila* (from here on, abbreviated as *DJA*), 231.

19.   Benedict XVI, "Address to the Pontifical Spanish College of St. Joseph in Rome" (May 10, 2012).

20.   This citation is taken from "Mensaje de Juan Pablo II en el encuentro-homenaje de los sacerdotes a San Juan de Ávila en el V centenario de su nacimiento," in *OC*, vol. 1, Montilla, 31 de mayo de 2000, 371. Francisco Martín credits the message as being from St. John Paul II but there is no record of this in any Vatican document. It is possible that it might have been sent for the occasion by the Secretary of State of the Vatican. When the person responsible for composing the *positio* for the doctorate of St. John of Avila listed papal honors and praises for the saint, this message was left out. The only message that appears from St. John Paul II for the occasion of the fifth centenary was a letter to the president of the Spanish episcopal conference—dated May 10, 2000. See María Encarnación González Rodríguez, *San Juan de Ávila, Doctor de la Iglesia universal* (Madrid: Biblioteca de Autores Cristianos, 2012), 142. The "message," however, is an excellent summary of the way in which St. John of Avila embodied the teachings found in *Pastores Dabo Vobis* in his own day.

21.   *Tratado del amor de Dios* (from here on, abbreviated as *TAD*) in *OC*, vol. 1, n. 7.

22.   Francis, *Misericordiae Vultus* (from here on, abbreviated as *MV*) (2015), sec. 6.

23.   Cachia, 12.

24.   *TAD* in *OC*, vol. 1, n. 8.

25.   *TSS* in *OC*, vol. 1, n. 12. See *PO*, sec. 12; *PDV*, sec. 21.

26.   *Pláticas* 7 in *OC*, vol. 1, n. 5.

27.   Sermon 55 in *OC*, vol. 3, n. 37.

28.   *Pláticas* 2 in *OC*, vol. 1, n. 4.

29.   Letter 8 in *OC*, vol. 4, 49.

30.   See Sermon 9, nn. 3-4; Sermon 32, n. 15; Sermon 33, n. 5.

31.   See Fulton J. Sheen, *Treasure in Clay: The Autobiography of Fulton J. Sheen* (San Francisco: Ignatius Press, 1993), 338.

32.   *Pláticas* 2 in *OC*, vol. 1, n. 3.

33.   See Luke 1:26-45.

34.   "Espiritualidad Mariana" in *DJA*, 376.

35.   Vatican II, *Lumen Gentium* (from here on, abbreviated as *LG*) (1964), sec. 65.

36.   *Pláticas* 2 in *OC*, vol. 1, n. 16.

37.   See *TSS* in *OC*, vol. 1, nn. 11, 36 and 39. Pope Benedict XVI also wrote of this fatherly and motherly affection in the act declaring St. John of Avila a doctor of the universal Church: "[A]cting *in persona Christi* demands that we humbly embody God's paternal and maternal love. This calls for a particular lifestyle, marked by regular recourse to the word of God and the Eucharist, by the adoption of a spirit of poverty, by preaching 'temperately', in other words, based on prior study and prayer, and by love for the Church as the Bride of Christ." "Apostolic Letter Proclaiming Saint John of Avila, diocesan priest, a Doctor of the Universal Church" (October 7, 2012), http://w2.vatican.va/content/benedict-xvi/en/apost_letters/documents/hf_ben-xvi_apl_20121007_giovanni-avila.html, (accessed January 15, 2016).

38.   Juan Esquerda Bifet, "Ser sacerdote desde los amores de Cristo. La herencia sacerdotal de San Juan de Ávila," in *San Juan de Ávila, Doctor de la Iglesia, Actas del Congreso Internacional*, eds. Juan Aranda Doncel and Antonio Llamas Vela (Cordoba: Ediciones y Publicaciones Diputación de Córdoba, 2013), 423.

39.   *PDV*, sec. 22.

40.   *Pláticas* 4 in *OC*, vol. 1, n. 7. Here, St. John includes "religious" because this conference was addressed to a community of Jesuits.

41.   Sermon 36 in *OC*, vol. 3, n. 99.

42.   Cachia, 13.

43.   Ibid., 19. The reference to St. John Chrysostom is *De Sacerdotio*, II.1.14-40.

44.   Sermon 35 in *OC*, vol. 3, n. 26.

45.   *Advertencias* in *OC*, vol. 2, nn. 6-7. It may seem interesting here that St. John speaks of the need for bishops to skip their siesta since the Spanish are known for it and St. John would actually recommend his disciples to take one. But, of course, what was at play was of much more importance. If bishops, indeed, had "motherly hearts," it would be difficult to think that they could actually get some sleep when their children were in danger. He speaks of this in a sermon for the feast of St. Nicholas. See Sermon 73 in *OC*, vol. 3, n. 10.

46.   Letter 182 in *OC*, vol. 4, 603.

47.   *Memorial Segundo al Concilio de Trento* (from here on, abbreviated as *MT2*) in *OC*, vol. 2, n. 10.

48.   *Advertencias* in *OC*, vol. 2, n. 5.

49.   *MT1* in *OC*, vol. 2, n. 12.

50.   Sermon 8 in *OC*, vol. 3, n. 28.

51.   Sermon 15 in *OC*, vol. 3, n. 31.

52.   Letter 10 in *OC*, vol. 4, 54. The reference to St. Augustine is: *Confess.* 1.10 c.27 n.38; *Patrologia Latina* 32, 795 (from here on, abbreviated as

PL). The translation is: "Late did I know you, beauty ever ancient; late did I know you, beauty ever new!"

53.   Francis, "Homily for Chrism Mass" (March 28, 2013).

54.   Letter 178 in *OC*, vol. 4, 592.

55.   *TSS* in *OC*, vol. 1, n. 40.

56.   Cachia, 21-22. The citation from Origen is from *Homilies on Joshua*, VII.6.

57.   An interesting insight found in this sermon is that the shepherd pays someone to care for the ninety-nine before he goes out to seek the lost one. In a way, this makes the parable more credible and it shows how much the shepherd is willing to invest to seek the fullness of the flock. See Sermon 19 in *OC*, vol. 3, n. 12.

58.   Ibid., n. 5 (italics in the original). The reference to St. John Chrysostom is *In Epist. 1 ad Tim.* C.1 hom.4,1: Patrologia Greca 62, 519-520 (from here on, abbreviated as *PG*).

59.   Ibid., n. 21.

60.   Letter 182 in *OC*, vol. 4, 603.

61.   See Luke 12:42.

62.   Letter 208 in *OC*, vol. 4, 675. The "zeal for souls" comes up frequently in the writings of St. John of Avila. See *Advertencias*, n. 34; *TSS*, n. 39; Sermon 81, n. 5.

63.   See *PDV*, sec. 82.

64.   Paul VI, *Evangelii Nuntiandi* (from here on, abbreviated as *EN*) (1975) in *Acta Apostolicae Sedis* 68 (1976): 1-76, English translation: Vatican City: Libreria Editrice Vaticana, 1976, n. 1.

65.   Ibid.

66.   Sermon 19 in *OC*, vol. 3, n. 26.

67.   Francis, *Evangelii Gaudium* (from here on, abbreviated as *EG*) (2013) sec. 271.

68.   Ibid., sec. 9.

69.   *Pláticas* 1 in *OC*, vol. 1, n. 13. It could also be argued that, besides the shortage of priests, the reason why many Catholic parishes operate more on a "maintenance mode" rather than being actively engaged in evangelization is that priests are overwhelmed with administrative duties. Archbishop Fulton Sheen, who lived closer to our day (d. 1979), had an observation in regard to this that may be worth pondering: "Was it not the failure of many priests to read the Council's distinction of the world as a theater of redemption and a spirit which is anti-Christ which prompted so many to abandon pastoral activities and to be more concerned with management as imitation and the industrial life of the world? Added to this is the number of meetings called by the bishops of various heads of departments which keep priests and religious away from their assigned duties, to enter into fruitless prolonged dialogues which manifest little light but much heat." Sheen, *Treasure in Clay*, 296.

70.   *MT2* in *OC*, vol. 2, n. 10.

71.   *TSS* in *OC*, vol. 1, n. 36.

72.   Ibid., n. 37. The reference to St. Gregory the Great is *Reg. pastor.* p.1. c.10: PL 77, 23; p.2 c.3.7: PL 77, 28.40 and to St. John Chrysostom is *De sacerdotio*, 1.3,6: PG 48, 643; cf. 1.2 c.2: PG 48, 633.

73.   Letter 11 in *OC*, vol. 4, 78.

74.   The fact that St. John lists all three virtues in just one paragraph is an indication that this was far from being an exhaustive treatment of the virtues. Besides temperance, which could come under St. John's idea of holiness in general and the need to give a good example, justice is also important. In parishes, many conflicts arise from groups or people who feel treated differently from others.

75.   *TSS* in *OC*, vol. 1, n. 37. For the reference to St. Gregory, see *Reg. past.* p.1.ch.1: PL 77, 14.

76.   Ibid., n. 39.

77.   "Prudencia" in *DJA*, 770-71.

78.   Letter 11 in *OC*, vol. 4, 77.

79.   *TSS* in *OC*, vol. 1, n. 37.

80.   Letter 27 in *OC*, vol. 4, 169 (although the letter was written to an abbess, the teaching applies to every Christian).

81.   *TSS* in *OC*, vol. 1, n. 37.

82.   Ibid. For a thorough treatment of the virtue of fortitude in the priesthood, see Archbishop José H. Gomez, *Men of Brave Heart: The Virtue of Courage in the Priestly Life* (Huntington: Our Sunday Visitor, 2009).

83.   Cachia, 12.

84.   See Letter 86. This is a beautiful epistle for the Villa de Utrera written by St. John upon learning that there were divisions in that city. Having been among them in the past and, as he says, grateful for the benefits received from them, he hopes that through his writing, he may be able to reconcile them to one another. The letter resembles those of St. Paul to the different Christian communities.

85.   *LG*, sec. 4.

86.   Vatican II, *Ad Gentes* (1965), sec. 3.

87.   *Directory*, n. 41.

88.   "Letter to Ephesians" (Nn. 2, 2-5, 2: Funk 1, 175-77), quoted in *The Liturgy of the Hours*, vol. 3 (New York: Catholic Publishing Book, 1975), 80-81 (Second Sunday in Ordinary Time).

89.   *PO*, sec. 6.

90.   *Pláticas* 1 in *OC*, vol. 1, n. 11. The "crown" he speaks about here was part of the minor orders before Vatican II. The hair of the cleric was cut to resemble a crown. What St. John says here still applies, though. The priest does share in the ministry of the bishop who is anointed with Chrism on the head to make him high priest, one who shares in the

fullness of Christ's priesthood. Though only bishops share in the fullness of Christ's priesthood, the priests share in the authority.

91. "Discourse Against the Pagans," (Nn. 42-43: PG 25, 83-87), quoted in *The Liturgy of the Hours*, vol. 3 (New York: Catholic Publishing Book, 1975), 71-72 (Friday of the First Week in Ordinary Time).

92. *LG*, sec. 4.

93. *New Outpourings of the Spirit: Movements in the Church*, trans. Michael J. Miller and Henry Taylor (San Francisco: Ignatius Press, 2007), 23.

94. *PO*, sec. 6. This "power" could be seen as the actualization of God's command to humanity to "subdue" the earth and care for it, to organize the whole world according to God's design—that is, to make his kingdom present (see Sir 17:3; Gn 1:28).

95. Daytime Prayer, Monday, Week 1, in *The Liturgy of the Hours*, vol. 3, 712 (first Psalm prayer).

96. Sermon 33 in *OC*, vol. 3, n. 16.

97. Sermon 81 in *OC*, vol. 3, n. 5.

98. *MT2* in *OC*, vol. 2, n. 40.

99. Ibid.

100. *LG*, sec. 4.

101. "This is the Day the Lord has Made!" *L'Osservatore Romano* 22 (June 3, 1998): 2 (n. 4).

102. John Paul II, *Redemptor Hominis* (1979) in *AAS* 71 (1979): 257-324, English translation (Vatican City: Libreria Editrice Vaticana, 1979), sec. 21 (from here on, abbreviated as *RH*). He also touches on charisms in *Pastores Dabo Vobis* (see sec. 31). See also *Catechism of the Catholic Church* (New York: Image, 1995), n. 2003 (from here on, abbreviated as *CCC*).

103. See "All the children of the Church should have a lively consciousness of their own responsibility for the world, they should foster within themselves a *truly catholic* spirit, they should spend themselves in the work of the Gospel." *AG*, sec. 36 (emphasis added).

104. *AG*, sec. 28.

105. *PO*, sec. 6.

106. Ibid., sec. 9.

107. Rev. Timothy Hepburn, "Fathering the Fire: Uncovering, Acknowledging, and Fostering Charisms," in *Spiritual Fatherhood: Living Christ's Own Revelation of the Father*, ed. Edward G. Mathews, Jr., Eighth Annual Symposium on the Spirituality and Identity of the Diocesan Priest (Omaha: The Institute for Priestly Formation, 2009), 54.

108. See John Paul II, *Catechesi Tradendae* (1979), sec. 19: "But in catechetical practice, this model order must allow for the fact that the initial evangelization has often not taken place. A certain number of children baptized in infancy come for catechesis in the parish without receiving any other initiation into the faith and still without any explicit

personal attachment to Jesus Christ; they only have *the capacity* to believe placed within them by Baptism and the presence of the Holy Spirit" (emphasis added).

109.   Sherry A. Weddell gives some alarming statistics. According to her, 71 percent of former Catholics who joined Protestant communities stated doing so because their "spiritual needs were not being met." Many others, she says, have become "nones," that is, those who do not practice anything. See Weddell, 28-33.

110.   *EG*, sec. 47. He also speaks of people's need to share their charisms with the community in *Gaudete et Exsultate* (from here on, abbreviated as *GE*) (2018) (see sec. 130).

111.   The Charismatic Renewal Movement in the Church has done much to tap into people's gifts for the good of the community. The only "monsters" that have led to some horror stories are those individuals that are not properly formed or supervised. When people understand that formation means to take the form of Christ in one's life (see Gal 4:19)—Christ the humble and obedient servant who gave His life out of love for others (cf. Phil 2:1-11)—and that, as St. Paul teaches, the gifts of apostleship, teaching, and administration come before some of the gifts frequently present in the Charismatic Renewal (see 1 Cor 12:28-31), then there should be no conflicts. A pastor in the Archdiocese of Los Angeles, for example, found out that having term limits (of a maximum of four years) in ministry for parish leaders heading Church groups prevented people from acquiring too much power or clinging to positions for a long time in an unhealthy manner. It also allowed others in the community to step forward and discover and develop their own gifts.

112.   Cachia, 13.

113.   Hepburn, 52. See Weddell: "It is critical that we understand that charisms are given to all the baptized, not just a few extraordinary Christians, and to individuals as well as to religious communities or movements. . . . Being open to these gifts of the Holy Spirit, discerning them, and then exercising them for the sake of others are critical acts of obedience. . . . After working with tens of thousands of Catholics in the discernment process, we have noticed something important: Not all charisms are welcomed and valued at the parish level. This is almost never intentional or bad-willed, but it hampers the work of the Kingdom all the same. For instance, the following charisms are typically welcomed and fostered in parochial settings: administration, craftsmanship, encouragement, giving, helps, hospitality, mercy, music, pastoring, service and wisdom. Why are these charisms particularly welcomed? These are spiritual gifts that are particularly useful in the liturgy, in caring for people, and when maintaining institutional structures. . . . Which charisms are we not likely to welcome? *The charisms primarily aimed at starting new initiatives, evangelizing and proclaiming Christ, forming disciples and apostles, and freedom for unusual*

ministry and prophetic change. Many of these gifts have been traditionally associated with religious communities rather than parish life" *Forming Intentional Disciples*, 229-31 (emphasis in the original).

114.   Ibid.

115.   It may be that priests have not always been good at helping others to develop their gifts because they just do not know how to do that. There are resources out there. Weddell speaks of the "Called and Gifted" discernment process offered by the Catherine of Siena Institute, a ministry of the Western Dominican Province of the United States. In pages 71-80 of her book, she shares some success stories of parishes who have offered the workshops to parishioners where many have become actively involved in the community and several have entered the seminary, the convent, or formation for the permanent diaconate. Another book that some priests have found helpful is Albert L. Winseman, Donald Clifton, and Curt Liesveld's *Living Your Strengths: Discover Your God-Given Talents and Inspire Your Community*, Catholic Edition (New York: Gallup, 2008). Though the pioneers of the research that led to this useful tool offered in the book to identify individual talents came from Protestant backgrounds, Gallup worked with Catholic leaders to produce this Catholic edition. Many parishes have already benefitted from those who have come forward to exercise their gifts in community. More tools can also be found with the Catholic Leadership Institute. As the name suggests, the "Good Leaders, Good Shepherds" program is all about helping Catholic bishops, priests, and lay people in leadership to know how to empower and inspire others as they work together for the good of the Kingdom.

116.   Hepburn, 52.

117.   *Pláticas* 7 in *OC*, vol. 1, n. 5.

118.   *Entre todos, Juan de Ávila: Elogio al Santo Maestro en el entorno de su proclamación como Doctor de la Iglesia Universal*, ed. María E. González Rodríguez (Madrid: Biblioteca de Autores Cristianos, 2011), 84-85.

119.   *OT*, sec. 2. See *PDV*, sec. 41.

120.   *PO*, sec. 11, (emphasis added).

121.   *PDV*, sec. 74.

122.   *Directory*, n. 43.

123.   See *PDV*, sec. 41.

124.   *Advertencias* in *OC*, vol. 2, n. 39.

125.   Sermon 76 in *OC*, vol. 3, n. 21.

126.   Documents exist that reveal the expenses of the University of Baeza, of which St. John of Avila was the rector. Besides paying for professors' salaries and for repairs, St. John would also give students financial assistance. Since the university was founded mainly to form future priests, there is no question that money was not an obstacle for him when he saw a good vocation. See Sala and Martín, *OC*, vol. 1, 89-90. See also Sermon 81, n. 8.

127. Vatican II, *Sacrosanctum Concilium* (from here on, abbreviated as *SC*) (1963), sec. 7.

128. *LG*, sec. 6. This is another indication of the indivisible three-fold role of Jesus that must be emulated in the spirituality of the diocesan priest. Jesus is priest, prophet, and king; and as such, He continues to be present in the person of His minister.

129. Cachia, 17.

130. *Sermo* 46, 29-30: *Code of Canon Law* (from here on, abbreviated as *CCL*) 41, 555-557, in *The Liturgy of the Hours*, vol. 4, 307 (Friday of the Twenty-Fifth Week in Ordinary Time).

131. John Paul II, "Letter to Priests for Holy Thursday" (March 7, 1984), accessed April 23, 2016, http://w2.vatican.va/content/john-paul-ii/es/letters/1984/documents/hf_jp-ii_let_19840307_priests.html, English translation: Cachia, 25 (italics in the original). In 1984, Pope John Paul II sent priests the homily he preached on February 23, 1984, for the conclusion of the World Jubilee of Clergy on the occasion of the Redemption Jubilee.

132. See Cachia, 15.

133. Ibid., 14.

134. *TSS* in *OC*, vol. 1, n. 12. See *PDV*: "By virtue of this consecration brought about by the outpouring of the Spirit in the sacrament of holy orders, the spiritual life of the priest is marked, molded and character-ized by the way of thinking and acting proper to Jesus Christ, head and shepherd of the Church, and which are summed in his pastoral charity" (sec. 21).

135. Cachia, 13-14. The author refers here to Walter Grundmann's article "Kalos" in the *Theological Dictionary of the New Testament*, ed. by Gerhard Kittel and Gerhard Friedrich, (Grand Rapids: Eerdmans, 1976), III.536-550. Cachia goes on to say that other authors give "kalos" other interpretations, such as "tending His flock tenderly," "being for," or even "attractive loveliness." Grundmann's explanation seems to be more appro-priate for our purposes. The healthier and more balanced a priest is, the better he will be able to serve his people.

136. *PDV*, sec. 26. See *EN*, sec. 15.

137. Cachia, 23.

138. Once again, this is the "Message" credited to St. John Paul II in the year 2000. See *OC*, vol. 1, 373. The quote in the message is from *PDV*, sec. 70. For some of St. John of Avila's recommendations for the continu-ing education of priests, see *MT2* (nn. 63-71) and *Advertencias* (nn. 44-46) in *OC*, vol. 1, as well as letters 244 and 233 in *OC*, vol. 4.

139. See the following Church documents for information about ongo-ing formation: *PDV* (sec. 70-81), *OT* (sec. 22), and *PO* (sec. 19). For a sample of a plan published by an episcopal conference, see United States

Conference of Catholic Bishops, *The Basic Plan for the Ongoing Formation of Priests* (Washington, D.C.: United States Catholic Conference, 2001).

140.   See *CCC*, n. 464.

141.   *PO*, sec. 9. See also *PDV*, sec. 74.

142.   Cachia, 23.

143.   *PDV*, sec. 22.

144.   In the *Song of Songs*, this dual aspect is also seen when the Groom calls the bride "my sister, my bride" (see 4:9-10, 5:1).

145.   See *PO*, sec. 3. Older generations of Catholics still remember the touching words of St. John XXIII the night of the opening of the Second Vatican Council. Upon gazing at a spontaneous crowd of faithful who had joyfully gathered to pray with candles at St. Peter's Square, it is reported that he came out of the balcony to greet them and said: "I am a brother who, by God's grace, has become your father." He concluded by asking them to go to their homes and kiss their children for him. The Italian papers the following morning had headlines about "the kiss of the Pope." It is common knowledge that by this point, the Pope knew of his terminal cancer. Mindful of his short days, he was eager to express to the world all the love he had in his heart. Given his permanent humble disposition and such expressions of affection, he endeared himself to the people; his love was reciprocated.

146.   Letter 4 in *OC*, vol. 4, 29.

147.   See *TAD* in *OC*, vol. 1, n. 11.

148.   *PO*, sec. 15.

149.   Ibid.

150.   Granada, 170.

151.   See *TSS* in *OC*, vol. 1, n. 37.

152.   Ibid., n. 36. The reference to St. John Chrysostom is *De sacerdotio* 1.3, 6: PG 48, 639-660.677-692, and to St. Augustine: *Epist. classis* I epist.21, 1ff: PL 33, 88.

153.   Cachia, 23. See *PDV*: "This same pastoral charity is the dynamic inner principle capable of unifying the many different activities of the priest. . . . Only by directing every moment and every one of his acts toward the fundamental choice to 'give his life for the flock' can the priest guarantee this unity which is vital and indispensable for his harmony and spiritual balance" (sec. 23). See also *PO*, sec. 14.

154.   Ibid., 8.

155.   See Congregation for Religious and Secular Institutes and Congregation for Bishops, *Mutuae Relationes: Directives for the Mutual Relations between Bishops and Religious in the Church* (May 14, 1978), (Washington, D.C.: United States Catholic Conference Publications, 1978), n. 7 (from here on, abbreviated as *MR*); Karl Rahner, S.J., "The Spirituality of the Priest in the Light of His Office," in *Theological Investigations*, vol. 19: Faith and Ministry, trans. Edward Quinn (New York: Crossroad, 1983), 124; Avery

Dulles, S.J., *The Priestly Office: A Theological Reflection* (New Jersey: Paulist Press, 1997), 7.
  156.   See John 4:34.

CHAPTER 4

THE PRIEST AND THE PEOPLE OF GOD: MUTUAL SANCTIFICATION

If it seems that little of what is covered in this chapter can be found in the writings of St. John of Avila, we must keep in mind what then-Cardinal Joseph Ratzinger observed years ago, before his election to the See of Peter. He said that since Vatican II, there has been a "marked insistence on interrelations in the Church and on the communal journey of the whole Church,"[1] a reality that was not yet present in the sixteenth century. Since the whole basis of St. John of Avila's theology—and specifically, his ecclesiology—is the Mystery of Christ, the living organism that has Christ as its head, the conclusions reached in this chapter are the normal development that has taken place in that body, in the Church. If the writings of the Apostle of Andalusia are to mean anything to us priests of the twenty-first century as we try to apply them to our own spirituality, this adaptation to today's reality is a must. We, too, need to take our rightful place in the Body of Christ and to "make it beautiful" with the graces entrusted to us.[2]

The Church as *"Communio"*

Pope Benedict XVI has been one of the greatest theologians the Church has had in modern times. As such, he often spoke and wrote of the reality of the Church as *communio.* "After the Second Vatican Council," he explains, "this term indeed became a central word of theology and of preaching, because it expresses all the dimensions of our being as Christians and of ecclesial life."[3] In another homily he gave as Pope, he said: "The dimension of community is an essential part of Christian faith and life. Christ came 'to gather into one the dispersed children of God' (cf. *Jn* 11:52). The 'we' of the church is a community in which Jesus draws us together to himself (cf. *Jn* 12:32): faith is necessarily ecclesial."[4] His successor, in continuity with this teaching, would add that "no one baptizes himself, just as no one comes into the world by himself."[5]

The Church is a community because she resembles the unity that is present in God Himself. *Lumen Gentium* states this: "The universal Church is seen to be 'a people brought into unity from the unity of the Father, the Son and the Holy Spirit."[6] In *Laudato Si*, Pope Francis speaks of how this Trinitarian reality is even present in the world itself: all things tend to unity,[7] not even atoms and particles can be considered separately[8] as it is the will of God that all things be interdependent.[9] The mission of Jesus, St. John of Avila concurs, was precisely to make present the unity found in the Godhead in the Church:

> Our Lord is in a great way a friend of unity; it is his task to join things that are separated and divided and to keep together what is united; this seemed good to him, he liked

unity. We will see in this, if we look closely, the very being of God, who is the essence of unity in all its simplicity, for nothing can be thought of which is more united, without a composition or division. From this we can see how unity would be so pleasing to him.[10]

In *Pastores Dabo Vobis*, St. John Paul II tells us what this this concept of *communio* means for priests and for those in preparation to serve in that ministry:

> Of fundamental importance is awareness that the Church is a "mystery," that is, a divine work, fruit of the Spirit of Christ, an effective sign of grace, the presence of the Trinity in the Christian community. . . .
>
> Awareness of the *Church* as "*communion*" will prepare the candidate for the priesthood to carry out his pastoral work with a community spirit, in heartfelt cooperation with the different members of the Church: priests and bishops, diocesan and religious priests, priests and lay people. Such a cooperation presupposes a knowledge and appreciation of the different gifts and charisms, of the diverse vocations and responsibilities which the Spirit offers and entrusts to the members of Christ's body. It demands a living and precise consciousness of one's own identity in the Church and the identity of others. It demands mutual trust, patience, gentleness and the capacity for understanding and expectation. It finds roots above all in the love for the Church that is deeper than love for self and the group or groups one may belong to.[11]

Indeed, as St. John of Avila states, we are "a Church and a unity in Jesus Christ. All those who serve Jesus Christ, who are in his service, all are one same thing, the Church of God and the congregation of Christians."[12]

The spirituality of the diocesan priest, therefore, if it is to be authentic, must be ecclesial. As Louis Bouyer states, "the spiritual life must be fully Catholic, that is, lived in the Church."[13] Along with all the members of the Church, priests must strive to be faithful in carrying out what is asked of them, to grow in holiness as they serve their brothers and sisters in the community. This is why we pray in the Liturgy of the Hours: "God our Father, work is your gift to us, a call to reach new heights by using our talents for the good of all. Guide us as we work and teach us to live in the spirit that has made us your sons and daughters, in the love that has made us brothers and sisters."[14] Clearly, we are called to "serve one another through love" (Gal 5:13).

Mutual Love, the Unifying Factor

It should come as no surprise that people have different ideas of what it means to be Catholic, what it means to be a member of the Church. In his foundational work *Models of the Church*, Cardinal Avery Dulles speaks of at least six different models that people in the Church tend to follow: the Church as institution, mystical communion, sacrament, herald of the Gospel, servant, and—added later—community of disciples.[15] And, even before Vatican II, Father Ronald Knox, in his book *Enthusiasm*, could speak of the tendency found in some to think that "their way" is the only way, that what they have to offer is the key to solving all the Church's and the world's problems.[16] But, as we read in Scripture, "the body is not a single part, but many. . . . The eye cannot say to the hand, 'I do not need you'" (1 Cor 12:14, 21). The answer, then, is in the whole, in all the members doing their part and being faithful to their calling.

In his treatment on the different parts of the Body of Christ, St. Paul concludes by saying that love is what keeps the individual parts together and, therefore, that they should pursue this most "excellent way" of love.[17] In *Galatians*, he also teaches: "the whole law is fulfilled in one statement, namely, 'You shall love your neighbor as yourself'" (5:14). Being familiar with these teachings, St. John of Avila would say in his preaching: "*If you do not have love* to love God and neighbor, *nothing is of value* (1 Cor 13:3); even if you sell yourself in Muslim territory and give to God whatever they can pay for you, it is not worth anything."[18] Therefore, St. John would exhort: all Christians "must go out of themselves and go to work in the Lord's vineyard, which is the Church."[19]

Seeking only personal interests leads to destruction, our saint says in one of his letters to a group of canons. The conflicts and envies in that unnamed Spanish community (possibly Cordoba) got so out of hand that they even reached the attention of Church officials in Rome. To them, then, the Apostle of those Andalusian cities would write about the errors of self-love: "It is pure lunacy that, thinking that we love ourselves, we actually despise ourselves, searching for what seems good to us and falling into all kinds of errors!"[20] The solution, he tells someone else while following the thought of Pseudo-Dionysius, is to have "the same love that is in God. Because, as St. Dionysius says, one of the effects of love is to unite the wills of those who love, that is, that they love and hate the same thing."[21]

In one of his lessons on the Epistles of St. John, St. John of Avila expounds the traditional teaching of the Church on love. Following the Angelic Doctor, he explains: "St. Thomas says that the perfection of the Christian life consists in keeping the commandments and in charity. If the married person has more charity than the cleric or the friar, he is better than them, because he does not do what the friar does."[22] In other words, the married person is holier than those who made a vow to seek Christian perfection because he is actually practicing it. And St. John warns:

> How many are there who think that they keep the commandments of God and they do not! That is a real deceit: to think that I am walking down the path of God and not to do it. . . . We must flee from this deceit, for so much is at stake here. . . . How careful people are so as not to be deceived with this or that merchandise! How much sleep they lose over that! How much work and care they put into it! But how careless if they are erring on the path of God . . . ![23]

Unity of Heart[24]

The Decree on Ecumenism that resulted from the Vatican II proceedings states that no unity can be hoped for except when there is a change of heart. The actual words from the Council Fathers are:

> There can be no ecumenism worthy of the name without interior conversion. For it is from newness of attitudes of mind, from self-denial and unstinted love, that desires of unity take their rise and develop in a mature way. We should therefore pray to the Holy Spirit for the grace to be genuinely self-denying, humble, gentle in the service of others and to have an attitude of brotherly generosity

toward them. The Apostle to the Gentiles says: "I, therefore, a prisoner for the Lord, beg you to lead a life worthy of the calling to which you have been called, with all humility and meekness, with patience, forbearing one another in love, eager to maintain the unity of the spirit in the bond of peace" (Eph 4:1-3).[25]

The same is true for unity within the Church among those of us that claim to be in full communion with Christ's Vicar and with each other. St. John of Avila speaks of that "unity of heart" in the letter that he wrote for a city from that southern region of Spain. There, he encourages the faithful to "guard the unity of heart, for Christ prayed to the Father saying: *Father, I want them to be one, as you and I are one* (cf. Jn 17:22)."[26] If people are at peace with themselves, if they have a "good" heart, a heart that is whole, pure, and full of love for others like the heart of the Good Shepherd, then, acting as His true followers, they will gravitate and work toward that unity for which Jesus prayed. If, on the contrary, their hearts are in turmoil, if there is no integrity on their part, if they are busy looking at the faults of others, as St. John tells the canons of the Spanish city mentioned earlier, then the grace of peace and unity can be taken away. Therefore, unity must be constantly sought; it is a conscious decision that we must make on a regular basis as we fight against our inner desires for having things our way and seek what we prefer. "This business" of unity, our saint says, "is not a business of words, but of actions."[27] Truly then, as the bishops at Vatican II quoted above said, we must pray "for the grace to be genuinely self-denying and humble." The love of God that was "poured out into our hearts" (Rom 5:5) at Baptism must be

manifested as we carry out concrete acts of service for one
another and for the greater glory of God.[28]

Communion with the Bishop

It is the teaching of the Second Vatican Council that the
unity between the priest and his bishop can actually be an
aid to the priest's sanctification.[29] Since priests "depend on
the bishops in the exercise of their own proper power,"[30]
they can respond to the universal call to holiness, we are told,
when they "grow in the love of God and of their neighbor
by the daily exercise of their duty."[31] As they carry out what is
asked of them, they will come to resemble the obedience and
humility of Jesus, *Presbyterorum Ordinis* tells us:

> The priestly ministry, being the ministry of the Church
> itself, can only be fulfilled in the hierarchical union of the
> whole body of the church. . . . They will accept and carry
> out in the spirit of faith the commands and suggestions
> of the Pope and of their bishop and other superiors. . . .
> By acting in this way they preserve and strengthen the
> indispensable unity with their brothers in the ministry
> and especially with those whom the Lord has appointed
> the visible rulers of his Church. They also work towards
> the building up of the Body of Christ, which grows
> "by what every joint supplies" (cf. Eph 4:11-16). . . . By
> this humility and by responsible and willing obedience
> priests conform themselves to Christ. They reproduce the
> sentiment of Jesus Christ who "emptied himself, taking
> the form of a servant . . . and became obedient unto
> death" (Phil 2:7-9), and who by this obedience overcame
> and redeemed the disobedience of Adam, as the apostle
> declares (cf. Rom 5:19).[32]

In *Pastores Dabo Vobis*, St. John Paul II also writes about the priest's unity with his bishop and the ways in which this relationship contributes to his own spirituality. There, we read:

> Like every authentically Christian spiritual life, the spiritual life of the priest has an *essential and undeniable ecclesial dimension* which is a sharing in the holiness of the Church herself, which we profess in the *Creed* to be a "communion of saints." The holiness of the Christian has its source in the holiness of the Church; it expresses that holiness and at the same time enriches it. This ecclesial dimension takes on special forms, purposes and meanings in the spiritual life of the priest by virtue of his specific relation to the Church, always as a result of his configuration to Christ the head and shepherd, his ordained ministry and his pastoral charity.
>
> In this perspective, it is necessary to consider the priest's membership in and dedication to a particular Church. These two factors are not the result of purely organizational and disciplinary needs. On the contrary, the priest's relationship with his bishop in the one presbyterate, his sharing in the bishop's ecclesial concern, and his devotion to the evangelical care of the People of God in the specific historical and contextual conditions of a particular Church are elements which must be taken into account in sketching the proper configuration of the priest and his spiritual life. In this sense, "incardination" cannot be confined to a purely juridical bond, but also involves a set of attitudes, as well as spiritual and pastoral decisions which help to fill out the specific features of the priestly vocation.

> The priest needs to be aware that his "being in a particular Church" constitutes by its very nature a significant element in his living a Christian spirituality. In this sense, the priest finds precisely in his belonging to and dedication to the particular Church a wealth of meaning, criteria for discernment and action which shape both his pastoral mission and his spiritual life.[33]

Indeed, the Council teaches that when bishops see their priests not only as their "helpers and advisers" but also as "brothers and friends,"[34] the priests "will find unity of life. . . . In this way they will be united with their Lord and through him with the Father in the Holy Spirit, and can be filled with consolation and exceedingly abound with joy."[35] In other words, when priests enjoy a close relationship with their bishop, they will feel loved and appreciated; and this becomes another avenue by which they find meaning for their lives; they will experience the love of God mediated by the one He has given them as a spiritual father and will be able to share it with others.

This is precisely the relationship that St. John of Avila longed to see in his day. In his writings for the Council of Trent, he says of bishops: "giving orders is easy and it can be done without charity; but carrying the weaknesses of others with a persevering heart that wants to help them and strengthen what is weak requires richness of charity."[36] And he would add, "prelates with clerics are like fathers with sons, not masters with slaves."[37]

In the last apostolic exhortation of his pontificate, *Pastores Gregis*, St. John Paul II reiterated the teaching of Vatican II between a bishop and his presbyterate. It is a two-way street, he wrote, that leads to holiness:

Each Diocesan Bishop has as one of his primary duties the spiritual care of his presbyterate: "The action of the priest who places his hands in the hands of the Bishop on the day of his priestly ordination, as he professes to him 'filial respect and obedience,' can at first sight seem a one-way gesture. In reality, the gesture commits them both: priest and Bishop. The young presbyter chooses to entrust himself to the Bishop and the Bishop for his part obliges himself to look after those hands."[38]

The Pope goes on to add that the bishop must also be attentive when there have been priests in his diocese with heroic virtues to promote their cause for canonization. But, of course, in order to assists his priests to reach that point, there must be "frequent meetings" with them,[39] friendly gatherings, in order for "Bishops to have direct and personal contact with [them] . . . , following the example of the Good Shepherd who knows his sheep and calls each by name."[40]

Obviously, this ideal relationship between the bishop and his priests is not always possible. Lest these words be a setup for disillusionment and discouragement, it must be remembered that—besides constraints of time and space—bishops are also human beings affected by original sin; their leadership and their relationships with others will most likely be lacking at times. In light of this, *Presbyterorum Ordinis* states: "Priests for their part should keep in mind the fullness of the sacrament of Order which bishops enjoy and should reverence in their persons the authority of Christ the supreme Pastor. They should therefore be attached to their bishop with sincere charity and obedience."[41] This applies even when priests themselves are not treated charitably by bishops; it may be part of the asceticism or "the cross" that may have to be carried. According to St. John of Avila, this, too, can be an aid to the priest's purification and sanctification.[42]

Communion with the Presbyterate

In a message for the five hundredth anniversary of the birth of St. John of Avila, it was said that: "John of Avila has known how to be faithful to this continual vocation from the Lord in the Church and in the society in which he lived and where he exercised his mission in fraternity. He understood that this mission had to be done *in fraternity with other evangelizers* and helping to awaken and unite the diverse charisms in the Church."[43] Although the concept of a "presbyterate" around the bishop had not yet developed in the sixteenth century,[44] the Apostle of Andalusia intuited that this unity and collaboration was essential. In Vatican II, with the emphasis on communion, the term "presbyterate" constantly appears in different documents.

The Council tells us that priests "constitute, together with their bishop, a unique sacerdotal college (*presbyterium*),"[45] "one priestly body and one family of which the bishop is the father."[46] This common bond can manifest itself "in a spontaneously and gladly given mutual help, whether spiritual or temporal, whether pastoral or personal, through the medium of reunions and community life, work and fraternal charity."[47]

It is the Church's belief that "the presbyterate is the privileged place where the priest should be able to find specific means of formation, sanctification and evangelisation [*sic*], and be helped to overcome the limits and weaknesses proper to human nature."[48] Therefore, even though every diocese will necessarily have different structures and means of support, priests will be there.[49] It may be helpful to look at some common elements that might assist priests in carrying out their ministry and developing a healthy spirituality.

Mentoring Newly Ordained Priests

Studies over the years have pointed out how essential it is to be attentive to the needs of newly ordained priests.[50] In *Pastores Dabo Vobis*, we read that the presbyterate "takes special care of the young priests."[51] But unfortunately, that is not always the case. Especially in an age where there is a shortage of priests, it has been pointed out that sometimes "our young priests are placed in situations of great stress with few personal supports" and that "newly ordained priests are often put in a parochial setting of tens of thousands of the faithful and there are few, if any, other priests for guidance and support."[52] Given this reality, "it is very opportune, and perhaps even absolutely necessary nowadays, to create a *suitable support structure*, with appropriate guides and teachers," we read in *Pastores Dabo Vobis*.[53] If a diocese is too small to provide this for its newly ordained priests, the exhortation goes on to say, it could join with neighboring bishops so that a program can be in place with mutual resources.

St. John of Avila was blessed to find a good mentor right from the beginning of his priesthood. After his ordination, he went to Seville where he hoped to take a ship that would take him to the New World; and it was there that he met the saintly priest Fernando de Contreras. Father Fernando was fifty-six years old at the time, and his zeal and creativity would mark the young John of Avila for the rest of his life. It was from Father Contreras that he learned some important methods for evangelization and to catechize, especially, children.[54]

After having had this foundational positive experience, St. John would return the favor: he, in turn, would spend the rest of his priesthood supporting others and helping them to discern their calling.

Living in an age where the family unit is not always available and where many times, seminarians have not had good father figures in their lives, the need for positive role models at the beginning of a priest's ministry cannot be underestimated.[55]

Spiritual Direction

Besides having role models for practical matters, a priest also needs a spiritual guide.[56] The book of Proverbs reveals the importance of not trusting in one's own judgment: "Those who trust in themselves are fools, but those who walk in wisdom are safe" (28:26). In his master work, *Audi, filia*, St. John of Avila points out that that there is a language of the world, a language of the flesh, a language from the devil, and God's voice, which is revealed through faith.[57] Part of submitting to God's will, St. John teaches, is having a good spiritual director who can help us in the ongoing process of discernment. He recommends having as *guía y padre* (guide and father) "someone who is learned and experienced in the things of God" since "one without the other does not suffice."[58]

It has already been said that St. John, following the teaching of St. Gregory the Great, believed that, for the most part, pastors of souls should not be very dependent on others for spiritual matters.[59] This, however, does not mean that they should not have a spiritual director or that St. John believed that priests did not need to go to confession.[60] What this suggests is that he hoped the formation in the seminary—along with the priest's own prayer life and spiritual practices—would equip him to make prudent decisions for the challenges that would come up on a normal basis. For critical issues, though, it is essential to have someone to turn to. He speaks of this in his *Audi, filia*:

> Since it is so helpful to find a good guide . . . , entrust your heart to him with great security. Do not hide anything from him, either good or bad: the good, so that he may direct and warn you; the bad so that he may correct you. *Do nothing important without his opinion*, trusting that God, who is a friend of obedience, will place in the heart and on the tongue of your guide what will be helpful for your salvation. In this way you will flee from two evil extremes. One is that of those who say, "I do not need advice from men; God teaches me and is enough for me." Others are so subject to men that they are included in that curse that says, "cursed be the man that trusts in man" (Jer 17:5). Subject yourself to a man, and you will have escaped the first danger. Do not trust in the knowledge or strength of a man, but in God, who *will* speak to you and strengthen you *by means of a man*. Thus, you will have avoided the second danger.[61]

And in one of his sermons, he adds: "The servant of God, the confessor and the preacher must not get in the way of the Holy Spirit; he must be a ladder so that you can go up to God."[62] Since the priest is called to be a man of communion, it is difficult to see how this ascent to God could be accomplished without the guidance of others. St. John clearly states that God "will speak to you and strengthen you by means of a man."[63]

While in today's Church, the laity is also involved in offering spiritual direction and some priests do believe that having the wisdom of a woman religious or a layman may be of benefit to them to offer a different perspective, there is something to be said for turning to a brother priest for spiritual guidance. Besides sharing the same life and having similar experiences in ministry, he can also offer the Sacrament of Reconciliation at some point during the session. Having the input or the wisdom of other members of Christ's Body can be received in other contexts, such as professional therapy or healthy friendships with groups of women religious and faithful Catholic families.

Common Life

The *Directory on the Ministry and Life of Priests* states that the "common life is an image of that *apostolica vivendi forma* of Jesus with his apostles."[64] It also mentions that bishops like St. Augustine practiced it with their priests and that it is a form of life which is "always supported by the Church."[65] Church and Magisterial documents confirm this encouragement,[66] and the common life is presently lived in several institutes of secular priests, as will be explained later.[67] In addition to being an aid "to safeguard them from possible dangers arising from loneliness,"[68] it can also help priests in their sanctification. Pope Benedict XVI put it like this:

> The common life expresses a form of help Christ gives to our existence, calling us, through the presence of brothers, to an increasingly deeper configuration of his person. Living with others means accepting the need for one's ongoing conversion, and especially discovering the beauty of such a journey, the joy of humility, repentance,

but also conversion, mutual forgiveness and reciprocal support. *Ecce quae bonum et quam iucundum habitare fratres in unum* (Ps 133:1).[69]

St. John of Avila recognized this need for conversion. As it has already been said,[70] he surrounded himself with other priests for mutual growth and study everywhere he went, and this is something he recommended for all particular churches, at least in major cities. He writes to the Spanish bishops with the following recommendation:

> It would be very edifying and it would solve many problems if, in every city where it is possible, there were a hospital with beds and all other essential services where all priests—and even those in first tonsure who have benefices—could live together so that they are not going from inn to inn where they face thousands of dangers and indecencies for those in this state. Or have a house of safe and trustworthy charitable people, like the house of a cleric or an elderly couple where there are no young women, in which everything can be found to house these men.[71]

In his retirement, St. John of Avila always lived with other priests. His faithful disciple, Father Juan de Villarás, for example, lived with him for sixteen years.[72] They were also in the habit of having a couple of virtuous students at a time living with them who would answer the door, copy the writings of the saint, or write letters that he would dictate. St. John called them "brothers," and many of them embraced the religious life after this experience.[73] Those of us who have had seminarians living in our rectories can also attest to the graces that can result from this beautiful exchange.

The common life is so important that it is even mentioned in the *Code of Canon Law*. In canon 550 section 1, we read: "A parochial vicar is obliged to reside in the parish or, if he has been appointed for different parishes jointly, in one of them. Nevertheless, for a just cause the local ordinary can allow him to reside elsewhere, especially in a house shared by several presbyters, provided that this is not detrimental to the performance of his pastoral functions." It also goes on to state: "The local ordinary is to take care that some manner of common life in the rectory is fostered between the pastor and the vicars where this can be done."[74] The latest edition of the *Directory on the Ministry and the Life of Priests* also adds: "In cases where there is only one priest in a parish, the possibility of a common life with other priests in neighbouring parishes is highly encouraged."[75]

Priestly Associations

Where living with other priests is not possible, it is very helpful to have fraternity groups where the brothers can gather to pray, share personal experiences, and encourage one another. The *Directory* also mentions this: "Worthy of praise in particular are those associations which support priestly fraternity, holiness in the exercise of the ministry, and communion with the Bishop and the entire Church."[76] In *Pastores Dabo Vobis*, St. John Paul II lists such associations as one of the means of ongoing growth and sanctification for priests. He writes:

> Another help can be given by *priestly associations*, in particular by priestly secular institutes—which have as their characteristic feature their being diocesan—through which priests are more closely united to their bishop, and

which constitute "a state of consecration in which priests by means of vows or other sacred bonds consecrate themselves to incarnate in their life the evangelical counsels." All the forms of "priestly fraternity" approved by the Church are useful not only for the spiritual life but also for the apostolic and pastoral life.[77]

Some religious orders or institutes offer priests the possibility of attaching themselves to their community in the form of a third order or by being an oblate or associate. While these are also worthy associations, it may be more beneficial to look for one where, besides the spiritual enrichment, the focus is on strengthening the relationships between their fellow priests and their bishop. The Sacrament of Holy Orders does call for this unity of purpose and fraternity. As St. John of Avila said to his brother priests: "If we, the head and the members join together in God, we will be so powerful that we will overcome the devil in us and we will free the people from their sins, because . . . God made the clerical state so powerful that, if it is as it ought to be, it can influence the people in virtue as heaven influences the earth."[78]

Healthy Friendships

Presbyterorum Ordinis states that priests "should also be delighted to gather together for relaxation, remembering the words by which the Lord himself invited his weary apostles: 'Come apart into a desert place and rest a little' (Mk 6:31)."[79] Older, wise priests do say that when a brother calls to see if they can share a coffee or a drink, the invitation implies more than just that. It may be a cry for help; it could also mean that the brother needs to vent about something, which he cannot do with anybody else at the parish, or simply get the opinion of another priest. It is good to be receptive and make time for these kinds of invitations. Again, citing *Presbyterorum Ordinis*, "under the influence of the spirit of brotherhood priests should not forget hospitality."[80]

Especially in areas where the distance or multiple responsibilities prevent priests from seeing each other more often, it is helpful if they spend their day off or go on vacation together. Some dioceses also allow for a monthly day of recollection. Besides the occasions for fraternity that annual priestly retreats sponsored by the diocese or local monasteries may offer,[81] these days can also be opportunities in which priests can plan to do things together.

Mutual Assistance and Fraternal Concern

Because we are human, most likely, we will also come across brother priests whom, for whatever reason, we find difficult and with whom we wish we did not have to interact. Since "no priest is sufficiently equipped to carry out his own mission alone,"[82] however, the bond of ordination calls us to do our best to interact with them. The Church does tell us that we must be mindful of "those laboring under difficulties" and that we "should offer timely help to them."[83] We must also "be particularly concerned about those who are sick, about the afflicted, the overworked, the lonely, the exiled, the persecuted."[84] Even in the case of those who have failed in some way, priests "should pray earnestly to God for them and never cease to show themselves genuine brothers and friends to them."[85]

It seems very revealing that when *Presbyterorum Ordinis* lists the spiritual requirements that can make this unity in the presbyterate and in the Church possible, the first one mentioned is humility.[86] The fact that priests renounce certain things in their lives makes them liable to the spirit of competition and thirst for power that was present even in the first disciples of our Lord.[87] St. John Paul II did state that in order for the spirituality of communion to be present, we must resist "the selfish temptations which constantly beset us and provoke competition, careerism, distrust and jealousy."[88] Here again, St. John of Avila is a safe model for us priests. Besides his personal witness of renouncing two bishoprics and the cardinalate[89] and choosing to remain only a priest, he emphasized humility in all his endeavors. He would say things like, "Whoever is with God is recognized in his humility. . . . Do not believe that sanctity is possible without humility, even if you are taken to the third heaven,"[90] and "there is no other art to escape the traps of the devil except in being small."[91] He was mindful that "the Son of Man did not come to be served but to serve and to give his life as a ransom for many" (Mt 20:28) and that nothing less was expected from the priest, His representative.

The Lord knew what He was doing when He sent out his disciples "two by two" (Mk 6:7). His actions suggest that, as the saying goes, he wanted them to know that "charity begins at home," with those closest to us.

Collaboration with Permanent Deacons

The Church teaches that "the divinely instituted ecclesiastical ministry is exercised in different degrees by those who even from ancient times have been called bishops, priests and deacons."[92] In *Pastores Dabo Vobis*, St. John Paul II also wrote:

In their turn, the apostles, appointed by the Lord, progressively carried out their mission by calling—in various but complementary ways—other men as bishops, as priests and as deacons in order to fulfill the command of the risen Jesus who sent them forth to all people in every age.

The writings of the New Testament are unanimous in stressing that it is the same Spirit of Christ who introduces these men chosen from among their brethren into the ministry. Through the laying on of hands (cf. *Acts* 6:6; 1 *Tm* 4:14; 5:22; 2 *Tm* 1:6) which transmits the gift of the Spirit, they are called and empowered to continue the same ministry of reconciliation, of shepherding the flock of God and of teaching (cf. *Acts* 20:28; 1 *Pt* 5:2).[93]

Much has evolved in the ministry of deacons since it was reinstituted at the Second Vatican Council.[94] Today, in some areas of the world, deacons actually outnumber priests in their dioceses.[95] Yet, it is not unusual to find priests who do not value or understand the ministry of deacons. Although it is true that it is to the bishop that deacons promise respect and obedience at ordination, the communal aspect of Holy Orders also puts them "in a special relationship with the priests."[96] Deacons are called to "serve the people of God in union with the bishop and his clergy."[97] The fact that *Lumen Gentium* left the competence of the restoration of the diaconate to episcopal conferences rather than individual bishops seems very revealing.[98] The universal Church, with the guidance of the Holy Spirit, was asking for this.

From the beginning, deacons were ordained so that priests would not "neglect the word of God to serve at table" (Acts 6:2). If deacons are allowed to serve the Church with their special charism and according to their calling, it is difficult to believe how this would not help priests to focus more on their spirituality and the ministry that is truly theirs.[99]

Communion with Religious

Religious life, likewise, "has its own place in relation to the divine and hierarchical structure of the Church."[100] We are told that, "while not entering into the hierarchical structure of the Church, [it] belongs undeniably to her life and holiness."[101] Members of religious communities "adorn the bride of Christ by the steadfast and humble fidelity of their consecrated lives and give generous service of the most varied kinds,"[102] especially in areas where the hierarchy may need their help. They are there to complement what bishops, priests, and deacons may not be able to do since the needs of humanity can be vast and the laborers may not be enough to gather the Lord's harvest.[103] As was mentioned before, St. John of Avila understood this need for religious even in his day. In one of his sermons, he observed: "The [Good Shepherd] ordered it that way: that the Pope stayed in his place, and that prelates succeed the apostles, and pastors the seventy-two disciples, as St. Jerome says; they are part of the intrinsic nature of the Church; and religious are added to help prelates and pastors."[104]

Even though both the hierarchical and charismatic aspects of the Church come from the same Spirit, it is not rare that, at times, there are tensions and conflicts between them.[105] In 1978, the Congregation for Religious and Secular Institutes and the Congregation for Bishops together published *Mutuae Relationes,* a declaration to express the communal relationship that must exist between both bishops and religious. Written for the purpose of solving some of the problems that arose after Vatican II, the document contributed to their common understanding. In it, we read the following:

> All pastors, mindful of the apostolic admonition never to be a "dictator over any group that is put in [their] charge, but [to] be an example that the whole flock can follow" (*1 Pt* 5:3), will rightly be aware of the primacy of *life in the Spirit*. This demands that they be at the same time *leaders* and *members*; truly *fathers*, but also *brothers*; *teachers* of the faith, but especially *fellow disciples* of Christ; those indeed, *responsible for the perfection* of the faithful, but also true *witnesses of their personal sanctification*.[106]

Because bishops and priests are the shepherds called to guide and care for all the gifts and charisms present in God's family, the document goes on to say, they "should be convinced advocates of the consecrated life, defenders of religious communities, promotors of vocations, firm guardians of the specific character of each religious family both in the spiritual and in the apostolic field."[107] Once the bishop has discerned and accepted the charism offered by the religious communities present in his diocese,[108] he is to "exhort the diocesan priests to recognize gratefully the fruitful contribution made by religious to their Church and to approve willingly their nomination to positions of greater responsibility, which are consonant with their vocation and competency."[109] In other words, both diocesan priests and religious men and women must work hand in hand to respond to the needs of the local Church. They each have their gifts to contribute for the good and vitality of the Church of God.

Almost forty years later, the *Directory on the Ministry and the Life of Priests* reaffirms this mutual collaboration. It states:

The priest will dedicate particular attention to relations with brothers and sisters engaged in the life of special consecration to God in all its forms, showing them sincere appreciation and a real spirit of apostolic collaboration, respecting and prompting their specific charisms. Moreover, he will cooperate so the consecrated life may appear even more luminous for the good of the entire Church, and increasingly persuasive and attractive for the new generations.[110]

Religious priests are especially a blessing in any diocese. Many local churches could not function without their assistance. Besides the priestly help that they are able to offer, their "different particular charisms . . . help to encourage and promote ongoing priestly formation."[111] Their presence "broadens the horizon of Christian witness and contributes in various ways to an enrichment of priestly spirituality . . . ,"[112] for they, in fact, take seriously the call to discipleship and the living out of the evangelical counsels. As is the case with deacons, then, when the priest works well with religious, many fruits can be gathered from this fraternal relationship.

Communion with the Faithful

The Second Vatican Council placed a great emphasis on the role of the laity in the Church.[113] The fact that *Lumen Gentium* presents a chapter on "The People of God" (Chapter Two) before it mentions that "The Church is Hierarchical" (Chapter Three) is a clear indication of this emphasis on laity, reminding us also of the fundamental vocation to holiness through our Baptism and the further specific call to become holy members of Christ's faithful laity, religious, or ordained ministers. In this dogmatic constitution, then, we read that

God "willed to make [humanity] holy and save them, not as individuals without any bond or link between them, but rather to make them into a people who might acknowledge him and serve him in holiness."[114] As mentioned earlier, priests have a primordial role in contributing to that unity that God wants to see among His children.

Common and Ministerial Priesthoods Ordered to One Another

The Church teaches that "the common priesthood of the faithful and the ministerial or hierarchical priesthood are . . . ordered one to another,"[115] that "the ordained ministry or *ministerial* priesthood is at the service of the baptismal priesthood."[116] Father Cachia also tells us: "the notion of the shepherd cannot be understood in itself but in reference to the sheep."[117] And he goes on to explain what this meant to early bishops like St. Augustine:

> Worth recalling is yet another Augustinian expression: *non tam praeesse quam prodesse* (not so much to preside over but to be useful). . . . After giving a list of what is expected of a good shepherd, he synthesizes everything in the phrase *omnes amandi*, loving all. Then he goes on to say: "In all the vast and varied activity involved in fulfilling such manifold responsibilities, please give me your help by both your prayers and your obedience. In this way I will find pleasure not so much in being in charge of you as in being of use to you."[118]

In other words, bishops and priests are to facilitate the "interconnection of relationships which arise from the Blessed Trinity and are prolonged in the communion of the Church," as St. John Paul II put it in *Pastores Dabo Vobis*.[119]

The Council clearly stated that the sanctification of the world was placed in the hands of the laity given their secular nature.[120] In his Post-Synodal Apostolic Exhortation *Christifideles Laici*—published in 1988 as a result of the 1987 Synod of Bishops on the Vocation and Mission in Church of the Laity—St. John Paul II reaffirmed the interconnection between the ministerial and common priesthood.[121] In *Pastores Dabo Vobis*, he speaks further of this "helping relationship," as he calls it:

> Finally, because their role and task within the Church do not replace but promote the baptismal priesthood of the entire People of God, leading it to its full ecclesial realization, priests have a positive and helping relationship to the laity. Priests are there to serve the faith, hope and charity of the laity. They recognize and uphold, as brothers and friends, the dignity of the laity as children of God and help them to exercise fully their specific role in the overall context of the Church's mission.[122]

In fact, at the beginning of the exhortation, the Pope mentions that it was the laity who was asking for holy and educated priests. He writes:

> Lay people themselves had asked that priests commit themselves to their formation so that they, the laity, could be suitably helped to fulfill their role in the ecclesial mission which is shared by all. Indeed, "the more the lay apostolate develops, the more strongly is perceived the need to have well-formed holy priests. Thus the very life of the People of God manifests the teaching of the Second Vatican Council concerning the relationship

between the common priesthood and the ministerial or hierarchical priesthood."[123]

If "the sinfulness of the clergy is a very efficient cause of the sinfulness of the laity,"[124] as St. John of Avila says, the opposite is also true: holy priests will necessarily translate into faithful and committed Christians.

Mutual Sanctification

Probably every priest has had the experience of being momentarily distracted at Mass and forgetting part of the Creed or some other prayer as he is reciting it with the community, especially if he is presiding at multiple celebrations on a given day. When this happens, it is the prayer of the congregation that puts him back "on track" as he catches up with them. In a way, this is a good image of what takes place spiritually between them: the priest is supposed to be the one leading; but at times, it is the faithfulness of the parishioners that brings him back to God's fold when he fails or goes through a difficult moment in his life.

The Church teaches that, because of the anointing of the Holy Spirit, all the baptized are infused with a supernatural faith, the *sensus fidei*, which guides them so as not to falter.[125] Although individually they can sin, the faith of the entire community cannot be wrong. Therefore, both priests and faithful "may be mutually encouraged by one another's faith" (Rm 1:12), as St. Paul wrote. The inspiration and encouragement can actually go in both directions. There is no way that any priest who is open to the work of the Holy Spirit can disagree with this point. Surely, we have all experienced it with the holy and unassuming people God has entrusted to our care. St. John Paul II speaks of this dynamic when he addresses the continuing formation of the priest. He writes:

> The very exercise of the pastoral ministry leads to a constant and fruitful mutual exchange between the priest's life of faith and that of the laity. Indeed *the very relationship and sharing of life between the priest and the community*, if it is wisely conducted and made use of, will be a *fundamental contribution* to permanent formation, which cannot be reduced to isolated episodes or initiatives, but covers the whole ministry and life of the priest.[126]

With this in mind, it is helpful to take a closer look to the ways in which the priest's relationship with the faithful can assist him in his own spirituality.

God Speaks Through Others

God's prophets did not end with John the Baptist. The prophetic mission of the Church continues in all the baptized "to allow the newness and the power of the Gospel to shine out everyday [*sic*]."[127] In *Christifideles Laici*, we read that "the lay faithful are given the ability and responsibility to accept the Gospel in faith and to proclaim it in word and deed, without hesitating to courageously identify and denounce evil."[128] Thus, a priest does well when he listens to his parishioners and tries to discern the voice of God in what he hears and sees in them. What Pope Francis says in *Laudato Si'* could also apply to God's minister:

> Human beings are not completely autonomous. Our freedom fades when it is handed over to the blind forces of the unconscious, of immediate needs, of self-interest, and of violence. In this sense, we stand naked and

exposed in the face of our ever-increasing power, lacking the wherewithal to control it. We have certain superficial mechanisms, but we cannot claim to have a sound ethics, a culture and spirituality genuinely capable of setting limits and teaching clear-minded self-restraint.[129]

Though here he speaks of technology, there is no question that a priest can benefit from that interaction and the "checks and balances" that the People of God can offer. They can be God's instruments to balance him out and keep him honest.

Since no one is beyond reproach, priests are always in need of conversion[130] and can benefit from the "prophets" they find along the way. King David learned the bitter lesson when he did not listen to Joab's concerns about his desire to take a census of his people. After going against the advice of his assistant, he and all the Israelites had to endure the consequences of his actions.[131]

Every priest has his share of stories of people who have helped him to see things differently and grow in his awareness of God's action in his life. Archbishop Fulton Sheen relates one of them in his autobiography. He writes: "I remember once meeting a doorman at the Great Southern Hotel in Killarney. I said to him as I came out of the hotel door: 'Oh, it's raining.' He put out his hand and said: 'You call that rain, Father. That's holy water from Heaven and it's blessing yourself you ought to be doing with it,' as he signed himself with the sign of the Cross."[132]

As mentioned earlier, this is the reason why St. John of Avila would tell a fellow theologian that "it will be good for you"[133] to visit the sick or those that were in need in the community. St. John Paul II reiterates this in *Pastores Dabo Vobis*. He writes:

> In particular, through coming to know and share, through making his own the human experience [of] suffering in its many different manifestations, from poverty to illness, from rejection to ignorance, loneliness and material or moral poverty, the priest can cultivate his own humanity and make it all the more genuine and clearly apparent by his increasingly ardent love for his fellow men and women.[134]

Surely, there is no question that such encounters can touch the heart of the priest, lead him to pray for his people, and be mindful of his own humanity and dependence on the Lord. The people can "preach to him" even without saying a word just by the way that they embrace their crosses and face their daily struggles with deep faith and trust in God.

Mutual Love and Support

St. John Paul II was a great contributor to modern humanism. On many occasions, he repeated the call for a "Civilization of Love" initiated by St. Paul VI.[135] In his writings, St. John Paul II spelled out that call. In his first encyclical, *Redemptor Hominis*, for example, he writes: "[A human being] cannot live without love. He remains a being that is incomprehensible for himself; his life is meaningless, if love is not revealed to him, if he does not encounter love, if he does not experience it and make it his own, if he does not participate intimately in it."[136] In *Mulieres Dignitatem*, he also says: "Being a person means striving toward self-realization, which can only be achieved 'through a sincere gift of self.'

The model for this interpretation of the person is God himself as Trinity, as a communion of Persons. To say that man is
created in the image and likeness of God means that man is
called to exist 'for' others, to become a gift."[137] Since the Pope
speaks of human realities, these apply both to the priest and
to the people to whom he ministers. Their relationship finds
meaning in the love that is shared between them, for when
we love, it is then that we become more like God, "for God is
love" (1 Jn 4:8).

Love does not need to be expressed in words. As the
saying goes, "actions speak louder than words." We can see
this in the life of St. John of Avila. Even though he lived a
very simple life, he accepted with gratitude the generosity
of benefactors. He did not take advantage of it, but he did
accept what was necessary for his sustenance. He trusted in
the words of the Gospel that the Lord would provide, since
"the laborer deserves his keep" (Mt 10:10).[138] Though he
would shy away from staying in mansions or palaces, he did
accept a small house for his retirement, as was mentioned
earlier.[139] And, despite not being "a friend of gifts,"[140] as his
biographers observe, he would turn to some of his neighbors
to ask them to prepare something for him to eat; but most of
the time, he would rather eat at the homes of priest friends.[141]

Call to Service

Every Christian has a vocation to service and love. The
Church tells us that God calls us not as individuals, but as a
people to "serve him in holiness."[142] Therefore, when speaking of a vocation, we must understand that "not only does it
derive 'from' the Church . . . but it also necessarily appears—
in fundamental service to God—as a service 'to' the Church.

Christian vocation, whatever shape it takes, is a gift whose purpose is to build up the Church and to increase the kingdom of God in the world."[143]

The priest and the People of God can help each other to live out their vocation. Since it is the priest's duty to preach, to sanctify, and to lead others, it is understandable that most of his ministry will take place with the people at his parish.[144] The Church says that priests are to be "defenders of the common good" and to bring about "agreement among divergent outlooks in such a way that nobody may feel a stranger in the Christian community."[145] He will, therefore, send parishioners to reach out to others and organize them in such a way that the needs of all in the community, both Catholics and non-Catholics, are met. This is what St. John of Avila recommended in forming confraternities—or groups of people that would work with the poor, with children in orphanages, and who would visit jails and hospitals.[146] This was, in his eyes, the way in which the Kingdom of God could be expanded in the world and people could experience the loving touch of Christ and the Church. And, just as he said to his theologian friend, such contact with others can also be helpful to their own spirituality. This is what happened in his case. It has been written of him: "John of Avila, in exercising his pastoral ministry, not only grew in his human formation, but also in his *spiritual life*."[147]

Because in the decades since Vatican II the lay faithful have assumed their rightful place in the mission of the Church, it is imperative that priests see to the laity's formation so that they can represent the Church properly in society. The *Directory on the Ministry and the Life of Priests* states: "One of the tasks that demands special attention is the formation of the laity . . . to expedite in full their role as Christian animators of the temporal order (political, cultural, economic, social)."[148] By having a body of well-formed disciples, the priest can also find there some of his greatest helpers and supporters to look after the life of the parish, as the *Directory* goes on to say:

> In this sense one of the important tasks for parish priests is to discover among the faithful persons with the skills virtues and coherent Christian life—for example, as regards matrimony—who can provide an efficient and helping hand in pastoral activities: the preparation of children for First Communion and first Confession or youngsters for Confirmation, the family apostolate, pre-marriage catechesis, etc.[149]

CHARITY MANIFESTED IN FRIENDSHIP

It has been established that the priest's pastoral charity must extend to everyone in the community. As a celibate man, he puts himself "at the service of all;"[150] he belongs to everyone and to no one in particular. In serving his people, however, many times friendships and special bonds develop with them. Even in the Gospel, we read how "Jesus loved Martha and her sister and Lazarus" (Jn 11:5). He would visit with them often, and He responded to their request to go see Lazarus when Lazarus was at the point of death. The Gospel of John tells us that it was at their home that Mary anointed the feet of Jesus in preparation for His Death.[151] She was also to be one of the few disciples who would stand faithfully by Him during the Crucifixion and, perhaps because of that faithfulness, she received the grace of being the first one to see the resurrected Lord.[152]

The Church praises these friendships and sees them as a "very useful means to overcome the negative effects of loneliness which the priest can sometimes experience,"[153] especially for priests who are far away from their families or who, because of their ministry, live in isolated places. Since no one can live without love, as St. John Paul II stated,[154] these relationships can be very beneficial in the life of the priest. They can also be opportunities for him to grow in his generativity and his creativity as he comes up with initiatives that may be helpful not just to his close friends, but to everyone in general. In the case of St. John of Avila, for example, it was one of those relationships that led to the writing of his masterpiece, the spiritual treatise *Audi, filia*. The work was written at the request of Sancha Carrillo, the sister of one of St. John's disciples, Pedro Fernandez de Cordoba.[155] When she asked our saint to write some recommendations for her spiritual growth, the work began to take shape. He would continue to add to it even after Sancha's death when he realized that it could be helpful to other people.

These friendships, then, often endure beyond the priest's assignment and, sometimes, even for life. If a priest begets "spiritual children" through preaching, as the Apostle of Andalusia wrote to his friend Louis of Granada, this is understandable.[156] So long as the priest remembers that his primary relationship must be to Christ[157] and he does not shy away from relating to other brothers in the presbyterate, these relationships with parish families can be very helpful.[158] Nonetheless, *Pastores Dabo Vobis* mentions them last and only after addressing the relationship that the priest must have with his bishop, his fellow priests, and others in the local Church. It is there, in the presbyterate, that a spirit of "a true family"[159] must exist.

The Role of the Priest's Own Family

Jesus wanted to establish His Church as a family, the family of God. He revealed God as "Father" (Mt 6:9), called his "brother, and sister, and mother" those who do the will of God (Mt 12:50); and finally, on the night before He died, He prayed that all believers might be one, just as the Father and the Son are one.[160] As a brother, He "chose us and predestined us in him for adoptive sonship."[161] That is why "priests . . . live with the rest of [human beings] as with brothers."[162]

The Church tells us that every family has natural and supernatural bonds. It is through the natural bond of "flesh and blood" that children are begotten and that they are raised and prepared to be active members of society.[163] But families also have a supernatural relationship with the rest of believers:

> The Christian family is also called to experience a new and original communion which confirms and perfects natural and human communion. In fact the grace of Jesus Christ, "the first-born among many brethren," is by its nature and interior dynamism "a grace of brotherhood," as St. Thomas Aquinas calls it. . . . The Christian family constitutes a specific revelation and realization of ecclesial communion, and for this reason too it can and should be called "the domestic Church."[164]

In *Pastores Dabo Vobis*, St. John Paul II mentions the importance of family in the life of the seminarian[165] and in

the ongoing formation of the priest.[166] It is a given that, in
the case of diocesan priests, unless they are incardinated in
a diocese that is not their own, they will spend most of their
lives close to their families. If the families are able to visit
the priest from time to time, they can become part of the
"extended family" of the parish community. This is a grace
that can be present only for diocesan priests. In the case of
religious and missionaries, they are called to "leave everything behind to follow the Lord."[167] For the diocesan priest,
though, the contact with his family of origin can become a
blessing for the entire parish community.[168] When he plays
with and holds his nephews and nieces, or when he embraces
his parents in a loving, tender way, parishioners can see a different side of him and experience his humanity in a deeper
level; they can also see him as "a brother" who shares the
same joys and life experiences as them, not just as "father" or
a distant Church figure who needs to be respected, feared, or
put on a pedestal.

And what to say of the days when the priest will be called
to care for his elderly parents? Or when he has to celebrate
the funeral Mass for them? These can also be moments in
which the life of the entire parish can be touched as they
grow in love and appreciation for each other. When the priest
experiences the comfort and support of the community,
then he can really understand what he is called to do for the
community—that together, they are called to be the family
of God, a cell imbued with love incorporated in the Body
of Christ.

Families also have a way of keeping us honest and humble. Most likely, every priest will have family members that are
not living the Church's teaching or that have fallen away from

the Church. By being a loving presence to them, the priest gains life experience in knowing what needs to be done in the world at large, how priests can treat those who may have stopped practicing the faith. Our family can be a microcosm of the larger arena where we are called to minister. If, in our families, we do not act in ways that are edifying or respectful, will we really have the credibility to do that with others? As St. Paul wrote to Timothy regarding bishops who had families in the early Church, "If a man does not know how to manage his own household, how can he take care of the church of God?" (1 Tm 3:5). Thus, above all, our families can help us remember that it is only through God's grace that we can hope to accomplish what is asked of us, weak and humble ministers of Christ.[169] Whatever seems impossible for us to handle can be possible when we kneel down in prayer and hand it over to the One who can make all things possible. In a way, this is the best lesson we can pass on to our "spiritual children" and to our family; we must do our part, for sure, but we must also be mindful of our limits and know when to leave things in the Lord's hands. Jesus alone is the Messiah.

The family of the priest, then, is an essential part of his spirituality.[170] He came from a "domestic Church," but now, as the representative of the Good Shepherd, he is to form the one family of God in the local parish community, in the local Church. In the case of St. John of Avila, he was deprived of enjoying the presence of his family because he was an only child and his parents died before he was even ordained a priest. This led him, though, to create community with other priests and with those who God sent to him along the way.

The Witness of Holiness [171]

Holiness is contagious. Even our Lord was touched by the witness of those who gave everything they had, as when the poor widow gave the two small coins in the Temple .[172] He also praised the faith of the Canaanite woman who did not give up until He healed her tormented daughter[173] and rejoiced at the conversion of Zacchaeus[174] and the sinful woman who washed His feet at the house of Simon the Pharisee .[175] If this is true for Him, who was perfect and never sinned, it must be even more so for the priest, who is always in need of conversion. The Church knows that "men and women saints have always been the source and origin of renewal."[176] God continues to raise souls of heroic virtue in every age; and many times, priests hear them in the confessional, see them in their RCIA groups, in church where they attend daily Mass, or out in the community, serving their brothers and sisters at soup kitchens or food banks.

Holy priests can lead to more holy souls in the Church— as was the case with St. John of Avila and the famous conversions of St. John of God and St. Francis Borgia. But lay people can also have a similar effect on priests. St. John Paul II wrote:

> The truth is that the Christian experience of persons who are simple and humble, the spiritual enthusiasm of people who truly love God, the courageous application of the faith to practical life by Christians involved in all kinds of social and civil tasks—all these things are embraced by the priest who, while illuminating them with his priestly service, at the same time draws from them a precious spiritual nourishment.[177]

Since "all the faithful are invited and obliged to holiness and the perfection of their own state of life,"[178] both priests and faithful can help and support each other in their journey of faith. And, as always, the best way they can do this is by simply living their faith to the fullest in their own walk of life.

Collaboration with the Community at Large

The Church expects her priests to be men "of mission and dialogue," pastors who promote "justice and peace" and who are able to work "with the brethren of other churches and Christian denominations . . . , [with] followers of other religions . . . , [and with] people of good will."[179] If Christians are to be a "yeast" that introduces the kingdom of God into the world (Mt 13:33), priests must also lead in establishing contacts with others so that Christ's mission can, in fact, continue in the different members of His body.[180]

The need for dialogue is especially urgent given the violent tendencies that are presently being witnessed in the Middle East and in some African countries where Christians are a minority. When people understand that no one is an island, as Thomas Merton reminded us through his writing,[181] and that even learned Islamic philosophers long for the unity that God wants to see in the world,[182] we have reasons to hope and do our part in alleviating fragmentation and indifference, in building "the family of God."[183]

Ecumenical and Inter-Faith Relationships

Much has happened since the sad days that St. John of Avila experienced when he saw Martin Luther breaking off from the Church in 1517.[184] The bishops at the Second Vatican Council said in the Decree on Ecumenism, *Unitatis*

Redintegratio, that the work of Christian unity is one of the main reasons that led to the Council in the first place.[185] They also mention, in a different document, that it is essential for all Christians to "join our forces and modify our methods in a way suitable and effective today . . . , [in order to] pattern ourselves daily more and more after the spirit of the Gospel and work together in a spirit of brotherhood to serve the human family which has been called to become in Christ Jesus the family of the sons [and daughters] of God."[186]

The work of building God's family is not an easy one, though, and it requires much dialogue and adaptation of general prescriptions. The work of Church leaders who are actively engaged in the ecumenical dialogue in order to come up with mutual agreements or joint declarations must be studied and applied at the local level through the leadership of bishops, priests, and other trained members of the Church. This is precisely what we read in *Gaudium et Spes*:

> Faced with the wide variety of situations and forms of human culture in the world, this conciliar program is deliberately general on many points; indeed, while the teaching presented is that already accepted in the Church, *it will have to be pursued further and amplified* because it often deals with matters which are subject to continual development. . . . Hence we entertain the hope that many of our suggestions will succeed in effectively assisting people, especially after they have been *adapted* to different nations and mentalities and put into practice by the faithful *under the direction of their pastors.*[187]

Beautifully crafted documents elaborated by those "at the top" will not have much effect if in our cities and neighborhoods, we are unkind or indifferent toward pastors or members of other ecclesial communities or make no effort to get to know them and work together for the common good. The priest, as a man of communion, can set the tone by participating in ministerial associations with pastors from other denominations or by joining in causes that benefit everyone in the community, regardless of their faith. Examples of these might be local food banks, Thanksgiving or Christmas banquets, and so on. People need to understand that we are not competitors but fellow workers of the Gospel. It seems appropriate that, at the very least, priests ought to be present for ecumenical prayer services offered during the annual Week of Prayer for Christian Unity or similar efforts.[188] We do need to join Christ, our High Priest, in praying that we "may all be one" (Jn 17:21). Similar recommendations are issued in *Nostra Aetate* in regard to relations with other religions. The Church calls for "bonds of friendship,"[189] "discussion and collaboration,"[190] and "mutual understanding and appreciation."[191]

Relationship with Civil Authorities

With Vatican II, the Church desired to join the movement "towards civil, economic and social unity" that it was witnessing in the world.[192] The Pastoral Constitution on the Church in the Modern World (*Gaudium et Spes*) lays out the vision of what it hoped, and still hopes, to offer to society. Having an obligation to serve all people, "especially those in need," the Church could show the world "that social and exterior union comes from a union of hearts and minds, from the faith and love" that can make humanity one.[193] It is her duty "to foster and elevate all that is true, all that is good, and all that is beautiful in the human community"[194] and to promote the dignity of the human person, which must be "the source, the focus and the end of all economic and social life."[195]

The Council further points out that both government and Church leaders can fulfill their mutual obligation of service to humanity "in so far as both institutions practice better cooperation according to the local and prevailing situation."[196] It is this "local situation" that gives priests their mandate. They must work in their communities to respond to whatever needs they find there, whether offering reconciliation after a violent crime, providing wholesome events to keep young people away from drugs and boredom, and so on.

St. John of Avila lived in an environment that was very favorable to the Catholic Church. Both the King and Queen of Spain were Catholic—as they still are today—and they actually used the Catholic religion as a means of bringing unity to the country. Because of this, all government officials were also Catholic, and they would turn to priests for guidance in order to carry out their public service. This interaction is reflected in Letter 11 of the epistles of St. John, written in response to an official's request for practical recommendations on how to carry out his office, for example. Other letters and sermons also abound with calls for governors to follow the example of Christ who "did not come to be served but to serve and to give his life as a ransom for many" (Mt 20:28).[197] As Monsignor Esquerda states, the saint could write to them "in a demanding and yet familial tone."[198]

Most priests nowadays cannot even begin to dream of serving in similar conditions. Governments, for the most part, operate in countries where there is a separation between Church and State or where there is a secular or even anti-Christian climate. Still, some parishes have found creative ways of reaching out to government officials and making themselves present in the community. Some, for example, offer Christmas luncheons for police officers, fire fighters, and emergency personnel for their cities. In cities that welcome the participation of religious leaders in the public life, priests may be called upon, along with representatives from other Christian denominations, to offer an invocation before a meeting or a memorial service of some sort. It would be good for priests to be available for these kinds of events. The one thing the Church emphasizes for priests in their relationships with the government or in their civic duties is not to take sides.[199] He is merely to be "a servant of the Church, which by virtue of its universality and catholicity cannot have ties with any . . . political party. . . . Just like Jesus (cf. *Jn* 6:15ff), the priest 'must . . . remain the man of all from the viewpoint of spiritual fraternity.'"[200]

Being a Light for Others

Christ is "the true light, which enlightens everyone" (Jn 1:9). If artists and philosophers in the world can "greatly contribute towards bringing the human race to a higher understanding of truth, goodness, and beauty,"[201] as *Gaudium et Spes* says, how much more the priest, the representative of Christ. Being configured to Christ through the Sacrament of Holy Orders, he can lead others "to be a leaven and, as it were, the soul of human society in its renewal by Christ and transformation into the family of God."[202] Even when interacting with non-believers, the priest and those he leads can plant seeds for evangelization through the love, kindness, and friendship they offer those around them. Mindful that it is one who sows and another one who waters ,[203] he can simply carry out faithfully what is asked of him in a Christ-like manner. Consequently, he will imitate the example of him who "went about doing good" (Acts 10:38).

As a man of God and a man of the Church, the priest can make his own the words found in the last paragraph of the Second Vatican Council's *Gaudim et Spes*:

> Christians can yearn for nothing more ardently than to serve the men [and women] of this age with an ever growing generosity and success. Holding loyally to the Gospel, enriched by its resources, and joining forces with all who love and practice justice, they have shouldered a weighty task here on earth and they must render an account of it to him who will judge all [human beings] on the last day. Not everyone who says "Lord, Lord," will enter the kingdom of heaven, but those who do the will of the Father, and who manfully put their hands to the work.[204]

St. John of Avila "manfully put [his] hands to the work" as a diocesan priest in his own day and brought many others to Christ. The Lord is counting on us, priests of the twenty first century, to do our part as well.

Conclusion

The Second Vatican Council revolved around the ecclesiology and spirituality of "communio." In a way, it is the normal development of understanding the Church as the Body of Christ, the mystery St. John of Avila professed in every aspect of his ministry. In that body, all the members are essential, and each one has a function.

The priest, as the representative of Christ in the community, has the responsibility of building up this body and sanctifying it through the Sacraments, of "making it beautiful," as the Apostle of Andalusia would say. Although every member must share his or her gifts and work for this unity, the priest offers a service that cannot be done without, a service conferred through the Sacrament of Holy Orders. In preaching the Word, sanctifying the faithful, and leading them to unity, he fulfills Christ's priestly ministry "until He comes again," as the Church prays during the Mass.

Regardless of where he is found, therefore, the priest must always be a man of communion. He is the bishop's collaborator in continuing the apostolic mission of restoring the unity and right relationship that humanity enjoyed with their Creator and with one another before the Fall, of establishing the Kingdom of God. The Church has recognized that, though she is holy because she is the bride of Christ, she is also imperfect in her human dimensions. Thus, she and her members, each one of them—the priest included—are always in need of conversion. The priest, therefore, will benefit tremendously from the friendly and respectful relationships he enjoys with other members in the community, both in the parish and in the community at large—including non-Catholics. He must be attentive to listen to God's voice in those he encounters and ready to discern the work of the Holy Spirit who is known for blowing "where it wills" (Jn 3:8).

There is a reason why at priestly ordinations, there is the need for someone in the community to testify to the candidate's "worthiness." While acknowledging that no one truly is,[205] it is the community of the Church that helps the candidate to discern his calling and to prepare for this office with the help of the seminary faculty. And, yes, it is also the community as a whole that has the responsibility of helping the priest to grow in his humanity, in his faith, and in his love for others, as expressed in *Pastores Dabo Vobis*.[206] The relationships the diocesan priest enjoys with others, therefore, are also an essential element of his spirituality. It is in them and through them that he fulfills his priestly calling as he assists others to live out their own vocation. We can, thus, speak of mutual sanctification, a sanctification the priest and the people offer each other in and through the Body of Christ.

NOTES

1. Joseph Ratzinger, "Ministry and Life of Priests," *Pilgrim Fellowship of Faith: The Church as Communion*, trans. Henry Taylor (San Francisco: Ignatius Press, 2005), 157.
2. See *Tratado del amor de Dios* (from here on, abbreviated as *AD*) in *Obras Completas* (from here on, abbreviated as *OC*), vol. 1, n. 8.
3. "Homily. Mass for the Episcopal Ordination of Five Archbishops" (February 5, 2011) in *Acta Apostolicae Sedis* (from here on, abbreviated as *AAS*) 103 (2011): 175-181, English translation (Vatican City: Libreria Editrice Vaticana, 2011). The awareness of this concept of *communio* as the synthesis of the Council became obvious at the Second Extraordinary General Assembly of the Synod of Bishops in 1985, at which Cardinal Ratzinger—as Pope Benedict was then known—was also present. St. John Paul II speaks of this in *Christifideles Laici* (see sec. 19).
4. "Homily. Ash Wednesday" (February 13, 2013) in *AAS* 105 (2013): 269-272, English translation (Vatican City: Libreria Editrice Vaticana, 2013).
5. Francis, *Lumen Fidei* (2013) in *AAS* 105 (2013): 555-596, English translation (Vatican City: Libreria Editrice Vaticana, 2013), n. 41.
6. Vatican II, *Lumen Gentium* (1964), sec. 4.
7. Francis, *Laudato Si* (from here on, abbreviated as *LS*) (2015), sec. 240.
8. Ibid., sec. 138.
9. Ibid., sec. 86. See *Catechism of the Catholic Church* (from here on, abbreviated as *CCC*) (New York: Image, 1995), n. 340.
10. Sermon 6, in *OC*, vol. 3, n. 2.
11. John Paul II, *Pastores Dabo Vobis* (from here on, abbreviated as *PDV*) (1992), sec. 59 (italics in the original). See also his words in his Apostolic Letter *Novo Millennio Ineunte*: "Before making practical plans, we need *to promote a spirituality of communion*, making it the guiding principle of education wherever individuals and Christians are formed, wherever ministers of the altar, consecrated persons, and pastoral workers are trained, wherever families and communities are being built up. A spirituality of communion indicates above all the heart's contemplation of the mystery of the Trinity dwelling in us, and whose light we must also be able to see shining on the face of the brothers and sisters around us. A spirituality of communion also means an ability to think of our brothers and sisters in faith within the profound unity of the Mystical Body, and therefore as 'those who are a part of me'. This makes us able to share their joys and sufferings, to sense their desires and attend to their needs, to offer them deep and genuine friendship. A spirituality of communion implies also the ability to see what is positive in others, to welcome it and prize it as a

gift from God: not only as a gift for the brother or sister who has received it directly, but also as a 'gift for me'. A spirituality of communion means, finally, to know how to 'make room' for our brothers and sisters, bearing 'each other's burdens' (*Gal* 6:2) and resisting the selfish temptations which constantly beset us and provoke competition, careerism, distrust and jealousy. Let us have no illusions: unless we follow this spiritual path, external structures of communion will serve very little purpose. They would become mechanisms without a soul, 'masks' of communion rather than its means of expression and growth." *Novo Millennio Ineunte* (January 6, 2001) in *AAS* 93 (2001): 266-309, English translation (Vatican City: Libreria Editrice Vaticana, 2001), n. 43 (from here on abbreviated as *NM*).

12. Sermon 27, in *OC,* vol. 3, n. 4.

13. Louis Bouyer, *Introduction to the Spiritual Life* (Notre Dame: Christian Classics, 2013), 385.

14. Midmorning Prayer, Monday, Week I, in *The Liturgy of the Hours,* vol. 4, 679.

15. See Avery Dulles, S.J., *Models of the Church,* Expanded ed. (New York: Doubleday, 2002).

16. See Ronald A. Knox, *Enthusiasm: A Chapter in the History of Religion* (Oxford: Clarendon Press, 1950).

17. See 1 Corinthians 12:12-13;13.

18. Sermon 8, in *OC,* vol. 3, n. 20. St. John mentions here "moros" (Muslims). Since the last Spanish city—Granada—was retaken from Muslim control in 1492, their presence was still very much in the mind of all Spanish people in the sixteenth century.

19. Ibid., n. 14.

20. Letter 148, in *OC,* vol. 4, 511. Sala and Martín speak of those conflicts in the introduction to the letter.

21. Letter 26, in *OC,* vol. 4, 160. The reference to Pseudo-Dionysius is *De divinis nominibus* c. 4, 15: PG 3, 713.

22. *Lecciones sobre 1 San Juan [I] (from here on, abbreviated as Lecc 1SJ[I]),* in *OC,* vol. 2, Lesson 7, 159. The reference to St. Thomas Aquinas is *Summa* II.II. q.184 a.1 ad 3.

23. Ibid., 160.

24. This insight is taken from Monsignor Juan Esquerda. See "Comunidad" in *Diccionario de San Juan de Avila* (from here on, abbreviated as *DJA*), 189. Along the same lines, but from a psychological perspective, Monsignor Stephen J. Rossetti speaks of the need for priests to have "a reconciled heart." He gives four aspects that lead to it and which are essential to creating community: 1) having a solid sense of self-identity and a secure self-image; 2) an integration of one's emotions and sexuality; 3) seeing the complexities and nuances in life, and 4) mature faith. See Stephen J. Rosetti, *The Joy of Priesthood* (New York: Ave Maria Press, 2005),

121-127. Pope Francis speaks of a "heart set at peace by Christ." See Francis, *Gaudete et Exsultate*, sec. 121.

25. Vatican II, *Unitatis Redintegratio* (1964), sec. 7 (from here on abbreviated as *UR*). The bishops of Latin America consider divisions to be the effects of original sin. In their *Documento de Santo Domingo* (1992), they speak of this and how only God's grace can lead people to conversion and to unity: "el hombre creado bueno . . . al pecar ha quedado enemistado con [Dios], *dividido en sí mismo*, ha roto la solidaridad con el prójimo y destruido la armonía de la naturaleza. . . . ¿Quién nos librará de estas fuerzas de muerte? (cf. Rom 7,24). Sólo la gracia de Nuestro Señor Jesucristo, ofrecida... como llamada a *la conversión del corazón*" (emphasis added). Consejo Episcopal Latinoamericano (CELAM), *Documento de Santo Domingo*, Cuarta Conferencia General (1992), n. 9, http://www.celam.org/conferencia_domingo.php, accessed November 15, 2015.

26. Letter 86, in *OC,* vol. 4, 370.

27. Letter 148, in *OC,* vol. 4, 513.

28. In his Apostolic Exhortation *Marialis Cultus*, Paul VI encouraged, along with Rosary, the daily recitation of the Angelus. See *Marialis Cultus* (February 2, 1974) in *AAS* 66 (1974): 113-168, (n. 41). In this prayer, besides making us mindful of Christ's unity with us through his Incarnation, we pray that God's grace may be "poured into our hearts." The emphasis on conversion of heart is also prominent in the Liturgy, especially during the season of Lent (see Jl 2:12; Ps 51:12). As always, approaching the Liturgy and other devotions with a receptive heart and mind can give us the strength and the tools we need to continue working toward that perfect unity Christ desires to see in us.

29. See Vatican II, *Lumen Gentium* (1964) (from here on, abbreviated as *LG*): "Let all priests, especially those who by special title of ordination are called diocesan priests, remember that their faithful union and generous cooperation with their bishop greatly helps their sanctification" (sec. 41). See also Vatican II, *Optatum Totius* (1965), (from here on, abbreviated as *OT*), sec. 8.

30. Ibid., sec. 28.

31. Ibid., sec. 41.

32. Vatican II, *Presbyterorum Ordinis* (1965) (from here on, abbreviated as *PO*), sec. 15.

33. John Paul II, *Pastores Dabo Vobis* (1992) (from here on, abbreviated as *PDV*), sec. 31 (italics in the original). See also sec. 17. In Italy, this belonging to the local church has been taken very much to heart. Some even speak not so much of the spirituality of the diocesan priest, but rather "the diocesan spirituality" in which the priest shares. See *La Spiritualitá Diocesana: il cammino nello Spirito della Chiesa particolare*, ed. by Erio Castellucci, Unione Apostolica del Clero (Rome: Elledici, 2004). However, while it is true that the Council calls bishops to assist priests, religious, and

lay people to seek holiness (See Vatican II, *Christus Dominus* [1965], sec. 15 [from here on, abbreviated as *ChD*]), there is nothing that prevents priests from trying to develop or understand their own spirituality. St. John Paul II merely speaks of the ecclesial "dimension" as being "a significant element" of that spirituality, but it does not entirely define it or replace it.

34. *PO*, sec. 7. See *ChD*: "In exercising his office of father and pastor the bishop should be with his people as one who serves, as a good shepherd who knows his sheep and whose sheep know him, as a true father who excels in his love and solicitude for all, to whose divinely conferred authority all readily submit. . . . His priests, who assume a part of his duties and concerns, and who are ceaselessly devoted to their work, should be the objects of his particular affection. He should regard them as sons and friends. He should always be ready to listen to them and cultivate an atmosphere of easy familiarity with them, thus facilitating the pastoral work of the entire diocese" (sec. 16). The *Directory* seems to go even further: "The Bishop must have the disposition of a father towards his priests, beginning from the seminarians, avoiding any distance or a personal style proper to a mere employer. By virtue of his function he must always be close to his priests and easily accessible. His *first concern* must be his priests, his collaborators in his Episcopal ministry" (n. 107; emphasis added).

35. Ibid., n. 14.

36. *Memorial primero al Concilio de Trento* (from here on, abbreviated as *MT1*) in *OC*, vol. 2, n. 5.

37. Ibid.

38. John Paul II, *Pastores Gregis* (2003) in *AAS* 96 (2004): 825-924, English translation: Vatican City: Libreria Editrice Vaticana, 2004, sec. 47 (from here on, abbreviated as *PGr*).

39. St. John of Avila speaks of this in a letter he wrote to the archbishop of Granada, Pedro Guerrero, in preparation for a regional synod. He reminds him: "Lo principal que deseo que se trate es . . . la obligación de los obispos así en predicar como en hacer pláticas a sus clérigos." Letter 244 in *OC*, vol. 4, 774.

40. *PGr*, sec. 28. See also sec. 22.

41. *PO*, sec. 7. See *Pláticas* 1 in *OC*, vol. 1, where St. John makes reference to the humility and obedience St. Peter recommends in 1 Pt 5:5-6.

42. See *Reglas* in *OC*, vol. 2, n. 6 ("4: Avisos para D. Diego de Guzmán y el Dr. Loarte para entrar en la Compañía"). Although this was written for two of St. John's disciples upon entering the Society of Jesus, the same is true for diocesan priests or anybody in the Church.

43. *OC*, vol. 1, 373 (emphasis added).

44. See Esquerda, "Presbiterio" in *DJA*, 763; Juan José Gallego Palomero, "San Juan de Ávila, actualidad de su doctrina, ministerio y fraternidad sacerdotal," in *San Juan de Ávila, Doctor de la Iglesia, Actas del*

Congreso Internacional, ed. Juan Aranda Doncel and Antonio Llamas Vela (Cordoba: Ediciones y Publicaciones Diputación de Córdoba, 2013), 129.

45. *LG*, sec. 28. See *PDV*, sec. 74.

46. *ChD*, sec. 28. See *PDV*: "The presbyterate thus appears as a *true family,* as a fraternity whose ties do not arise form flesh and blood but from the grace of holy orders. This grace takes up and elevates the human and psychological bonds of affection and friendship, as well as the spiritual bonds which exist between priests" (sec. 74; emphasis in the original).

47. *LG*, sec. 28.

48. *Directory*, n. 36.

49. Rev. J. Ronald Knott has written different works on presbyterates and their work in communion with their bishop. See *Intentional Presbyterates: Claiming Our Common Sense of Purpose as Diocesan Priests* (Louisville: Sophronismos Press, 2003); *A Bishop and his Priests Together: Resources for Building More Intentional Presbyterates* (Louisville: Sophronismos Press, 2011).

50. See Dean R. Hoge, *The First Five Years of the Priesthood: A Study of Newly Ordained Catholic Priests* (Collegeville: Liturgical Press, 2002); Mary L. Gautier, Paul M. Perl, and Stephen J. Fichter, *Same Call, Different Men: The Evolution of the Priesthood since Vatican II* (Collegeville: Liturgical Press, 2012).

51. *PDV*, sec. 74.

52. Stephen Rossetti, "The Need for Connections" in *The First Five Years of the Priesthood,* 133-34.

53. *PDV*, sec. 76 (emphasis in the original).

54. See Granada, 131; Llin, 423; Sala and Martín, *OC*, vol. 1, 30-33. A cause for the canonization of Father Fernando Contreras was opened, but he has not yet been canonized.

55. It is praiseworthy that many bishops, mindful of the need of this foundational experience, assign their newly ordained priests not where they are needed, but where they know they will have a good experience. This can make all the difference if the young priest ever has doubts about his calling or his fitness for ministry. If the support needed is readily there, this will make it easier for him to trust in God's faithfulness and ever-loving providence.

56. See *PDV*, sec. 81; *PO*, sec. 18.

57. St. John of Avila, *Audi, filia,* trans. Joan F. Gormley. The Classics of Western Spirituality (New York: Paulist Press, 2006). See chapters 2-4, 5-16, 17-30, and 31-44.

58. *Audi Filia [II]* (from here on, abbreviated as *AF [II]*)in *OC*, vol. 1: ch. 55, n. 3 (Gormley's translation). The same recommendations on spiritual directors can be found in St. Teresa of Avila. It is possible that she might have learned this from St. John of Avila.

59. See *Tratado sobre ell sacerdocio* (from here on, abbreviated as *TSS*) in *OC*, vol. 1, n. 39.

60.   In his *Reglas de espíritu*, St. John makes frequent confession his fourth recommendation. He also gives similar qualities for the right confessor as for a spiritual director: he must be learned and a man of God. See *Reglas* in *OC*, vol. 2: "3: Diez documentos," 849. The reference to St. Bernard is *Ep*. 113, 4ff: *Patrologia Latina* (from here on, abbreviated as *PL*) 182, 258.

61.   *AF[II]* in *OC*, vol. 1: ch. 55, n. 5 (Gormley's translation; emphasis added). The instruction of "not hiding anything" from the spiritual director is in line with the practice of *exagóreusis* (revealing one's thoughts) recommended by Greek spiritual fathers. See Thomas Spidlík, *La spiritualitá dell'Oriente cristiano: Manuale sistematico* (Milan: Edizioni San Paolo, 1995), 231.

62.   Sermon 27 in *OC*, vol. 3, n. 17.

63.   *AF[II]* in *OC*, vol. 1: ch. 55, n. 5.

64.   *Directory*, n. 40. Jordan Aumann writes on the common life: "Bishop Eusebius of Vercelli (+307) and St. Augustine (+430) introduced the common life among their clergy; in 535 the Council of Clermont defined canons as priests or deacons assigned to a church; Bishop Chrodegang of Metz drew up a rule for his clergy (c. 755) which was based on the Rule of St. Benedict; and the Synod of Aix-la-Chapelle (816-817) promulgated the new *Regula Canonicorum* requiring common life and obedience to a superior but allowing possession of goods. . . . Between the ninth and the eleventh centuries the *vita canonica* was proposed and then imposed on diocesan priests as a means of reform, to protect them against avarice and lust. The Synod of Rome (1059) proposed the *vita canonica*, a common life in poverty, as a means to return to the apostolic life of the primitive Christians. . . . The mendicant orders [in the thirteen century, especially with St. Dominic] . . . were a response to vital needs in the Church: the need to return to the Christian life of the Gospel (*vita apostolica*); the need to reform religious life, especially in the area of poverty; the need to extirpate the heresies of the time; the need to raise the level of the diocesan clergy. . . . " *Christian Spirituality*, 114-15, 126. These reforms from the Middle Ages led to what today we know as "canon regulars," orders like the Norbertines and the Augustinians. The *apostolica vivendi forma*, however, can also be found in secular institutes.

65.   Ibid., n. 38.

66.   See *PDV*, sec. 81; *ChD*, sec. 30; Paul VI, *Sacerdotalis Caelibatus* (1967) in *AAS* 59 (1967): 657-697, English translation (Vatican City: Libreria Editrice Vaticana, 1967), sec. 80; *Code of Canon Law, AAS* 75, Part 1 (1983): 1-317, English Translation (Vatican City: Libreria Editricine Vaticana, 1983), c. 550 (from here on, abbreviated as *CCL*).

67.   Secular institutes of clergy are not to be confused with secular institutes of lay people or with religious orders. Diocesan priests can belong to a secular institute by taking vows and following a specific

spirituality while continuing to owe obedience and affiliation to the diocesan bishop. See *PDV*, sec. 81.

68.   *PO*, sec. 8.

69.   "Private Audience with the Priests of the Fraternity of St. Charles on the Occasion of the XXV of Foundation" (February 12, 2011), http://w2.vatican.va/content/benedict-xvi/en/speeches/2011/february/documents/hf_ben-xvi_spe_20110212_borromeo.html (accessed January 10, 2016).

70.   See His "Priestly School" in ch. 2.

71.   *Algunas advertencias al sínodo de Toledo* in *OC*, vol. 2, n. 80.

72.   See Sala and Martín, *OC*, vol. 1, 6. It was this disciple who acted as his secretary and who published the works of St. John of Avila after the saint died.

73.   See Ibid., 200-01.

74.   *CCL*, c. 550 sec. 2.

75.   *Directory*, n. 39. See *CCL*, c. 533 sec. 1.

76.   Ibid. See *PO*, sec. 8; *PDV*, sec. 68, 81.

77.   *PDV*, sec. 81 (emphasis in the original).

78.   *Pláticas* 1 in *OC*, vol. 1, n. 13. The life and the writings of the Apostle of Andalusia have inspired several priestly associations in the Church, especially in his native Spain. For the International Apostolic Union of the Clergy, see www.uac-int.org.

79.   *PO*, sec. 8.

80.   Ibid.

81.   *PDV*, sec. 80.

82.   *PO*, sec. 7.

83.   Ibid., sec. 8.

84.   Ibid.

85.   Ibid.

86.   Ibid., sec. 15.

87.   See Luke 22:24-27.

88.   *NM*, sec. 43. Pope Benedict XVI repeats this same phrase in his Post-Synodal Apostolic Exhortation *Africae Munus*. See *Africae Munus* (2011) in *AAS* 104 (2012): 239-314, English translation (Vatican City: Libreria Editrice Vaticana, 2012), sec. 35. Pope Francis has used stronger language to refer to these tendencies among the clergy. In an address he gave to the Pontifical Ecclesiastical Academy in Rome shortly after his election, he said: "Careerism is a form of leprosy, a leprosy. No careerism, please." "Address to the Pontifical Ecclesiastical Academy" (June 6, 2013), http://w2.vatican.va/content/francesco/en/speeches/2013/june/documents/papa-francesco_20130606_pontificia-accademia-ecclesiastica.html (accessed April 18, 2016).

89.   See Muñoz, lib. 3, c. 4.

90.   Sermon 66 in *OC*, vol. 3, n. 10.

91. Letter 105 in *OC*, vol. 3, 419.

92. *LG*, sec. 28.

93. *PDV*, sec. 15.

94. The Council of Trent actually called for the restoration of the diaconate in its Twenty-Third Session (ch. 17 on Reform), but the prescription, for whatever reasons, was not carried out. See "Introduction," *Basic Norms for the Formation of Permanent Deacons*, Congregation for Catholic Education (Vatican City: Libreria Editrice Vaticana, 1998), n. 2.

95. In the Archdiocese of San Juan in Puerto Rico, the *Annuario Pontificio* for 2015 indicates that there are 142 priests and 202 deacons. In Chicago, the number of both ministers is almost equal: 885 priests and 652 deacons. See *Annuario Pontificio* (Vatican City: Libreria Editrice Vaticana, 2015).

96. *Basic Norms for the Formation of Permanent Deacons*, n. 8.

97. *ChD*, sec. 15.

98. See *LG*, sec. 29.

99. In Southern California, for example, there are permanent deacons who are assigned as full-time administrators of parish communities. They are responsible for the day-to-day activities, and priests are responsible only for celebrating Mass and offering the Sacraments. With the shortage of priests, more and more dioceses seem to be moving in this direction so that the spiritual needs of the people are not neglected.

100. *LG*, sec. 43.

101. Ibid., sec. 44.

102. Ibid., sec. 46.

103. See Luke 10:2.

104. Sermon 81 in *OC*, vol. 3, n. 5. The reference to St. Jerome is *Ep.* 78 mans. 6: PL 22, 704.

105. Basil Cole, O.P. and Paul Conner, O.P. compare the relationship between these two aspects of the Church to the relationship of husband and wife. It is complementary, but not free of healthy arguments which are in themselves good for the sake of the family. See *Christian Totality: Theology of the Consecrated Life* (New York: Alba House, 1997), 47.

106. Congregation for Religious and Secular Institutes and Congregation for Bishops, *Mutuae Relationes: Directives for the Mutual Relations between Bishops and Religious in the Church* (1978), sec. 9b (emphasis in the original).

107. Ibid., sec. 28.

108. Ibid., sec. 52.

109. Ibid., sec. 55.

110. *Directory*, n. 42.

111. *PDV*, sec. 74.

112. Ibid.

113. See John Paul II, *Christifideles Laici* (1988), sec. 2 (from here on, abbreviated as *CL*): "The Council, in particular, with its rich doctrinal,

spiritual and pastoral patrimony, has written as never before on the nature, dignity, spirituality, mission and responsibility of the lay faithful."

114.   *LG*, sec. 9.

115.   *LG*, sec. 10.

116.   *CCC*, n. 1120 (emphasis in the original).

117.   Nicholas Cachia, "The Good Shepherd: Living Christ's Own Pastoral Authority," *Good Shepherd: Living Christ's Own Pastoral Authority*, ed. Edward G. Mathews, Jr., 7-30. Fifth Annual Symposium on the Spirituality and Identity of the Diocesan Priest (Omaha, NE: The Institute for Priestly Formation, 2006), 14.

118.   Ibid., 20.

119.   *PDV*, sec. 12. See *LG*, sec. 28.

120.   See *LG*, sec. 31; Vatican II, *Gaudium et Spes* (1965), sec. 43 (from here on, abbreviated as *GS*).

121.   See *CL*, sec. 22: "The ordained ministries, apart from the persons who receive them, are a grace for the entire Church. . . . On the other hand, the ministerial priesthood, as the Second Vatican Council recalls, essentially has the royal priesthood of all the faithful as its aim and is ordered to it. . . . The lay faithful, in turn, must acknowledge that the ministerial priesthood is totally necessary for their participation in the mission of the Church."

122.   *PDV*, sec. 17. See *PO*, sec. 9.

123.   Ibid., sec. 3.

124.   Pláticas 1 in *OC*, vol. 1, n. 13.

125.   See *CCC*, nn. 91-92.

126.   *PDV*, sec. 78 (emphasis in the original).

127.   *CL*, sec. 14.

128.   Ibid.

129.   *LS*, sec. 105.

130.   See *PDV*, sec. 26, 70, 79.

131.   See 1 Chronicles 21:1-13.

132.   Fulton J. Sheen, *Treasure in Clay: The Autobiography of Fulton J. Sheen* (San Francisco: Ignatius Press, 1993), 298.

133.   Letter 5 in *OC*, vol. 4, 37. See The "Priestly School" of St. John of Avila in Chapter 3.

134.   *PDV*, sec. 72.

135.   See John Paul II, *Dives in Misericordia* (1980), sec. 14. St. John Paul II cites here the words of his predecessor pronounced at the closing of the Holy Year in 1975: see *Insegnamenti*, XIII (1975), p. 1568 (close of the Holy Year, December 25, 1975).

136.   John Paul II, *Redemptor Hominis* (1979), sec. 10 (from here on, abbreviated as *RH*).

137.   John Paul II, *Mulieris Dignitatem* (1988) in *AAS* 80 (1988): 1653-1729, English translation (Vatican City: Libreria Editrice Vaticana, 1988), sec. 7.

138.   It is noteworthy that the Apostle of Andalusia never preached a sermon on tithing. However, he did preach on the proper use of riches and care for the poor: See Sermons 1[1], n. 4; 2, n. 13; 4, n. 19; 12, n. 13; 15, n. 14; 18, n. 6; 76, n. 20, all in *OC*, vol. 3. See "Riquezas" in *DJA*, 809-11.

139.   See "Poverty" under Evangelical Counsels in Chapter 2.

140.   Sala and Martín, *OC*, vol. 1, 257.

141.   Ibid., 257-58.

142.   *LG*, sec. 9.

143.   *PDV*, sec. 35.

144.   The *Directory* states: "Like Christ, [the priest] must make Christ 'visible in the midst of the flock' entrusted to his care, creating a positive relationship between himself and the lay faithful; recognising their dignity as children of God, he fosters their role in the Church and places at their service everything of his priestly ministry and pastoral charity. This attitude of love and charity is far removed from the so-called "laicisation of priests. . . . ' Moreover, entrusted in certain cases to laypersons with sufficient formation and a sincere desire to serve the Church may be some tasks—in accord with the laws of the Church—that do not pertain exclusively to the priestly ministry, and which they can perform on the basis of their professional and personal experience. In this manner the priest will be freer in attending to his primary commitments such as preaching, the celebration of the Sacraments and spiritual direction" (n. 41).

145.   *PO*, sec. 9.

146.   See *Advertencias* in *OC*, vol. 2, nn. 27-30.

147.   "Mensaje en el V centenario de su nacimiento" in *OC*, v. 1, 372 (emphasis in the original).

148.   *Directory*, n. 41.

149.   Ibid. *Christifideles Laici* does speak against the "clericalization" of the laity and the lax use of the word "ministry" for apostolic works that are done on behalf of the Church. It suggests a clear distinction between those tasks that are proper to the office of the priest and those that fall to the competence of the lay faithful (see n. 23). There is no question of the lay faithful participating in the ministry of the Church—the exhortation makes this clear on paragraph 20—but only of making sure that "ministry" is, indeed, being commissioned by and done on behalf of the Church. One issue that is not addressed in the exhortation is the tendency in some developed countries to pay people for any work that they do for the Church, especially when it comes to music, liturgy, technology, etc. While a just compensation does need to be paid to contractors and people in full-time ministry, it seems that a greater spirit of volunteerism

and stewardship needs to be promoted among Catholics. This is where the formation mentioned in the *Directory* is important. Everyone needs to understand that all the baptized are part of the mission of the Church and that the gifts and charisms received are for the good of the community. The passage "the laborer deserves his payment" from the gospel of Luke (10:7) must be balanced with that of Matthew: "Without cost you have received; without cost you are to give" (10:8). While it may seem that the latter applies only to the Apostles, St. Peter clarifies that it applies to all believers: "As each one has received a gift, use it to *serve one another as good stewards* of God's varied grace. Whoever preaches, let it be with the words of God; whoever serves, let it be with the strength that God supplies, so that in all things God may be glorified . . . " (1 Pt 4:10-11; emphasis added).

150.   Congregation for the Clergy: *The Priest, Pastor and Leader of the Parish Community* (Vatican City: Libreria Editricine Vaticana, 2002), n. 5.

151.   See John 12:1-3.

152.   See John 20:11-18.

153.   *PDV*, sec. 74. See Cachia, 18. St. Thomas Aquinas also says that it is normal and praiseworthy to love those closest to us more than others. See *Summa*, II.II.q.26, art. 7.

154.   See *RH*, sec. 10.

155.   See Sala and Martín, *OC*, 33-34, 171. Most likely, Sancha was only a half-sister of Pedro Fernandez de Cordoba since they have different last names.

156.   See Letter 1 in *OC*, vol. 1, 6. As I wrote this, I received a message on Facebook from a young father thanking me for posting a quote from St. Zelie Martin, the mother of St. Therese of Lisieux, on the rewards and sacrifices of raising children. He shared how, when he is tired or overwhelmed, a simple hug or a drawing from his children is enough to lift him up and keep going. Priests, no doubt, feel the same way about their spiritual children.

157.   St. John Paul II reminds priests that loneliness is not always a bad thing since it can lead to a closer relationship to God and it can be "a help for sanctification and also for human growth." See *PDV*, sec. 74.

158.   The book of Sirach praises spiritual relationships of kindred souls, which can only be experienced with certain priests: "associate with a religious person, who you know keeps the commandments; who is likeminded with yourself . . . " (37:12).

159.   *PDV*, sec. 74. This is the reason why the practice of moving the priests to new assignments is a helpful one. The feeling of family must extend beyond parish boundaries to the diocese and to the world at large. That is what it means to be "catholic."

160.   See John 17:20-21.

161.   *LG*, sec. 3.

162.   *PO*, sec. 3. See *PDV*, sec. 17.

163.   John Paul II, Familiaris Consortio (1981) (from here on, abbreviated as *FC*), sec. 21.

164.   Ibid.

165.   See *PDV*, sec. 68.

166.   Ibid., sec. 79.

167.   Some theologians suggest that the fact that bishops and priests are in apostolic succession means that they are to live just as the apostles did. In *Vita Consecrata*, St. John Paul II speaks of religious life as being the *apostolica vivendi forma*. See John Paul II, *Vita Consecrata* (1996) in *AAS* 88 (1996): 377-486, English translation (Vatican City: Libreria Editrice Vaticana, 1996), sec. 93. This seems to suggest that the apostles lived the way they did because they were missionaries; they had to go and proclaim the good news to the world. While the Church must always remain missionary, once local churches were established and the Church's institutional aspect was born, bishops and priests acquired a different life-style. Yes, they should continue to live a simple life and have the universal aspect of the Church in mind, but their main calling now is to make the Church present in their local community, to form the local Church family. The Lord Himself seems to have suggested that different circumstances in the Church would call for a different way of life when He said in Luke, "But now one who has a money bag should take it, and likewise a sack . . . " (22:36).

168.   Pope Francis said in one of his audiences: "A priest cannot lose his roots. . . . Our roots help us to remember who we are and where Christ has called us. We priests do not drop from above, but instead we are called, called by God, who takes us 'from among men', so as to be 'for men'. Allow me to share an anecdote. In the diocese, years ago. . . . No, not in the diocese, it was in the Society, there was a very good priest, he was young, and had been a priest for two years. He became confused, and spoke with his spiritual director, with his superiors and with the doctors, saying: 'I'm leaving, I can't any more, I am leaving'. After thinking things over—I knew his mother, they were humble people—I said to him: 'Why don't you go to your mom and talk with her about this?'. He went and he spent the whole day with his mother, and he came back changed. His mother gave him two spiritual 'slaps', she told him three or four things, put him in his place, and he went on. Why? Because he went to the root. This is why it is important to never remove the roots of where we come from." "Discorso per Convegnio 'Una vocazione, una formazione, una missione'" (November 20, 2015), http://w2.vatican. va/content/francesco/it/speeches/2015/november/documents/papa-francesco_20151120_formazione-sacerdoti. Html (accessed February 20, 2016). English translation (Vatican City: Libreria Editrice Vaticana, 2015).

169.   See 2 Corinthians 12:9.

170.   The "giving up of everything" to follow the Lord from the first apostles (see Mt 19:27) must now be balanced out with the "honoring of father and mother" (Mk 7:10) of those who are in a position to help them. As Pope Francis says in one of his exhortations, "the verb 'to honour' has to do with the fulfilment of family and social commitments; these are not to be disregarded under the pretence of religious motives (cf. *Mk* 7:11-13)." *Amoris Laetitia* (Vatican City: Libreria Editrice Vaticana, 2016), sec. 17. Since diocesan priests do receive a stipend, part of it must go to help their parents or extended family when they are in need. St. John of Avila did speak against using one's resources or Church funds to enrich one's relatives (See *Advertencias* in *OC*, vol. 2, n. 25), but mindful of what was "essential," he would, most likely, support assisting one's family as necessary.

171.   The first saints in the Church were martyrs, "witnesses," as that word states in the original Greek (*mártyras*). With time, those who witnessed to the faith in other ways, even if they were not killed for it, also were declared saints. See Bouyer, 173. Holiness necessarily requires an integral—both internal and external—commitment to God and to the Christian faith. Although good deeds must not be done in order for others to see them (see Mt 6:2), they are indeed necessary: "Faith of itself, if it does not have works, is dead" (Jas 2:17).

172.   See Luke 21:3.

173.   See Matthew 15:28.

174.   See Luke 19:9.

175.   See Luke 7:36-50.

176.   *CL*, sec. 16.

177.   *PDV*, sec. 78.

178.   *LG*, sec. 42.

179.   *PDV*, sec. 18. See Vatican II, *Gaudium et Spes* (1965), sec. 3 (from here on, abbreviated as *GS*).

180.   See *GS*: "Today there is an inescapable duty to make ourselves the neighbor of every man, no matter who he is" (sec. 27).

181.   "We do not exist for ourselves alone, and it is only when we are fully convinced of this fact that we begin to love ourselves properly and thus also love others. . . . Only when we see ourselves in our true human context, as members of a race which is intended to be one organism and 'one body,' will we begin to understand the positive importance . . . which is God's love living and acting in those whom He has incorporated in His Christ." See *No Man is an Island* (New York: Harcourt, Brace and Company, 1955), xx-xxiii. See *GS*, sec. 12, 24, 25.

182.   The height of Islamic philosophy was in the Middle Ages. One of the philosophers, known by his Spanish name Avempace (Abū Bakr Muhammad Ibn Bājjah, d. 1138), wrote: "man is political by nature, and it was explained in political science that all isolation is evil." See "The

Governance of the Solitary" in *Medieval Political Philosophy*, ed. Ralph
Lerner and Muhsin Mahdi, trans. Lawrence Berman (New York: Cornell
University Press, 1963), 132.

183.   *GS*, sec. 40.

184.   NB: The works of the Apostle of Andalusia are not the place
in which one can find inspiration for ecumenical relationships. This is
understandable because he was actively engaged in defending the Catholic
faith from his contemporaries and there was a much heated ambience of
mistrust as one can ascertain even in reading the decrees of the Council
of Trent. In referring to Luther and his followers, therefore, St. John of
Avila speaks of "heretics." See "Luteranos" in Esquerda, *DJA*, 575-78.
Many years would have to go by before the Church could acknowledge
her own need for conversion and could accept responsibility for some of
its "sins against unity." See *UR*, sec. 7.

185.   See *UR*, n. 1.

186.   *GS*, sec. 92.

187.   Ibid., sec. 91 (emphasis added).

188.   See *UR*, sec. 24.

189.   Vatican II, *Nostra Aetate* (1965), sec. 1.

190.   Ibid., sec. 2.

191.   Ibid., sec. 4.

192.   *LG*, sec. 28.

193.   *GS*, sec. 42.

194.   Ibid., sec. 76.

195.   Ibid., sec. 63.

196.   Ibid., sec. 76.

197.   See Sermon 38 in *OC*, vol. 3, n. 40. Along the same lines, see
Sermons 50 and 78, and Letters 12-18 in *OC*, vol. 4. Especially interest-
ing is the long list of recommendations that St. John of Avila wrote for
Spanish bishops in regard to their relationship with the King and Queen.
The monarchs too, he says, had to help with the implementation of the
Council of Trent. It deals with the appointment of bishops (n. 3), support
for religious orders (n. 20), good values in citizens (n. 25) and even the
prayer life of the royalty (n. 27). See *Advertencias necesarias para los reyes* in
OC, vol. 2, 629-43.

198.   See "Gobernantes, gobierno" in *DJA*, 444.

199.   See *GS*, n. 76.

200.   *Directory*, n. 44. As mentioned earlier, Ross Douthat has pointed
out the damaging results of religious leaders who have not acted prudently by getting too involved in politics. Sadly, the ones who were supposed to bring unity have contributed to creating more scorn and division.
See *Bad Religion*, 66.

201.   *GS*, sec. 57.

202.   Ibid., sec. 40.

203.   See 1 Corinthians 3:6.
204.   *GS*, sec. 93.
205.   See Hebrews 5:4.
206.   See *PDV*, sec. 74.

CONCLUSION

The Church teaches that "priests will acquire holiness in their own distinctive way by exercising their functions sincerely and tirelessly in the Spirit of Christ."[1] St. John of Avila would agree with this idea, not just for priests, but for all Christians. He would say that "there is no safeguard as secure for goodness and virtue as work."[2] As a spiritual master, he knew that selfishness and sloth are the perennial weapons of the enemy to introduce vice into the body of Christ and interfere with God's will, with the love and unity that He wants to see in His family.

Yet, being himself a holy priest, St. John understood that the strength the Christian needs to serve can be obtained only through prayer, in the time that one spends with the Lord, the Master of the vineyard.[3] It is during those moments of contemplation that the priest receives his mandate so that he does not labor in vain, so that, following the Master's instructions, he can obtain an abundant catch of fish.[4] The Apostle of Andalusia "united constant prayer to apostolic action," as Pope Benedict XVI said of him.[5]

The unity between prayer and action points to the unity between the three different aspects of the priest's office—his prophetic, priestly, and shepherding roles—as attested by Christ, the High Priest. A priest can be effective in his ministry only if he safeguards those moments of prayer and if he sets aside his personal preferences to do that which is required of him. A healthy balance of the three roles will avoid reductionisms in understanding his priestly identity or his ministry, as Benedict XVI reminded us. This is the reason why, beginning in the seminary, candidates for the priesthood are asked to preserve an appropriate balance between the four pillars of formation—human, spiritual, academic, and pastoral. As future priests who, "with a conscious and free response of adherence and involvement of their *whole person* [turn to] Jesus Christ . . . ," they will share in "intimacy of life with him and . . . share in his mission of salvation."[6] The Church, therefore, asks diocesan priests to be mindful that it is in this "joining of themselves with Christ in the recognition of the Father's will and in the gift of themselves to the flock entrusted to them"[7] that they find unity of life, that they find and live out their own specific spirituality.

Since love of God and love of neighbor are what leads to holiness, the hallmark of a holy priest is making himself available for whatever it is that the Church, through the direction of the diocesan bishop and the needs of the faithful in the local community, requires of him. Monsignor Patrick Thompson, a revered pastor from the Archdiocese of Los Angeles, for example, used to say that, when he was in the seminary in the 1950s, their rector would say to them: "Gentlemen, let the Church decide your life." This is similar to the words expressed by Pope Benedict XVI at the beginning of his Petrine ministry. Speaking of the vision he had for his pontificate, for his office of high priest, he said on that day: "My real programme of governance is not to do my own will, not to pursue my own ideas, but to listen, together with the whole Church, to the word and the will of the Lord, to be guided by Him, so that He himself will lead the Church at this hour of our history."[8]

Being the main collaborators of the bishop, diocesan priests belong to the hierarchical structure; it is their task as parish priests to nurture and support all other vocations, including religious, for the good of the Church. Those in religious life, in their turn, assist bishops and diocesan priests in carrying out their ministry, as St. John of Avila would teach, especially in areas where the efforts of the local Church cannot reach the faithful or where the charism offered by the specific religious community can benefit the people. Comparing priesthood to the medical field, it could be said that diocesan priests are "general practitioners" while religious are specialists. Both are needed since they are complementary.

It is not helpful to compare the spirituality of the diocesan priests with those of religious communities; they are different, and both have a place in the Body of Christ. In the Scriptures, besides the image of the Body of Christ to speak about the Church, St. Paul speaks of "God's building" (1 Cor 3:9), an image St. Peter picks up to instruct Christians to be "living stones" (1 Pt 2:5). Thus, in saying that diocesan priests belong to the hierarchical structure of the Church, the Church seems to convey the image that they are part of the walls, the "structure" of that building. Their ministry, though seemingly ordinary, is essential. While it is true that when we admire the beauty of a house, we may not necessarily be looking at the beams or the wooden frames behind the walls, it is those walls that make it stand. That is what diocesan priesthood offers: the solid structure of the regular proclamation of the Word of God, the celebration of the Eucharist and the Sacraments, and the shepherding of the People of God in the local parish. This solid presbyteral structure provides the spiritual context where the rest of Church life can take place. Religious, for their part, having received special and specific charisms from the Holy Spirit, adorn the Body of Christ, the building, and make it beautiful with what they can offer. Again, both are essential and complementary.

The spirituality of the diocesan priest, then, is lived in the faithful carrying out of his ministry. As he exercises his priestly, prophetic, and kingly office, he himself is transformed by the sacred realities that he handles and offers the rest of the community. And, given that all the baptized share in the common priesthood of Christ, the priest's constant interaction with them also serves for his sanctification. Their priesthoods are ordered to each other, the Church teaches, and, together, they grow individually and as a community; they engage in mutual sanctification.

St. John of Avila lived out his priesthood in a specific location and during a specific era. Yet, because "Jesus Christ is the same yesterday, today, and forever" (Heb 13:8), this saintly priest, who configured himself to Christ the High Priest and spent his whole life working for the formation of priests, has much to teach us today. That is why St. John was canonized at a time when the priesthood was in need of good role models and why the Church has bestowed on him the additional title of Doctor of the Universal Church. Jesus rightly taught that lamps are not lit to be put under bushel baskets but so they can shine before others .[9] The figure of the Apostle of Andalusia remained in hiding for a long time. Given his extreme humble disposition, that was probably in keeping with his wishes. But now, his lamp also must shine so that, just as in his day, he led so many others to holiness, he can continue to be a light for us.

The day St. John of Avila was canonized, St. Paul VI said of him: "May this saint, whom we have the joy of exulting before the Church, be a favorable intercessor of the graces that she seems to need today: firmness in the true faith, authentic love for the Church, holiness of the clergy, fidelity to the Council, and the imitation of Christ as it must be at all times."[10] With the Church, we continue to say: Amen!

NOTES

1.   Vatican II, *Presbyterorum Ordinis* (from here on, abbreviated as *PO*) (1965), sec. 13.

2.   Sermon 19 in *Obras Completas*, (from here on, abbreviated as *OC*) vol. 3, n. 16.

3.   See Matthew 20:1.

4.   See Luke 5:6 and John 21:6.

5.   "Homily at Mass Declaring St. John of Avila Doctor of the Church" (October 7, 2012) in *Acta Apostolicae Sedis* (from here on, abbreviated as *AAS*) 104 (2012): 874-878, English translation (Vatican City: Libreria Editrice Vaticana, 2012).

6.   John Paul II, *Pastores Dabo Vobis* (from here on, abbreviated as *PDV*) (1992), sec. 42 (emphasis added).

7.   *PO*, sec. 14. See also *PDV*, sec. 23.

8.   "Homily. Inauguration Mass of the Petrine Ministry" (April 24, 2005) in *AAS* 97 (2005): 707-712, English translation (Vatican City: Libreria Editrice Vaticana, 2005).

9.   See Matthew 5:15.

10.   *OC*, vol. 1, 362.

APPENDIX

SPIRITUAL PLAN FOR PRIESTS ACCORDING TO ST. JOHN OF AVILA

The *Directory on the Ministry and the Life of Priests* states the hope that every priest should "draw up a concrete plan of personal life in concord with his spiritual director."[1] As a spiritual master, St. John of Avila recommended the same, not just for priests, but for all believers.[2] In his *Reglas de Espíritu*, he gives suggestions that people can practice in order to grow in their spirituality.[3] The following are some recommendations for priests taken from these rules and from St. John's writings.

Personal Prayer

St. John believed that a priest cannot live without prayer. It is in prayer that he truly understands who he is and what he is called to do for the good of the people he serves. St. John recommended having two main periods of prayer, one in the morning and one in the evening, before going to sleep.[4]

Besides praying the Office—the Liturgy of the Hours—in the morning, St. John recommends meditating on some aspect of the Lord's Passion. This is helpful, he says, for three reasons: it helps us to understand God's love for us and to hope in Him; it leads us to greater charity with others since Jesus was willing to give His life for them; and it helps us to imitate the virtues of Christ, such as His patience, His fortitude and His great charity.[5]

St. John recommends an examination of conscience at night in which one recalls the events of the day and asks God for forgiveness for one's failures. Along with it, he also suggests reflecting on the final judgement so that one does not take one's actions lightly and is mindful that the joys of the world are ephemeral.[6]

Daily Mass

The recommendation for the daily celebration of the Eucharist is also found in the letters of St. John to his disciples. This recommendation applies even for those priests who are professors or have special ministries where they are not responsible for the direct pastoral care of souls.[7] It must be done even when one is lacking devotion, St. John of Avila would say;[8] the power of the Sacraments cannot be underestimated. Were a priest not assigned to a parish, he could offer his Masses for the souls in purgatory, for the reform of the Church, or for other worthy intentions.[9]

Frequent Confession

The practice of frequent confession and Communion is the third recommendation of St. John of Avila for all the faithful.[10] Following the teaching of St. Bernard, St. John would prescribe frequent confession as a "very good medicine" for the soul and a helpful incentive so that, out of the shame of embarrassment of confessing the same thing over and over again, the person may be converted.[11] In his view, this is also true for priests. As the rest of the baptized, priests also need to acknowledge their sins and believe in the "great sweetness and safety" of the Sacrament of Reconciliation.[12]

Spiritual Reading

In his letters to his disciples, St. John also mentions reading books that lead to devotion and to the edification of the soul. The lives of the saints or meditations written by spiritual masters were excellent options that he recommended to priests.[13] Specific suggestions varied, depending on the needs and circumstances of each disciple.

Sufficient Rest

Probably every priest has had the experience of saying something foolish or handling a situation in an undesirable manner because he was tired or frustrated. Our humanity cannot be denied, nor can the needs of the body. Rest and nourishment are essential in order for the priest to be at his best with those he serves.[14]

In the same letters mentioned earlier, St. John also speaks of taking a bit of rest after the midday meal.[15] Coming from a culture that treasures that famous *siesta*, this is not surprising. But again, as a spiritual master, he could see the benefits of it. Action can flow only from being, and those brief periods of rest can help to keep one's devotion strong, as he would say.[16] In other words, it is desirable that we always act from the center of our being, doing things wholeheartedly, and not just halfway or out of obligation; we must also discern whether or not what is being asked of us is a true need.[17]

But the above recommendation needs to be balanced with diligence and the zeal for serving others. In the experience of St. John of Avila, the body cannot always be trusted or given everything it asks for since "the flesh has desires against the Spirit, and the Spirit against the flesh" (Gal 5:17). Mindful of this truth, he would give the following rules for priests:

- Do not leave for tomorrow the good that you are able to do today, for each day has its own tasks.

- Do not believe your body after you have given it its proper portion (avoiding that which is unnecessary), even if it wants to persuade you that it is weak or in need.

- When the body pretends to be tired, seeks comforts, or is slothful in ordinary work, it is then that you must be more alive and make a greater effort, seeking to do that which must be done.

- Never be totally idle.[18]

Again, prudence and willingness to cooperate with God's will are key here.

Acts of Penance

Meditating upon the Lord's Passion, as St. John of Avila recommends, leads to the realization that we, too, must be willing to bear certain crosses along the way. Certainly, the disciple is not greater than the Master[19]; and if we are one with Christ, we too will be called upon to bear a heavy cross, at least occasionally. Therefore, carrying injuries with joy is also among St. John of Avila's recommendations.[20]

Besides accepting everyday challenges and trials with faith and fortitude, the Church has always praised voluntary penances as a way to ongoing conversion.[21] Having practiced these from an early age, St. John would also recommend them to other priests. To one of them, for instance, he suggests sleeping on a wooden board rather than on a regular bed on Thursdays and Fridays as a way of accompanying Jesus who suffered on those days.[22] But regardless of what one decides to do, Christ crucified must be the mirror on which we need to see ourselves and to which we should always strive to conform, as our saint would say.[23]

Pastoral Charity

It is appropriate to mention once again the unity of life that a diocesan priest must experience in the different aspects of his being and his responsibilities. Being "spiritually fit" is necessary not only for the priest's own sake, but for the good of Christ's flock. The advice St. John gives in another one of his letters is laudable: "Many times people serve God more in desiring a state of recollection and not having it than in actually having it, because sometimes—and this happens frequently—God wants us to leave the delight of being only with Him in order to care for his children."[24] As diocesan priests, then, servants of the Lord do benefit from a structured plan for their everyday life, but it must be flexible enough to respond to what is needed at the moment since their vocation places them at the forefront of Church life.

Church documents mention the importance of retreats and days of recollection for the spiritual life of the priest.[25] The aforementioned recommendations by St. John of Avila compliment these other activities. Together, they can help shape a spiritual plan that is appropriate and adapted to the needs of every priest in whatever circumstances he finds himself.

NOTES

1.   Congregation for the Clergy, *Directory on the Ministry and Life of Priests* (Vatican City: Libreria Editrice Vaticana, 2013), sec. 94. NB: This is in addition to the diocesan plan for ongoing formation mentioned in John Paul II, *Pastores Dabo Vobis* (from here on, abbreviated as *PDV*) (1992), sec. 79. The latter is the responsibility of the bishop; the former, the priest's own initiative.

2.   See "Plan de vida" in Juan Esquerada Bifet, *Diccionario de San Juan de Avila* (from here on, abbreviated as *DJA*) (Burgos: Monte Carmelo, 1999), 739-40. St. John also says that this must be done in consultation with one's "guide" or "spiritual father." See Rule 9 in Juan de Avila, *Obras Completas* (from here on, abbreviated as *OC*), ed. Luis Sala Balust and Francisco Martin Hernandez (Madrid: Biblioteca de Autores Cristianos, 2007), vol. 2, 845-46.

3.   There are different versions of St. John's *Reglas de espíritu*. The first *Reglas* were included with the unauthorized publication of his *Audi, filia* in 1556 with the title "Breve regla de vida cristiana" (Brief Rule of Christian Life). It consisted of ten rules that spelled out St. John's recommendations for all believers (see *OC*, vol. 2, 839-43). Another version was published in 1588, after the death of the saint. It consists of thirty-two rules, and it mixes recommendations for all the baptized and for priests (see Ibid, 843-48). The fact that some of the rules use the third person and others, the second indicates that they were taken from St. John's writings and letters to different disciples, some of whom were priests. This second version has the name of *Reglas muy provechosas para andar en el camino de nuestro Señor* (Very Beneficial Rules to Walk Down the Lord's Path). Another version entitled *Diez documentos* presents a corrected, simpler version of the first original rules (see Ibid., 848-50). Besides these and other recommendations that he wrote specifically for religious (see Ibid., 851-53, 856-57), other versions were published under different titles and translated into Italian, French, German, and Greek. See "Reglas de espíritu" in *DJA*, 793-94.

4.   The fact that these two periods of prayer are listed as the first of the ten rules in the original version points to their importance. See *OC*, vol. 2, 839.

5.   See Letter 236 in *OC*, vol. 4, 762. It is noteworthy that St. John here says "*mientras la devoción no pidiere otro paso o misterio.*" He provides a structure for these periods of meditation in case it is needed (and he even has recommendations for each day of the week—see page 753 of that same letter), but the emphasis is on the time spent with the Lord, not on the method itself. What matters is the relationship that is created between God and the believer. Meditation on the Passion of Christ, in his

view, was very beneficial, but he did not prescribe this as an absolute. The priest's personal devotion or the circumstances of his life could call for something else.

6. Ibid., 756-62. See also Letter 5 in *OC*, vol. 4, 33-35. On the daily examination of conscience, see also Vatican II, *Presbyterorum Ordinis* (from here on, abbreviated as *PO*) (1965), sec. 18.

7. See Letter 5, written for St. John of Avila and theologian García Arias. *OC*, vol. 4, 33ff.

8. Ibid., 39.

9. See Letter 8 in *OC*, vol. 4, 50. The daily celebration of the Mass is also prescribed by the Magisterium. See *Directory*, sec. 67; Benedict XVI, *Sacramentum Caritatis* (2007) in *Acta Apostolicae Sedis* (from here on, abbreviated as *AAS*) 99 (2007): 105-180, sec. 80.

10. See *OC*, vol. 2, 840. At a time when people received Holy Communion only once a year, this is significant. St. John makes reference in this third "rule" to the original Church, where the faithful would gather every Sunday to partake in "the breaking of the bread."

11. See *OC*, vol. 2, 849. In this version, confession is addressed under rule four. The reference to St. Bernard is *Ep.* 113, 4ff: *Patrologia Latina* (from here on, abbreviated as PL) 182, 258.

12. See Letter 5 in *OC*, vol. 4, 39. The writings of St. John reveal that he was concerned about the poor catechesis he saw among the faithful regarding the Sacrament of Penance. One of his Spiritual Conferences to priests is entirely dedicated to this topic (see *Pláticas* 5 in *OC*, vol. 1, 833-50), as is also a small treatise on the subject that has been partially preserved (see *Dialogus inter confessarium et paenitentem* in *OC*, vol. 2, 769-97). See "Confesión" in *DJA*, 199-203.

13. See Letter 5 and 8 in *OC*, vol. 4, 39 and 51, respectively. Also Letter 225, 724-25.

14. St. John writes of "eating well" in a letter he sent to another one of his disciples. See Letter 225 in *OC*, vol. 4, 726. See also *Directory*, sec. 101.

15. In Letter 8, he speaks of that afternoon siesta as a matter of fact. See *OC*, vol. 4, 50. In Letter 5, he says a rest can be taken "by all means" if needed. See *OC*, vol. 4, 36.

16. See Letter 8 in *OC*, vol. 4, 50.

17. The prudent advice of St. John of Avila to Fra Luis of Granada is fitting here. The very first recommendation he gives him is not to give himself entirely to the people. See Letter 1 in *OC*, vol. 4, 9.

18. *Reglas muy provechosas* 25-28 in *OC*, vol. 2, 848.

19. See John 15:20.

20. See Number 6 in St. John's "Avisos" for the disciples that were about to enter the Society of Jesus. *Reglas de espíritu* in *OC*, vol. 2, 853.

21. See Catechism of the Catholic Church (from here on, abbreviated as *CCC*) (New York: Image, 1995), sec. 1430-39.

22.   See Letter 8 in *OC*, vol. 4, 51. Thursdays and Fridays always had a privileged place in the life of St. John. He himself would keep long vigils on those days and practice other penances. See the biographical study by Sala and Martín at the beginning of the *Obras completas*, *OC*, vol. 1, 222-23.

23.   Ibid.

24.   Letter 55 in *OC*, vol. 4, 261. Although the letter is addressed to a woman who longed for those moments of recollection in the midst of all her activities, this also applies to diocesan priests, given our secular character.

25.   See *PDV*, sec. 80 and *Directory*, sec. 103.

CPSIA information can be obtained
at www.ICGtesting.com
Printed in the USA
FFHW020710241019
55716356-61586FF